On Being Included

On Being **Included**

Racism and Diversity in Institutional Life

Sara Ahmed

Duke University Press
Durham and London   2012

© 2012 Duke University Press

All rights reserved

Printed in the United States of
America on acid-free paper ∞

Designed by Heather Hensley

Typeset in Monotype Dante by
Keystone Typesetting, Inc.

Library of Congress Cataloging-in-
Publication Data appear on the last
printed page of this book.

This book is dedicated to
all diversity workers
who keep going
no matter what they
come up against.

Contents

Acknowledgments

Thanks to all the diversity practitioners who gave me their time, including those I interviewed as well as those I spoke to at conferences and workshops. My aim has been to retell the many stories you told me. This book is thus the product of our collective labor.

My appreciation goes to the diversity research team who worked together between 2003 and 2005 and from whom I learned a great deal: Elaine Swan, Shona Hunter, Sevgi Kilic, and Lewis Turner.

I am indebted to all those who participate in Black British feminism, including Suki Ali, Avtar Brah, Yasmin Gunaratnam, Gail Lewis, Heidi Mirza, Ann Phoenix, Nirmal Puwar, and Shirley Tate. As I completed this book, I benefited greatly from queer of color networks. Thanks especially to Paola Bacchetta, Campbell, Jin Haritaworn, Camel Gupta, Shamira A. Meghani, Pratibha Parmar, Jasbir Puar, and Sara Wajid. I am also grateful to my colleagues in Media and Communications: the good nature of our department makes it a special place to work.

Thanks to the team at Duke University Press, especially Ken Wissoker and Leigh Barnwell for your enthusiasm for the project and help in bringing it to completion. My appreciation also to two anonymous readers for their helpful feedback.

A special thanks to Clare Hemmings, Shona Hunter, Jonathan Keane, Elena Loizidou, Elaine Swan, and Beverley Skeggs for traveling in shared worlds. We need our co-travelers!

My appreciation goes to Sarah Franklin, whose questions keep me thinking and whose jokes (good and bad!) keep me laughing.

On Arrival

What does diversity do? What are we doing when we use
the language of diversity? These questions are ones that I
pose *in* this book as well as *to* diversity and equality practitioners working in universities. These questions can be
asked as open questions only if we proceed with a sense
of uncertainty about what diversity is doing and what we
are doing with diversity. Strong critiques have been made
of the uses of diversity by institutions and of how the
arrival of the term "diversity" involves the departure of
other (perhaps more critical) terms, including "equality,"
"equal opportunities," and "social justice." A genealogy
of the term "diversity" allows us to think about the appeal
of the term as an institutional appeal. We might want to
be cautious about the appealing nature of diversity and
ask whether the ease of its incorporation by institutions
is a sign of the loss of its critical edge. Although this book
is written with a sense of caution about diversity, I am
also interested in what diversity can and does do. The
more I have followed diversity around, the more diversity
has captured my interest.

How did I come to be following diversity around?

Every research project has a story, which is the story of an arrival. The arrival of this book is a significant departure for me as it is the first book I have written that draws on qualitative empirical research. There are at least two ways of telling the story of the arrival of this book: one focuses on research practice, the other on institutional practice.

The first version: I had previously written about questions of race and difference, although, thinking back, it took time for me to get to the point when I could write about race. My initial research was on feminist theory and postmodernism. When I was working on my doctoral thesis in 1993, I remember searching for an example to ground the chapter I was writing on subjectivity. I can recall actually looking around the room, as if an object, one that I might find lying around, could become my subject.[1] At this moment of looking around, I recalled an experience, one that I had "forgotten." It came to me as if it were reaching out from the past. The very reach of the past shows that it was not one I had left behind. It was a memory of walking near my home in Adelaide and being stopped by two policemen in a car, one of whom asked me, "Are you Aboriginal?" It turned out that there had been some burglaries in the area. It was an extremely hostile address and an unsettling experience at the time. Having recalled this experience, I wrote about it. The act of writing was a reorientation, affecting not simply what I was writing about but what I was thinking and feeling. As memory, it was an experience of not being white, of being made into a stranger, the one who is recognized as "out of place," the one who does not belong, whose proximity is registered as crime or threat. As memory, it was of becoming a stranger in a place I called home.[2]

Why had I forgotten about it? Forgetting has its uses; unpleasant experiences are often the ones that are hard to recall. I had not wanted to think about race; I had not wanted to think about my experiences growing up, as someone who did not belong. Allowing myself to remember was a political reorientation: it led me to think and write about the politics of stranger making; how some and not others become strangers; how emotions of fear and hatred stick to certain bodies; how some bodies become understood as the rightful occupants of certain spaces. Throughout the course of my writing, I have tried to write from this experience of not belonging, to make sense of that experience, even when it is not the explicit subject of recall.

One of my aims in this book is to show that to account for racism is to offer a different account of the world. I thus do not begin with the category of race but with more apparently open terms. The racialization of the stranger is not immediately apparent—disguised, we might say—by the strict anonymity of the stranger, who after all, we are told from childhood, could be anyone. My own stranger memory taught me that the "could be anyone" points to some bodies more than others. This "could be anyone" only appears as an open possibility, stretching out into a horizon, in which the stranger reappears as the one who is always lurking in the shadows. Frantz Fanon ([1952] 1986) taught us to watch out for what lurks, seeing himself *in* and *as* the shadow, the dark body, who is always passing by, at the edges of social experience. In seeing the stranger, we are most certainly seeing someone; in some cases, we are seeing ourselves.

We can think from the experience of becoming a stranger. A stranger experience can be an experience of becoming noticeable, of not passing through or passing by, of being stopped or being held up. A stranger experience can teach us about how bodies come to feel at home through the work of inhabitance, how bodies can extend themselves into spaces creating contours of inhabitable space, as well as how spaces can be extensions of bodies (see Ahmed 2006). This book explores the intimacy of bodily and social space: it develops my earlier arguments about "stranger making" by thinking more concretely about institutional spaces, about how some more than others will be at home in institutions that assume certain bodies as their norm.

There is another story of arrival. I became co-director of the Institute for Women's Studies at Lancaster University in 2000. I began to attend faculty meetings. I was the only person of color at these meetings.[3] It is important to note that I noticed this: whiteness tends to be visible to those who do not inhabit it (though not always, and not only). During the discussion of one item at a faculty meeting on equality, the dean said something like "race is too difficult to deal with." I remember wanting to challenge this. But the difficulty of speaking about racism as a person of color meant that I did not speak up during but after the meeting, and even then I wrote rather than spoke. Saying that race is "too difficult" is how racism gets reproduced, I put in an email to the dean. The belief that racism is inevitable is how racism becomes inevitable, I pointed out. (One of the favorite arguments made by senior management was that the university was "very white" because of geography—and that you can't do anything about geography.) Do something about it, he replies. It shouldn't be up to me, I answer.

How quickly we can be interpellated! My correspondence with the dean took place in 2000 just before the Race Relations Amendment Act came into effect, which made race equality into a positive duty under law, and required all public institutions to write a race equality policy. The dean spoke to the director of human resources. She got in contact with me, offering an invitation to become a member of the newly formed race equality team responsible for writing our university's race equality policy. There were two academics on the team, both people of color. There are problems and pitfalls in becoming a diversity person as a person of color. There is a script that stops anyone reading the situation as a becoming. You *already* embody diversity by providing an institution of whiteness with color.

It is certainly the case that responsibility for diversity and equality is unevenly distributed. It is also the case that the distribution of this work is political: if diversity and equality work is less valued by organizations, then to become responsible for this work can mean to inhabit institutional spaces that are also less valued.

We can get stuck *in* institutions by being stuck *to* a category. This is not to say that we cannot or do not value the work of these categories. But we can be constrained even by the categories we love. I had experienced already what it can mean to be "the race person." Indeed, both academic positions I have held in the United Kingdom were advertised as posts in race and ethnicity, the first in Women's Studies, the second in Media and Communications. In both cases, the experience felt like being appointed by whiteness (even if the appointment was intended as a countering of whiteness). There we can find ourselves: people of color being inter-viewed for jobs "on race" by white panels, speaking to white audiences about our work. In both cases the experience was one of solidarity with those who have to face this situation. Whiteness can be a situation we have or are in; when we can name that situation (and even make jokes about it) we recognize each other as strangers to the institution and find in that estrangement a bond. Of course, at the same time, I should stress that we do want there to be posts on race and ethnicity. We also want there to be more than one; we want not to be the one. Becoming the race person means you are the one who is turned to when race turns up. The very fact of your existence can allow others not to turn up.

Although being part of the race equality group made me uneasy for these reasons, the experience of being in the group was nevertheless inspiring. I learned from our conversations, and they provided me with a framework I later developed in the research project on diversity upon which this book is based. What was important and reorienting for me was the experience of working closely with practitioners from human resources. The conversations we had about how to write our race equality policy taught me about what it means to pose questions strategically: to think, for example, about words as tools for doing things, and to think of strategy not as the absence or bracketing of thought (as strategy is often thought) but as the unfolding of thought. The experience of working "on" the institutions "at" which I worked also brought my own thinking closer to home.

At this point I had no intention of writing about those experiences. If anything I welcomed being involved in institutional work that was not related to my academic scholarship. The imperative to transform all experience into writing can reduce the value of an experience by treating experience as a means to this end (though, as I have suggested, writing as a prompter for recollection can be reorienting). Doing this kind of work allowed me to think more about my relationship to institutional worlds. I had imagined that my task as an academic in the race equality working group was to bring a critical vocabulary into the wording of the document. I realized very quickly that critique is not something that academics bring; those employed to write policies and frameworks can be just as (if not more) critical given their very involvement in policy worlds. I realized how the presumption of our own criticality can be a way of protecting ourselves from complicity. As Fiona Probyn-Ramsey has observed, complicity can be a starting point; if we start with complicity, we recognize our "proximity to the problems we are addressing" (2009: 161).

I also came to realize that documents, once written, acquire lives of their own. In my previous work I had offered close and critical readings of multicultural policy documents (see Ahmed 2000, 2004). I began to appreciate the importance of focusing not so much on what documents say but what they do: how they circulate and move around. Indeed, when I began the research, one of my questions was about a diversity and equality policy published in Australia in 1996.[4] I asked the first practitioner I interviewed about it. She described it as "an amazing document." But she then said, with an intonation that gave the impression of qualifying the value statement: "We changed government and it got buried; it's virtually never been dealt with that I know of in any arena I know." The document thus acquires no force. It ceases to have an official existence, even if it still exists in electronic and paper form. To read the document for what it is saying would be to miss this point by making it the point.

In this project I ended up following diversity documents around. But it still took time to get to this point. How did I end up doing an empirical study of diversity work? As with much research, the story of an arrival is a story of our encounters. I began to work more closely with scholars from the Management School at Lancaster University. It happened that Elaine Swan, based in the Management School, was involved in a major bid with colleagues to be the research arm for a new center being set up by the Department for Further Education and Skills on leadership in the Further Education sector (what became the Centre for Education and Leadership). So much research is premised on the "hap" of a happening! They were successful in the bid, which meant they had a budget to support a number of research projects on leadership. Elaine asked me if I would be interested in working with her on a project on leadership and diversity. I saw so much potential in this opportunity: to talk to diversity practitioners across a range of institutions about what they do, to support the Institute for Women's Studies by bringing research funding into it,[5] and to work with a team of feminist and critical race theorists on a project about institutional change. The story of what happened to the project is part of the story of this book. It unfolds, as the book does.

The Research Project

My aim in this project was to talk to diversity practitioners about their experiences of doing diversity work within the higher education sector.[6] Overall, I conducted twenty-one interviews, including ten semi-structured interviews in Australia in 2003 and 2004 and eleven in the United Kingdom (all of these took place in 2004 and 2005, except for the eleventh, which I undertook in 2009).[7] All of these interviews took place in the office of a diversity practitioner based in a higher educational institution, except for two interviews with those working at a policy level: in Australia, with one member of staff responsible for equality policy from what was then the Department for Education, Science and Training, and two staff members from the Equality Challenge Unit (ECU), which has responsibility for overseeing equality in higher education in the United Kingdom. For all semi-structured interviews, I arranged to meet and interview an individual person. However, in Australia, three of the interviews ended up being with two people; in the United Kingdom, four interviews ended up being with two people, and one with three. My decision in all cases was to "go with the flow" and make explicit my willingness to listen to anyone who wanted to talk to me. I actually learned a great deal from conducting interviews with more than one person, as it gave me the opportunity to listen to the ways diversity gets talked about. Where possible, I have tried to preserve the conversational flow of a group discussion in my use of data from these interviews.

My project was originally framed as a comparative study of diversity work in higher education in the United Kingdom and Australia. I soon realized that a properly national comparison would require more interviews than I would be able to complete myself. The project became reframed about the experiences of practitioners in a range of different universities: my aim was to ensure that the data set included old and new universities, urban and rural, and research-led and teaching-led. I was particularly keen to speak to practitioners in institutions that had diversity as central to their educational missions and those that did not.

My experiences of doing the research in Australia and the United Kingdom were quite different, which could be because of the timing of the research, as well as the contrasting national environments.[8] My early interviews in Australia were very much focused on questions of language and strategy, as my own starting points in the research (chapters 1 and 2). In the United Kingdom, the focus became more on the relationship between diversity, equality, and performance culture; my interviews took place after the process of writing race equality policies as a result of a change in legislation (chapters 3 and 4).[9] Changes in legislation instituted what I call a "new equality regime" premised on the redefinition of equality as a positive duty. The Race Relations Amendment Act (RRAA) of 2000 was followed by the Disability Discrimination Act (2005), the Equality Act of 2006 (which introduced gender equality as a positive duty), and most recently the Equality Act of 2010, which requires that all public institutions have a single equality scheme.[10]

Together these acts have changed in significant ways the kind of labor involved in doing diversity work: in effect, since 2000, practitioners in the public sector in the United Kingdom have been writing documents to comply with the law. We can ask about the relationship between the new equality regime and what the sociologist Joan Acker calls "the inequality regimes": the "interrelated practices, processes, action and meanings that result in and maintain class, gender and race inequalities" (2006: 443). To pose this question as an open question requires not only that we do not assume that an equality regime is necessarily aimed at the overcoming of an inequality regime but also that we recognize that an equality regime *can be* an inequality regime given new form, a set of processes that maintain what is supposedly being redressed.

My interviews in the United Kingdom offered an opportunity to reflect with practitioners on the experience of this process and address the question of what the effects of this new equality regime are. The experience of this process offers us the opportunity to "thicken" our description of institutions. The philosopher Gilbert Ryle suggests that "thicker descriptions" require more than describing an action; it would locate an individual action in terms of its wider meaning or accomplishment. He suggests that a thin description of what a person is doing (such as doodling) requires thickening "before it amounts to an account of what the person is trying to accomplish" (Ryle 1971: 498).[11] This book is premised on the assumption that we can thicken our description of institutions by offering an account of what diversity practitioners are trying to accomplish.

The experience of conducting the interviews was quite nerve-racking: as a text-based researcher by training, I found working with "living subjects" a challenge. Texts can and do talk to us, but their voices are less audible. At the same time, I loved doing these interviews: they became opportunities to have a dialogue with practitioners, to hear their voices. I learned so much from practitioners in both Australia and the United Kingdom who, in giving me their story, also gave me the story of their institutions. As I have already suggested, in arranging the interviews, my explicit aim was to speak to practitioners from different kinds of institutions (a project on diversity needs to think from and with a diversity of institutions). And indeed, unsurprisingly, in most of the interviews, practitioners related their work directly to the kinds of institutions they work in: diversity work often involves "working out" what works given the workplace. I became particularly interested in how diversity workers aim to associate the word "diversity" with the terms that are already valued by organizations. The story of diversity thus becomes a story of diversity's inclusion into the terms of an institution.

For me, the experience of doing the research was as much about visiting different universities to conduct the interviews, which gave me an opportunity to attend to the different kinds of spaces they offer. In my field notes after my first interview, I noted the following:

> This is a very different environment than Sydney University [where I was based on sabbatical]. There is no sandstone. Somehow that goes with the kind of bodies that populate its lawns and buildings. There are lots of black and brown bodies; I can really see the difference. In the student union, the atmosphere is lively. The socialist workers are visible outside, and posters cover the walls about women's space, queer groups and anti-violence campaigns. Although we can't stick all of this together (buildings, bodies, politics) somehow it goes together.

The process of visiting different university campuses in Australia and the United Kingdom allowed me to revisit my arguments about the politics of diversity and think more about how diversity becomes associated with certain bodies, shaping how the university comes to appear *as* body. Although I feel at home in the body of the university, entering it as a researcher of the environment was a new experience. The university reappears when you see it from the viewpoint of a stranger, as someone who is looking "at" rather than "from" its environment. I do not intend to privilege my own vision here, or to imply that a view from a stranger is necessarily more objective. But I suggest that the research process is a process of estrangement, which creates an orientation in which some things come into view that had previously been obscured.[12]

Given that this study involved a relatively small number of interviews, it is important for me to note that I cannot generalize my findings. The research was never intended to generate the kind of findings that can be generalized. The desire for findings can even reduce or limit what can be found. Practitioners across the public sectors repeatedly said to our diversity team that too much research in this field is premised on findings that institutions *want found*: from toolboxes to good practice. Too much research thus becomes translated into mission speech, turning stories of diversity and equality into institutional success stories. There is much less research describing the complicated and messy situations in which diversity workers often find themselves. When description gets hard, we need description.

It was thus very important to guarantee anonymity for both the interviewees and their institutions. Anonymity was necessary to create a certain freedom within the interview to discuss institutional failures and bad practice. I noticed in some of the interviews how accounts of bad practice "came out" gradually: to work for institutions, as practitioners do, can require that you develop a habit of talking in mission talk, what we can call "happy talk," a way of telling a happy story of the institution that is at once a story of the institution as happy. Over the temporal course of the interview, the happier languages seemed to wear out, and a very different account of the institution was generated. We need space that is not designated as institutional space to be able to talk about the problems with and in institutions.

The research process helped me to think more about the difficulty of equality as a politics: of how in legislating for equality (and against inequality), it can be assumed that equality is achieved *in the act*. As I explore in more detail throughout this book, it is as if having a policy becomes a substitute for action. To challenge this substitution (which can work to conceal the inequalities that make the law necessary in the first place), I began to think more explicitly about social action. I came to ask whether there is an investment in both law and policy as "performatives": as if they do what they say, as if they bring something into existence. If what they do depends on how they get taken up, then the action of policy (as law or letter) is unfinished.

Recognizing the unfinished nature of a social action can be thought of as a methodological challenge. In meeting this challenge, I wanted not only to talk to diversity practitioners about diversity but also to inhabit the world of diversity, to offer an ethnography of this world.[13] In addition to my interviews with diversity practitioners, I draw on my participation in what we can describe as "the diversity world" (meetings, conferences, and workshops on diversity and equality within higher and further education, as well as some events run by the then Commission for Racial Equality [CRE][14] that were aimed at all the public sectors) and my own experiences as a diversity practitioner. An ethnographic approach to diversity is necessarily "multi-sited" given that the diversity world is a world of mobile subjects and objects, of the networks and connections that are necessary for things to move around. As Mark-Anthony Falzon observes, "the essence of multi-sited research is to follow people, connections, associations, and relationships across space" (2009: 1–2; see also Marcus 1998).

In reflecting on diversity within the university, this book provides a different lens through which to see the environment of the university. I have been influenced by the work of the social anthropologist Marilyn Strathern (2000, 2004, 2006), who draws on her own experience as a university administrator to consider the university as a field of knowledge. The book could thus be considered part of a growing body of literature that offers an ethnographic approach of the university (see also De Bary 2009). To provide such descriptions of the university as a field site is a way of bringing academic knowledge "back home."

To describe a world that is emerging and to account for the experience of that world from the points of view of those involved in it are the tasks of ethnographers who participate in worlds they also observe. In writing from and about my involvement, I am both an insider and outsider to the world I am describing. As an academic, I am at home in the environment of the university in a way that many diversity practitioners are not; as someone who has been involved in equality work (as a member of a race equality group, as a participant in equality and diversity committees, as well as my experience as "diversity champion" for my department), I experience the institution in ways that I share with those appointed as diversity practitioners. This is why the task of description became for me not only about giving an account of what practitioners are doing but also to show how much the experience of practitioners can teach us about how we inhabit institutions, what we can simply call "institutional life."

I should note that in inhabiting this rather vast and fuzzy world of diversity, many of my accounts are premised on "fleeting encounters" with individual actors rather than the more lasting encounters we (rightly) associate with ethnographic research. Perhaps a more precise description of my methodology would be "an ethnography of texts." To ask what diversity does, we need to follow diversity around, which is to say, we need to follow the documents that give diversity a physical and institutional form. Following documents is also about *following the actors who use these forms*. The question of what diversity does is also, then, a question of where diversity goes (and where it does not), as well as in whom and in what diversity is deposited (as well as in whom or in what it is not). The book draws on the conversations I have had at conferences and meetings on diversity and equality in the past ten years, which taught me a great deal about what does and does not tend to "come up" when diversity and equality are the explicit objects of conversation. It also draws on my own experience of equality and diversity committees at the two institutions in which I have worked, including some description of the conversations we had, when I think it is legitimate to do so (legitimacy becomes an important question when the anonymity of the institution and thus of participants cannot be guaranteed).

By following diversity around, my aim is certainly to describe the world that takes shape when diversity becomes used as a description. It is also important for me to locate this study in terms of intellectual worlds. I consider this book part of the specific tradition we can call, following Heidi Mirza, "Black British feminism."[15] I was very lucky in the early 1990s to meet Mirza and have one of my first academic essays be included in the collection she edited, *Black British Feminism* (1996). To be part of a collection can be to become a collective. Working as women of color in British higher education does provide us with a shared political and intellectual horizon.[16] To borrow Nirmal Puwar's (2004) wonderfully evocative expression, we share experiences of being treated as "space invaders," as invading the spaces reserved for others. We might even experience ourselves as space invaders, a way of experiencing spaces as if they are not reserved for us (and, indeed, they are not).

Yet it might be noticeable to readers that this book does not systematically address the gendering of institutional processes and organizations.[17] In what ways, then, can this book be thought of as a feminist project? Feminist theory has generated a body of knowledge of gendering as social process. However, that does not mean that feminism is necessarily *about* gender; as Judith Butler has argued, gender does not provide feminism with a proper object (2004: 181). In reflecting about gender as a relation, feminist theorists offer critical insight into the mechanisms of power as such and, in particular, how power can be *redone* at the moment it is imagined as *undone*. This book offers a set of feminist reflections on the subtle and not-so-subtle forms of institutional power.

Feminists of color have offered some of the most cogent critiques of the language of diversity (Davis 1996; Carby 1999; Bannerji 2000; Lewis 2000; Mohanty 2003; Puwar 2004; Alexander 2005; Anzaldúa and Keating 2009). Feminists of color have explored the relationship between diversity and power by showing how diversity is incorporated by institutions: "diversity management" becomes a way of managing or containing conflict or dissent. In particular, Chandra Talpade Mohanty's *Feminism without Borders* and M. Jacqui Alexander's *Pedagogies of Crossing* are important precursors to *On Being Included*. In these books, Mohanty and Alexander attend to the grammar of diversity and offer substantive critiques of diversity as a practice within educational institutions (Mohanty 2003: 208–16; Alexander 2005: 133–44). Mohanty shows how diversity is a discourse of "benign variation," which "bypasses power as well as history to suggest a harmonious empty pluralism" (2003: 193). Alexander explores how diversity documents have an ideological function in the "manufacture of cohesion" and create the impression of "more diversity" than "actually exists" (2005: 135). Following both these authors, this book interrogates diversity as a set of practices, asking how diversity can participate in the creation of an idea of the institution that allows racism and inequalities to be overlooked.

Furthermore, feminism of color provides us with a ways of thinking through power in terms of "intersectionality,"[18] to think about and through the points at which power relations meet. A body can be a meeting point. A concern with meeting points requires that we attend to the experiential: how we experience one category depends on how we inhabit others. It is important to note that the language of intersectionality is now associated with diversity. As Rachel E. Luft and Jane Ward observe, "the distinction between intersectionality and diversity remains blurry" (2009: 14). We need to think about how this blurriness can do things, such that the terms, in pointing to each other, can also obscure each other. If, as I have suggested, the focus on intersectionality within feminism of color meant a concern with the points at which power relations meet, then it is worth noting that these points often recede from view. This is why when we attend to intersectionality we are actually making a point. There is labor in attending to what recedes from view.

We can ask: what recedes when diversity becomes a view? If diversity is a way of viewing or even picturing an institution, then it might allow only some things to come into view. Diversity is often used as shorthand for inclusion, as the "happy point" of intersectionality, a point where lines meet. When intersectionality becomes a "happy point," the feminist of color critique is obscured. All differences matter under this view. Yet diversity in the policy world still tends to be associated with race. The association is sticky, which means the tendency is reproduced by not being made explicit. This book investigates what diversity does by focusing on what diversity obscures, that is, by focusing on the relationship between diversity and racism as a way of making explicit a tendency that is reproduced by staying implicit.

My concern with what recedes from general view also signals the importance of phenomenology to this project. I would not describe the research itself as phenomenological, although I do make a case in my conclusion for thinking about diversity work as a phenomenological practice. Nevertheless, phenomenological models have shaped some of my orientations, including my concern with orientation (Ahmed 2006), as well as my concern with describing how the most ordinary aspects of institutional life are often those that are least noticeable. Phenomenology provides a critical lens through which to think about "institutional life."

This book can be read in relation to the interdisciplinary literature on diversity, which includes scholarship in education, sociology, management, and organizational studies. I was struck in reading this academic literature by how little research into diversity has involved speaking to diversity and equal opportunities practitioners.[19] We have important studies of equal opportunities from the 1980s and 1990s that focus on the costs and difficulties of doing this kind of organizational labor, including Cynthia Cockburn's (1991) pioneering work, as well as Sarah Neal's (1998) study of equal opportunities within British universities. More recently, Gill Kirton, Anne-Marie Greene, and Deborah Dean (2007) conducted an interview-based study of diversity practitioners from private and public sector organizations within the United Kingdom.[20] They suggest that the shift from the framework of equal opportunities to that of diversity has involved a corresponding change in how practitioners understand their relationship to institutions. Kirton, Greene, and Dean argue that as diversity becomes more professionalized, practitioners are less likely to mobilize an activist framework. They suggest that diversity practitioners have an *ambivalent* relationship to institutions, as captured by their use of the phrase "tempered radical" to describe the attitude of practitioners (2007: 1981), a term they borrow from the earlier work of Deborah E. Meyerson and Maureen A. Scully (1995).[21] My interviews are full of similar accounts of ambivalence. We learn from this ambivalence about institutions and the ways practitioners can simultaneously experience themselves as working "for" and "against" them (see chapter 2).

It is important for me to address the politics of location in terms of the location of the research project. The study is of diversity practitioners based in Australia and the United Kingdom, two countries in which I have lived and worked myself. However, the arguments and accounts have a wider relevance. I argue that the languages of diversity are mobile, and the story of diversity's inclusion within and by institutions is transnational. We could take as an example the group Diversity in Organizations, Communities and Nations. They organize a conference (which in 2012 will be in its twelfth year), a journal, and a book series and function (in their terms) as "a knowledge community" that is "brought together by a shared interest in diversity in one or another of its manifestations, in organizations, communities and nations."[22] Although the significance of diversity can be described as international, the means by which diversity manifests itself will be local. We need to have conversations with each other from our specific locations. An example of this kind of conversation about diversity is offered in the edited collection *Doing Diversity in Higher Education* (Brown-Glaude 2009) in which faculty based in universities in the United States talk about their experience as diversity leaders within different kinds of institutions. When diversity becomes a conversation, a space is opened up. I have indeed learned from my conversations with academics and practitioners who are "doing diversity" across a range of locations.

I should note that although this book is very much a conversation with diversity practitioners, we should not assume that practitioners form a single community of actors. They do not. Although in both Australia and Britain there are professional associations for diversity practitioners in higher education, not all practitioners participate in these associations.[23] My conversations with practitioners both in interviews and informally at meetings or conferences gave me a very clear sense of the many different biographical as well as social routes into diversity work.[24] My task has been to engage with and analyze how practitioners describe the work they do.

Organization of the Book

The first chapter reflects on the institutional nature of diversity work exploring how practitioners aim to embed diversity such that it becomes an institutional given. I reflect on the relationship between diversity and institutional whiteness. I also ask what happens when the language of institutional racism becomes institutional language. In the second chapter, I turn to the significance of the word "diversity" itself, asking how practitioners use (or do not use) the term. The chapter aims to explain what appears as paradox between, on the one hand, the ubiquitous use of diversity as an official language by institutions and, on the other, how practitioners experience those institutions as resistant to their work. I am especially interested in how practitioners describe diversity as a tool that allows them to do things. These first two chapters are concerned with how practitioners describe their own work and with the strategies and tactics used for getting messages through to different actors within an institution.

As I have suggested, a key purpose of this book is to offer an account of the changing equality frameworks in the United Kingdom in terms of their effect on practice. The third chapter reflects specifically on the impact of the new equalities regime on what gets counted as equality and diversity, which includes a discussion of equality as a system for counting. In particular, I discuss some of the problems that follow when equality becomes a performance indicator. In the fourth chapter, I turn specifically to the question of commitment as that which is described as missing when diversity and equality become "paper trails." I offer a thesis that statements of commitment are non-performatives: they do not bring about the effects they name.

The final chapter offers a reflection on some of the consequences of diversity becoming a form of public relations. I reflect on how racism is heard as an injury to an institution and as damaging to an institutional reputation for "being diverse." I suggest that diversity can be offered as a narrative of repair, as what allows us to "recover" from racism by recovering the very signs of injury. In exploring the risks and necessity of speaking about racism, as both my starting point and conclusion, my aim is not to suggest that we should stop doing diversity, but that we need to keep asking what we are doing with diversity. If diversity is to remain a question, it is not one that can be solved. Indeed the critiques offered in this book are critiques of what follows when diversity is offered as a solution.

What is an institution? I want to start my reflections on racism and diversity within institutional life by asking what it means to think about institutions as such. We need to ask how it is that institutions become an *object* of diversity and antiracist practice in the sense that recognizing the institutional nature of diversity and racism becomes a goal for practitioners. Diversity work is typically described as institutional work. Why this is the case might seem obvious. The obvious is that which tends to be unthought and thus needs to be thought. We can repeat the question by giving it more force: what counts as an institution? Why do institutions count?

These questions are foundational to the social sciences. Émile Durkheim's definition of sociology is "the science of institutions, of their genesis and functioning" ([1901] 1982: 45). If the institution can be understood as the object of the social sciences, then the institution might be how the social derives its status as science. Durkheim's description was derived from Marcel Mauss and Paul Fauconnet's 1901 contribution on sociology to *La Grand Encyclopédie* (see M. Gane 2005: xii). The history of sociology is indeed a history of institutional thought.

Durkheim's innovative sociological method suggested that social facts can be approached as things. Arguably, treating institutions as an object of sociological inquiry, as social facts, can risk stabilizing institutions as things. We might stabilize institutions by assuming they refer to what is already stabilized. Within the humanities, the turn to thinking on the question of institutions has been predicated on a critique of sociological models. Samuel Weber's *Institutions and Interpretation* (2001), for example, cites with approval the work of René Lourau, who suggests that the sociological theories of institutions tend to assume their stability. Institutions, Lourau suggests, have been:

> increasingly used to designate what I and others before me have called the *instituted* (*l'institué*), the established order, the already existing norms, the state of fact thereby being confounded with the state of right (*l'état de droit*). By contrast, the *instituting* aspect (*l'instituant*) . . . has been increasingly obscured. The political implication of the sociological theories appears clearly here. By emptying the concept of institution of one of its primordial components (that of instituting, in the sense of founding, creating, breaking with an old order and creating a new one), sociology has finally come to identify the institution with the status quo. (Weber 2001: xv)

This reading of sociological work on institutions could be described as presuming the stability of its object (can all "sociological theories" of institutions be reduced to this identification?). Across a range of social science disciplines, including economics and political science as well as sociology, we have witnessed the emergence of "the new institutionalism," concerned precisely with how we can understand institutions as processes or even as effects of processes. Indeed, Victor Nee argues that the new institutionalism "seeks to explain institutions rather than simply assume their existence" (1998: 1). To explain institutions is to give an account of how they emerge or take form. Such explanations require a "thick" form of description, as I suggested in the introduction, a way of describing not simply the activities that take place within institutions (which would allow the institution into the frame of analysis only as a container, as what contains what is described, rather than being part of a description) but how those activities shape the sense of an institution or even institutional sense. The organizational studies scholars James G. March and Johan P. Olsen suggest that a thick approach to institutions would consider "routines, procedures, conventions, roles, strategies, organizational forms, and technologies" (1989: 22). The new institutionalism aims to think through *how* institutions become instituted over time (to "flesh out" this how): in other words, to think how institutions acquire the regularity and stability that allows them to be recognizable as institutions in the first place. Institutions can be thought of as verbs as well as nouns: to put the "doing" back into the institution is to attend to how institutional realities become given, without assuming what is given by this given.[1]

The new institutionalism allows us to consider the work of creating institutions as part of institutional work. Although this chapter does not engage with the "new institutionalism" literatures in a general sense, I consider how phenomenology can offer a resource for thinking about institutionality.[2] My arguments thus connect with some of the sociological literature on institutions insofar as the new institutionalism in sociology has been influenced by phenomenology.[3] Phenomenology allows us to theorize how a reality is given by becoming background, as that which is taken for granted. Indeed, I argue that a phenomenological approach is well suited to the study of institutions because of the emphasis on how something becomes given by not being the object of perception. Edmund Husserl (often described as the founder of phenomenology) considers "the world from the natural standpoint" as a world that is spread around, or just around, where objects are "more or less familiar, agreeing with what is actually perceived without themselves being perceived" ([1913] 1969: 100). To be in this world is to be involved with things in such a way that they recede from consciousness. When things become institutional, they recede. To institutionalize x is for x to become routine or ordinary such that x becomes part of the background for those who are part of an institution.

In his later work, Husserl ([1936/54] 1970) came to denote the "world of the natural attitude" as "the life-world," the world that is given to our immediate experience, a general background or horizon, which is also a world shared with others. To share a world might be to share the points of recession. If the tendency when we are involved in the world is to look over what is around us, then the task of the phenomenologist is to attend to what is looked over, to allow what is "overed" to surface.[4] In this chapter, I hope to offer this kind of attention. My primary aim is to offer an ethnographic approach to institutional life that works with the detail of how that life is described by diversity practitioners. Diversity work could be described as a phenomenological practice: a way of attending to what gets passed over as routine or an ordinary feature of institutional life.[5] We could even say that diversity workers live an institutional life. Dorothy E. Smith suggests that an institutional ethnography "would begin in the actualities of the lives of some of those involved in the institutional process" (2005: 31). Diversity workers work from their institutional involvement. Diversity practitioners do not simply work *at* institutions, they also work *on* them, given that their explicit remit is to redress existing institutional goals or priorities.

This chapter considers why institutions matter for diversity practitioners and explores how an *explicit* attention to institutions teaches us about their *implicit* significance and meaning. I want to think specifically about institutional life: not only how institutions acquire a life of their own but also how we experience institutions or what it means to experience something as institutional. We might also need to consider how we experience life within institutions, what it means for life to be "an institutional life." If the life we bracket as our working life is still a life, we need to attend to the form of this life by attending to what is bracketed by becoming institutionalized.

Institutionalizing Diversity

A typical goal of diversity work is "to institutionalize diversity." A goal is something that directs an action. It is an aiming for. However, if institutionalizing diversity is a goal for diversity workers, it does not necessarily mean it is the institution's goal. I think this "not necessarily" describes a paradoxical condition that is a life situation for many diversity practitioners. Having an institutional aim to make diversity a goal can even be a sign that diversity is *not* an institutional goal.

We could say that practitioners are given the goal of making diversity a goal. In most of my interviews, practitioners began their story with the story of their appointment. In the U.K. context, the appointment of officers is often about the appointment of a writer, of having someone who can write the policies that will effectively institutionalize a commitment to diversity.[6] Let's take the following account: "I came to [xxx] three and a half years ago and the reason that they appointed someone, I think, was because of the compliance with the Race Relations Amendment Act . . . you come into a position like this and people just don't know what kind of direction it's going to go in, you're not sort of, there's nobody helping to support you, this job does not have support mechanisms and you know maybe you're just there, because if you're not there then the university can't say that its dealing with legislation." An appointment becomes a story of not being given institutional support, as if being "just there" is enough. An appointment of a diversity officer can thus represent the absence of wider support for diversity.

The institutional nature of diversity work is often described in terms of the language of integrating or embedding diversity into the ordinary work or daily routines of an organization. As one practitioner explains, "My role is about embedding equity and diversity practice in the daily practice of this university. I mean, ideally I would do myself out of a job but I suspect that's not going to happen in the short term, so I didn't want to do that and I haven't got the staff or money to do it anyway." The diversity worker has a job because diversity and equality are not already given; this obvious fact has some less obvious consequences. When your task is to remove the necessity of your existence, then your existence is necessary for the task.

Practitioners partly work at the level of an engagement with explicit institutional goals, that is, of adding diversity to the terms in which institutions set their agendas—what we might think of as an institutional purpose or end. To agree on your aims is to offer an institutional attitude: a set of norms, values, and priorities that determine what is granted and how. Edmund Husserl suggests that "an attitude" means "a habitually fixed style of willing life comprising directions of the will or interests that are prescribed by this style, comprising the ultimate ends, the cultural accomplishments whose total style is thereby determined" ([1936/54] 1970: 280). To define or agree on the ends of an institution can thus shape what is taken for granted by it and within it. A phenomenology of institutions might be concerned with how these ends are agreed on, such that an individual accomplishment becomes an institutional accomplishment. An institution is given when there is an agreement on what should be accomplished, or what it means to be accomplished.

An institution gives form to its aims in a mission statement. If diversity work is institutional work, then it can mean working on mission statements, getting the term "diversity" included in them. This is not to say that a mission statement simply reflects the aims of the university: as Marilyn Strathern has shown, mission statements are "utterances of a specific kind" that mobilize the "international language of governance" (2006: 194–95). Giving form to institutional goals involves following a set of conventions. This is not to say that mission statements are any less significant for being conventional; the aim of a convention is still directive. When I participated in an equality and diversity committee, some of our discussions were based on how to get "equality" and "diversity" into the university's mission statement and other policy statements that were supposed to derive from it. We aimed not only to get the terms *in* but also to get them *up*: to get "equality" and "diversity" cited as high up the statement as possible. I recall the feeling of doing this work: in retrospect or in abstract, what we achieved might seem trivial (I remember one rather long discussion about a semicolon in a tag line!), but the task was still saturated with significance. The significance might be thought of as a distraction (you work on something you can achieve as a way of not focusing on—and thus being depressed by—what you cannot) but could also point to how institutional politics can involve the matter of detail; perhaps diversity provides a form of punctuation.

However, institutionalization was not simply defined by practitioners in terms of the formal or explicit goals, values, or priorities of an institution. Many spoke about institutionalization in terms of what institutions "tend to do," *whatever it is they say they are doing or should be doing.* The very idea of institutionalization might even denote those tendencies or habitual forms of action that are not named or made explicit. We can thus think of institutions in terms of how some actions become automatic at a collective level; institutional nature might be "second nature." When an action is incorporated by an institution, it becomes natural to it. Second nature is "accumulated and sedimented history," as "frozen history that surfaces as nature" (Jacoby 1975: 31).[7] When history accumulates, certain ways of doing things seem natural. An institution takes shape as an effect of what has become automatic. Institutional talk is often about "how we do things here," where the very claim of a "how" does not need to be claimed. We might describe institutionalization as "becoming background," when being "in" the institution is to "agree" with what becomes background (or we could speculate that an agreement is how things recede). This becoming background creates a sense of ease and familiarity, an ease that can also take the form of incredulity at the naiveté or ignorance of the newly arrived or outsiders. The familiarity of the institution is a way of inhabiting the familiar.

Institutionalization "comes up" for practitioners partly in their description of their own labor: diversity work is hard because it can involve doing *within* institutions what would not otherwise be done *by* them. As one interviewee describes, "You need persistence and I think that's what you need to do because not everyone has an interest in equity and diversity issues, so I think it needs to be up there in people's faces, well not right in their faces, but certainly up there with equal billing with other considerations, so that it's always present, so that they eventually think of it automatically and that it becomes part of their considerations." The aim is to make thought about equality and diversity issues "automatic." Diversity workers must be persistent precisely because this kind of thought is *not* automatic; it is not the kind of thought normally included in "how institutions think," to borrow an expression from the anthropologist Mary Douglas (1986). Or as Ole Elgström describes in a different but related context, such thoughts have to "fight their way into institutional thinking" (2000: 458). The struggle for diversity to become an institutional thought requires certain people to "fight their way." Not only this—the persistence required exists in necessary relation to the resistance encountered. The more you persist, the more the signs of this resistance. The more resistance, the more persistence required.

The institution can be experienced by practitioners *as* resistance. One expression that came up in a number of my interviews was "banging your head against a brick wall." Indeed, this experience of the brick wall was often described as an intrinsic part of diversity work. As one practitioner describes, "So much of the time it is a banging-your-head-on-the-brick-wall job." How interesting that a job description can be a wall description (see figure 1). The feeling of doing diversity work is the feeling of coming up against something that does not move, something solid and tangible.[8] The institution becomes that which you come up against. If we recall that most diversity practitioners are employed by institutions to do diversity (though not all: some have "equality" and "diversity" added to their job descriptions), then we can understand the significance of this description. The official desire to institutionalize diversity does not mean the institution is opened up; indeed, the wall might become all the more apparent, all the more a sign of immobility, the more the institution presents itself as being opened up. The wall gives physical form to what a number of practitioners describe as "institutional inertia," the lack of an institutional will to change.

Perhaps the habits of the institutions are not revealed unless you come up against them. When something becomes a habit, as the psychologist William James shows, it saves trouble and energy ([1890] 1950: 105):[9] you do not have to attend to something, it does not have to command your attention. In a classical work on the sociology of knowledge, Peter L. Berger and Thomas Luckmann identify the origins of institutionalization in the very mechanisms of habituation: "by providing a stable background in which human activity may proceed with a minimum of decision-making most of the time, it frees energy for such decisions as may be necessary on certain occasion. In other words, the *background* of habitualized activity opens up a *foreground* for deliberation and innovation" (Berger and Luckmann 1967: 71; emphasis added).[10] We can see the immediate difficulty of diversity work: to persist by making diversity into an explicit institutional end, by bringing diversity to the foreground, stops

Figure 1. A job description.

diversity from becoming habitual. While habits save trouble, diversity work creates trouble.

Diversity would be institutionalized when it becomes part of what an institution is already doing, when it ceases to cause trouble. Some universities in the United States now have "offices of institutional diversity." We need to stay surprised by this; we need the fact of such offices to be surprising. We need an account of the conditions in which such offices of institutional diversity make sense. In this formulation, the institutional is an adjective, as if institutional diversity is a particular kind of diversity. Such offices are also where institutional diversity happens: they institute institutional diversity. How does the institutional diversity get instituted? There is no doubt there is work involved. An example:

A commitment to diversity is an integral part of the University's educational mission. The institution's mission statement says in part that the University "endeavors to prepare the university community and the state for full participation in the global society of the 21st century.

Through its programs and practices, it seeks to foster the understanding of and respect for cultural differences necessary for an enlightened and educated citizenry." The mission of the Office of Institutional Diversity is to lead a focused institutional effort to evaluate existing programs and develop new initiatives to support diversity and equity at the University. The Office of Institutional Diversity seeks to ensure a University where people of many different backgrounds and perspectives join together to actively advance knowledge. As a community dedicated to scholarship, research, instruction, and public service and outreach, we recognize the importance of respecting, valuing and learning from each other's differences while seeking common goals. The Office of Institutional Diversity will provide the leadership to establish the University as a national and international model in creative ways to address diversity and equity issues in an academic setting.

Note how this statement directly quotes from the mission statement that describes the purpose of the institution. The Office of Institutional Diversity is set up by the institution to institute its commitment to diversity, proving leadership, shaping values, and enabling conversations. The office promotes a culture in which diversity is valued as part of an educational mission. The fact of this office is both an expression of the institution's commitment to diversity and how that commitment will be expressed. The office will "lead a focused institutional effort." To institutionalize diversity requires institutional effort within an institution. We might even say that the university *as* an institution will do diversity through what the office does; it provides the "institutional" in "institutional diversity."

To embed diversity within an institution involves working with the physicality of the institution: putting diversity into the organizational flow of things. I noticed how diversity practitioners often use the metaphor of the institution as an organic body. This metaphor has a long history as the idea of the social body (see Poovey 1995). The institution, in being imagined as an organic body, is understood as a singular entity made of multiple interrelated parts, all of which contribute to the health or well-being of that body.[11] Indeed, organic and mechanical metaphors are used simultaneously as ways of describing the institution. Both metaphors work to convey an entity that is made up of parts, where the communication between parts is essential to an overall performance. Structures of governance make an institution into a body or machine: there is a system of distribution, with paths that transfer materials to each part, each assumed to have their own function or purpose, each participating in the overall health of the body or machine. Practitioners do not simply aim for diversity to become part of an organizational body or machine; they want diversity *to go through the whole system.*

Diversity practitioners thus develop techniques for embedding diversity or making diversity given. As one practitioner described to me: "There are different ways that you can make diversity a given because it's actually part of the way you do things. Before it becomes that you have to recognize the value of it and I suppose that's what I mean by it becoming a given: the university is aware of the value of it on a range of levels and that it wants to benefit from the community of voices that can be heard and act through that diversity." This comment might remind us that all givens must become given. Perhaps when givens are given, we can forget about this becoming; to quote from Hannah Arendt, when something is given it "loses the air of contingency" (1978: 30).[12] If the task of embedding diversity is to find ways to make diversity become given, then diversity has an "air of contingency." Note as well that to make diversity a given requires achieving institutional recognition of the value of diversity. Such recognition involves an appreciation not only of the value of the term but also of a "community of voices." To value diversity is to value those who can "be heard and act" under its name.

To recognize diversity requires that time, energy, and labor be given to diversity. Recognition is thus material as well as symbolic: how time, energy, and labor are directed within institutions affects *how they surface.* Diversity workers aim to intervene in how the institution surfaces. Doing diversity work can mean passing "diversity" around, both *as* a word and *in* documents, as I discuss further in the following two chapters. As one practitioner describes, "I have a general circulation that goes to a diverse group of people, and if it doesn't get through one way it will get through another, by using about two or three different strategies of the circulation pool, in the end it must get there." Diversity work is about getting diversity into circulation, such that it can reach diverse people. Circulating diversity can be the aim of diversity work, which of course can bypass the question of what is being circulated. You get "it" out one way or another. Doing diversity requires expanding one's means of circulating information; for practitioners, diversity work is often about developing diverse communication strategies. We might even say that diversity workers *are* communication workers. You do diversity by working out how to circulate the matter of diversity around.

The importance of circulation systems to diversity work should not be underestimated. Arguably all institutional work involves the gradual refinement of systems for getting information through to those employed by the institution. My discussions with practitioners taught me that communication becomes an end as well as a means for certain kinds of work within universities. When your task is to get out information that is less valued by an organization, the techniques for moving information around become even more important. You have to persist because there is a resistance to the information getting through: to refer back to an earlier quote, "You need persistence and I think that's what you need to do because not everyone has an interest in equity and diversity issues." This practitioner usefully describes diversity work in terms of getting it "up there." Other practitioners talk about diversity work as putting stuff or material in the right places: "She is vigilant about constantly putting the stuff up on the table, so she is raising the awareness and putting it on the executive agenda so it's being seen to be part and parcel of university, so that I think is an extraordinarily important thing." To be part of the university requires tabling: diversity workers have to put stuff "on the table." I consider how the language of diversity offers a way of getting people to the table in the following chapter.

Organizations can be considered as modes of attention: what is attended to can be thought of as what is valued; attention is how some things come into view (and other things do not). Diversity work involves the effort of putting diversity into the places that are already valued so that diversity can come into view. Because "looking at equity groups is something that doesn't grab people's attention," practitioners suggest you have to "promote it" so that "it is about being cognizant of the diversity in front of you in a whole range of ways." One practitioner based in the United Kingdom describes her main problem as "competing for institutional attentions, the RAE[13] has been right in front of people's faces." Institutions have faces not simply in the sense that they are pictured but also in the sense that they have a direction; to have a direction is to face a certain way. To make diversity given thus requires institutional redirection.

Practitioners also describe their task as finding out who within the organization will speak up for diversity as a way of getting it into institutional conversations: "We've got some people on the senate, which is our governing body, and they have been interested in diversity. I don't think previously they ever saw it as particularly part and parcel of the central business of the university, so there's a combination of things that have happened. Since I've been here I've also totally restructured the university's equity and diversity committee structure. That has involved people at the senate level and debate at [the] senate about the university's equity and diversity strategies. That's put equity and diversity on the agenda for [the] senate in a way that it's never been before." Putting equality and diversity on the agenda can be about getting or keeping certain people in the important committees, as well as getting important people on the diversity committees. Having diversity people—those interested in diversity—in the governing bodies of the institution allows diversity to become "part and parcel" of what the institution is doing, to become "central business."

Diversity workers thus spend a lot of time identifying the people in an organization who are willing to speak up about diversity in meetings. They have to be very mobile: willing to speak to all university employees, willing to attend any meetings, at any time. One practitioner describes this labor in a vivid way: "Well you do, you do, and that's one of the things about our sort of jobs is that you are traveling around the university and you are in and out of many, many different forums and talking to all sorts of people, going to meetings that involve the vice chancellor or running a training program for teachers, you go across the whole range of the university and it can be quite challenging. . . . It is a unique position within the university, there's no other section of the university that is across the whole university in quite the same way that we are. You get sick of driving between campuses." Diversity work thus requires an intense form of phys-

May 24-28, 2010

DIVERSITY WEEK

OUR GLOBAL COMMUNITY

Figure 2. Diversity Weeks have become part of the official calendar of events. Graphic produced for the University of Queensland Diversity Week 2010. DESIGN BY JENELLE PHILLIPS, FROM THE UNIVERSITY'S OFFICE OF MARKETING AND COMMUNICATIONS.

ical and institutional mobility. To keep diversity moving, diversity workers have to be on the move.

Diversity workers thus align their own offices (if they have an office), and their own bodies, with the official lines of the institution. Diversity becomes physically embedded within the university through these multiple alignments: in some cases, leading to diversity weeks, prizes, and events becoming part of an official calendar of events (see figure 2). Diversity workers have to work with the organization as a physical body, working out the mechanisms of distribution through which it reproduces the conditions of its existence. This is why diversity workers are often extremely knowledgeable about how universities work, where things go, and where things get stuck. I am referring here not only to knowledge about the nature or character of specific institutions (which I discuss in more detail in the next chapter) but also to a more practical knowledge about the informal mechanisms and influences that allow some things to become institutional priorities rather than others. As one practitioner described, "There are informal influences that act as blocking agents that stop conversations from even taking place." Diversity workers are institutional plumbers: they develop an expertise in how and where things get stuck. Diversity strategies could be described as techniques for unblocking institutional blockages. The mechanical aspect of diversity work is revealed most explicitly when the institution is working: when diversity is blocked, institutional conversations stop diversity from becoming part of the conversation.

Institutional Whiteness

We learn from the pragmatics of organizations: how they circulate matter is a reflection of what matters. Diversity work is thus pragmatic work: you work with the very matter of an institution when you institutionalize diversity. How does diversity work relate to the project of challenging institutional whiteness? Nirmal Puwar argues that diversity has come "overwhelmingly to mean the inclusion of people who look different" (2004: 1). The very idea that diversity is about those who "look different" shows us how it can keep whiteness in place. If diversity becomes something that is added to organizations, like color, then it confirms the whiteness of what is already in place. Alternatively, as a sign of the proximity of those who "look different," diversity can expose the whiteness of those who are already in place. To diversify an institution becomes an institutional action insofar as the necessity of the action reveals the absence or failure of diversity.

Our diversity research team noticed this: the organization we worked for wanted to picture our team in picturing the organization. When our team was their picture, it created the impression that the organization was diverse. Arguably this was a false impression: the other teams were predominantly white. On the other hand, when our team was pictured, it helped expose the whiteness of the other teams. Even if diversity can conceal whiteness by providing an organization with color, it can also expose whiteness by demonstrating the necessity of this act of provision.

We need to think about the relationship between diversity and what we might call "institutional whiteness." We can think about how diversity involves a repicturing of an institution. The institution might not have an intrinsic character, but it is given character in part by being given a face. Diversity might create a new image of the institution or even a new institutional face. In the diversity world, there is a great deal of investment in images. Diversity might even appear as image, for example, in the form of the multicultural mosaic, as Elaine Swan (2010b) has carefully analyzed. An institutional image is produced in part for external others. The investment in diversity images might teach us about the importance of diversity as a way of managing the relationship between an organization and external others (as I explore later, diversity becomes a form of public relations).

Organizations manage their relation to external others by managing their image. This management can take the form of what speakers in a 2005 conference organized by the Commission for Racial Equality referred to as "perception data," that is, data collected by organizations about how they are perceived by external communities. In one interview with staff from a human resources department, we discussed such a research project:

> It was about uncovering perceptions, um, about the [xxx] as an employer. . . . [xxx] was considered to be an old boys' network, as they called it and white male–dominated and they didn't have the right perceptions of the [xxx] in terms of what it offers and what it brings to the academia. I think most of the external people had the wrong perceptions about the [xxx].

> And I mean, quotes, there were such funny quotes like librarians, they were sitting there with their cardigans you know. They were shocking reports to read, really, about how people, external people, perceive the [xxx] so we have to try to achieve. We have to try to make the [xxx] an attractive employer.

> There are issues of perception amongst certain communities, which are stopping them from reaching us.

Diversity work becomes about generating the "right image" and correcting the wrong one. I was quite interested that they were shocked by this image, given what I knew of the staffing profile of this university. What organizes this shock is the presumption that the perception is the problem. According to this logic, people have the "wrong perception" when they see the organization as white, elite, male, old-fashioned. In other words, behind the shock is a belief that the organization does not have these qualities: that whiteness is "in the image" rather than "in the organization." Diversity becomes about *changing perceptions of whiteness rather than changing the whiteness of organizations*. Changing perceptions of whiteness can be how an institution can reproduce whiteness, as that which exists but is no longer perceived.

I think the final comment, "there are issues of perception amongst certain communities, which are stopping them from reaching us," is particularly suggestive. The "certain communities" is an implicit reference to communities of color: race often appears under the euphemism of community, an appearance that is a disappearance (see Ahmed et al. 2006: 30). The implication is that the institution does not reach such communities—it does not include them—*because* they perceive the institution as excluding them. The problem of whiteness is thus redescribed here not as an institutional problem but as a problem with those who are not included by it.

What would it mean to talk about whiteness as an institutional problem or as a problem of institutions? When we describe institutions as being white, we point to how institutional spaces are shaped by the proximity of some bodies and not others: white bodies gather and create the impression of coherence. When I walk into university meetings, this is just what I encounter. Sometimes I get used to it. At one conference we organized, four Black feminists arrived. They all happened to walk into the room at the same time. Yes, we do notice such arrivals. The fact that we notice them tells us more about what is already in place than about "who" arrives. Someone says, "It is like walking into a sea of whiteness." This phrase comes up, and it hangs in the air. The speech act becomes an object, which gathers us around.

When an arrival is noticeable, we notice what is around. I look around and re-encounter the sea of whiteness. I had become so used to this whiteness that I had stopped noticing it. As many have argued, whiteness is invisible and unmarked, as the absent center against which others appear as points of deviation (Dyer 1997; Frankenberg 1993). Whiteness could be described as a habit insofar as it tends to go unnoticed (Sullivan 2006: 1).[14] Or perhaps whiteness is only invisible to those who inhabit it or those who get so used to its inhabitance that they learn not to see it, even when they are not it.

If we get used to inhabiting whiteness (it can be a survival strategy to learn not to see it, to learn not to see how you are not reflected back by what is around), it does not mean whiteness does not still affect us. One of the pleasures of doing this research was going to policy events on equality and diversity where I did *not* encounter a sea of whiteness.[15] I encountered a sea of brownness. I am well aware of the dangers of what Gayatri Chakravorty Spivak calls—in the context of a critique of the assumption of the "transformativity" of global feminism—"the body count" (2000: 128, see also Alexander 2005: 135). But numbers can be affective. It can be surprising and energizing not to feel so singular. When you inhabit a sea of brownness as a person of color, you might realize the effort of your previous inhabitance, the effort of not noticing what is around you. It is like how you can feel the "weight" of tiredness most acutely as the tiredness leaves you. To become conscious of how things leave you is to become conscious of those things. We might become even more aware of whiteness as wearing when we leave the spaces of whiteness.

The labor required to leave whiteness is also worth noting: in some institutional contexts, it is hard work not to reproduce the whiteness of events. I attended a conference on sexuality in 2011 that was a very white event (this is not unusual for academic events in the United Kingdom—whiteness is the norm). So, yes, I looked around the audience and encountered a sea of whiteness. The event was also structured around whiteness; all the plenary speakers were white. I had pointed out the problem with having all white plenary speakers to the conference organizers in advance of the event, hoping they might do something about it (but as I note in my conclusion, being asked to make up numbers after an event has been advertised can be a problem: we need not to be in the position of making such points or making up the numbers in the first place). When I turned up at the event, all the plenary speakers were white (is there a "still" before this "white"? Is whiteness something that can be described as "still"?). I was relieved that a black caucus had been set up by someone in the organizing team who was an activist of color; at the same time, I was cautious. Did giving the people of color a space allow the event to stay white? The caucus was explicitly framed as a space for all participants of color; whatever my caution, I was relieved to have the space when the time came; it can be tiring, all that whiteness.

What happened? Who turned up? All in all, ten people came to the black caucus, four of whom identified themselves as white. The organizer handed out a description of the event that made explicit that it was for people of color. No one left after reading the description. For understandable reasons, the organizer did not want to insist on anyone leaving. We sat in a circle and took turns speaking about why we had come to the event. I was very uncomfortable. I had expected this time and space to be a chance to talk to other people of color. It felt as if the one space we had been given—to take a break from whiteness—had been taken away. From the accounts offered, there were clearly different ways that white people had given themselves permission to turn up at a black caucus: being interested in questions of race; a sense of solidarity, alliance, and friendship; a desire to be at a workshop rather than a traditional academic session; a belief that race didn't matter because it shouldn't matter. Those of us of color tried hard—in different ways—to speak about why we wanted this event to be a person of color event. Someone mentions that it was interesting that a black caucus would have 40 percent white people; she used percentages, I think, because numbers can be affective. I talked about the relief of entering queer space after the fatigue of being in straight space as a way of making an implicit analogy, an appeal for recognition. Eventually, a white person left in recognition—and gave recognition—that we needed a space of relief from whiteness. A second person followed, but aggressively, saying we had made her unwelcome, forced her to leave. One by one the white people left, each offering an account of leaving, and a different account of why they had come. When the black caucus became itself, such joy, such relief! Such humor, such talk! What I learned from this occasion was the political labor that it takes to have spaces of relief from whiteness. I also realized the different ways that whiteness can be "occupying." Although the aggressive way of leaving was the most obviously difficult to deal with, we also need to account for the more sympathetic or caring ways of leaving the space. They may help us explore how whiteness can be occupying through or as care (what we might call simply a caring whiteness or even a sorry whiteness). I was struck how apology can be a form of permission: how apologizing for turning up at a person of color event as a white person might be a way of giving oneself permission to do so. The struggle against the reproduction of whiteness is a struggle against these forms of permission.

When bodies gather, it creates an impression. We can think of the "convene" in convention. A convention is a meeting point, a point around which bodies gather. Whiteness is a name we give to how some gatherings become conventions. Nirmal Puwar describes in *Space Invaders* (2004) how white bodies become somatic norms within spaces and how nonwhite bodies can feel "out of place" within those spaces. An institutional norm is a somatic norm when it takes the form of a white body. Institutional norms can refer to the explicit rules or norms of conduct enforced by an institution (through a system of awards and sanctions). If we think of institutional norms as somatic, then we can show how by assuming a body, institutions can generate an idea of appropriate conduct without making this idea explicit. The institute "institutes" the body that is instituting, without that body coming into view. If institutional whiteness describes an institutional habit, then whiteness recedes into the background.

Researching diversity involved me in lots of conversations about whiteness as a kind of surround or just as what is around. You can feel estranged from an around. In an informal conversation, one practitioner talked about her sense of alienation from her college. She talked about the experience of being surrounded by whiteness: "It's not just the people here now. They even name the buildings after dead vcs [vice chancellors]." Acts of naming, of giving buildings names, can keep a certain history alive: in the surroundings you are surrounded by who was there before. A history of whiteness can be a history of befores.

This practitioner also talked about a decision made by her institution to include photographs of the senior management team on the university website. The photographs were all of white men of a certain age. She relayed how when she was looking at the website, a friend of hers looked over her shoulder and asked, "Are they related?" When she told me this story, we couldn't stop laughing. There is a lot of humor in sharing the world of diversity, based on the shared recognition of and alienation from what is reproduced as an institutional given. An institutional logic can be understood as kinship logic: a way of "being related" and "staying related," a way of keeping certain bodies in place. Institutional whiteness is about the reproduction of likeness. Whiteness is a form of likeness that is not always revealed: precisely given that whiteness is often individuated or made "quirky."

Institutions are kinship technologies: a way of "being related" is a way of reproducing social relations. They also function to generate what we might call likability. It is not just a question of "being like" what an organization is like. It is not just an appearance of likeness that shapes the terms of an appearance. In an equal opportunities workshop I attended, someone made a comment that stuck with me. She said how a common talk during appointment panels is about whether such-and-such a candidate would "fit in" with the department. The measure of fitting in is indicated by the expression "the kind of person you could take down to the pub." Wanting to work with those who can inhabit a shared social space might seem like a rather ordinary aspiration. But the very desire for a shared social space can be a desire that *restricts to whom an institutional space is open* by imaging a social space that is not open to everyone. The likable candidate (the one we would like to "hang out" with) might be determined as a relation of likeness. In turn, the reference to a leisure space as a measure of recruitability shows how organizational habits are revealed in casual and informal conduct. When the rules are relaxed, we encounter the rules.

The institutionalization of whiteness involves work: the institution comes to have the form of a body as an effect of this work. It is important that we do not reify institutions by presuming they are simply given and that they decide what we do. Rather, institutions become given, as an effect of decisions made over time, which shapes the surface of institutional spaces. Recruitment functions as a technology for the reproduction of whiteness. We can recall that Althusser's model of ideology is based on recruitment:

> ideology "acts" or "functions" in such a way that it "recruits" subjects among the individuals (it recruits them all), or "transforms" the individuals into subjects (it transforms them all) by the very precise operation which I have called *interpellation* or hailing, and which can be imagined along the lines of the most commonplace everyday police (or other) hailing: "Hey you there." (1971: 163)

The subject is recruited by turning around, which immediately associates recruitment with following a direction, one that takes the line of an address. To recruit can suggest both to renew and to restore. The act of recruiting new bodies can restore the body of the institution. Becoming part of an institution, which we can consider as the demand to share in it or have a share of it, requires not only that one inhabits its buildings but that one follows its lines. We might start by saying "we"; by mourning its failures and rejoicing in its successes; by reading the documents that circulate within it, creating vertical and horizontal lines of communication; by the chance encounters we have with those who inhabit the grounds. To be recruited by an institution is not only to join up but also to sign up: to inhabit is to turn around as a return of its address.

Furthermore, recruitment creates the very idea of the institution, what it imagines as the ideal that working there means working toward. When we begin to think about the institutionalization of whiteness, we are asking how whiteness becomes the ideal of an organization. As scholars in critical management studies have shown us, organizations "tend to recruit in their own image" (Singh 2002: 3). One of the diversity workers I interviewed in Australia spoke directly about cloning as an institutional logic. As she describes: "Cloned groups are the people where we actually want to replicate ourselves and are only employing people who are like us because of our comfort zone and familiarity because we believe they are the same as us with that whole projecting stuff when actual fact they probably aren't—people do grow to be similar or more alike." The "hey you" is not just addressed to anybody: some bodies more than others are recruited, those that can inherit and reproduce the character of the organization, by reflecting its image back to itself, by having a "good likeness." There can be comfort in reflection. Note that there is an invitation in proximity—to become more alike, to acquire a better likeness. The word "comfort" suggests well-being and satisfaction, but it can also suggest an ease and easiness. Comfort is about an encounter between bodies and worlds, the promise of a "sinking" feeling. If white bodies are comfortable it is because *they can sink into spaces that extend their shape.*

To inhabit whiteness as a nonwhite body can be uncomfortable: you might even fail the comfort test. It can be the simple act of walking into the room that causes discomfort. Whiteness can be an expectation of who will turn up. A person of color describes: "When I enter the room there is shock on people's faces because they are expecting a white person to come in. I pretend not to recognize it. But in the interview there is unease because they were not expecting someone like me to turn up. So it is hard and uncomfortable and I can tell that they are uneasy and restless because of the way they fiddle and twitch around with their pens and their looks. They are uncomfortable because they were not expecting me—perhaps they would not have invited me if they knew I was black and of course I am very uncomfortable. I am wondering whether they are entertaining any prejudice against me" (cited in Ahmed et al. 2006: 77).[16] They are not expecting you. Discomfort involves this failure to fit. A restlessness and uneasiness, a fidgeting and twitching, is a bodily registering of an unexpected arrival.

The body that causes their discomfort (by not fulfilling an expectation of whiteness) is the one who must work hard to make others comfortable. You have to pass by passing your way through whiteness, by being seamless or minimizing the signs of difference. If whiteness is what the institution is oriented around, then even bodies that do not appear white still have to inhabit whiteness. One person of color describes how she minimizes signs of difference (by not wearing anything perceived as "ethnic") because she does not want to be seen as "rocking the boat" (cited in Ahmed et al. 2006: 78; see also chapter 5). The invitation to become more alike as an invitation of whiteness is about becoming more comfortable or inhabiting a comfort zone.

Bodies stick out when they are out of place. Think of the expression "stick out like a sore thumb." To stick out can mean to become a sore point, or even to experience oneself as being a sore point. To inhabit whiteness as a not-white body can mean trying not to appear at all: "I have to pretend that I am not here because I don't want to stick out too much because everybody knows I am the only black person here" (cited in Ahmed et al. 2006: 77). When you stick out, the gaze sticks to you. Sticking out from whiteness can thus reconfirm the whiteness of the space. Whiteness is an effect of what coheres rather than the origin of coherence. The effect of repetition is not then simply about a body count: it is not simply a matter of how many bodies are in. Rather, what is repeated is a very style of embodiment, a way of inhabiting space *by the accumulation of gestures of "sinking" into that space.* As George Yancy describes, "white bodies move in and out of these spaces with ease, paying no particular attention to their numbers or looking for bodies that resemble their own. They are at home" (2008: 40). If whiteness allows some bodies to move with comfort, to inhabit that space as home, those bodies take up more space.

It might seem problematic to describe whiteness as something we "pass through." Such an argument could make whiteness into something substantive, as if it has an ontological force of its own, which compels us and even "drives" action. It is important to remember that whiteness is not reducible to white skin or even to something we can have or be, even if we pass through whiteness. When we talk about a "sea of whiteness" or "white space," we talk about the repetition of the passing by of some bodies and not others. And yet nonwhite bodies do inhabit white spaces; we know this. Such bodies are made invisible when spaces appear white, at the same time as they become hypervisible when they do not pass, which means they "stand out" and "stand apart." You learn to fade in the background, but sometimes you can't or you don't.

That the arrival of some bodies is more noticeable than others reveals an expectation of who will show up. The word "expect" derives from the Latin verb *spectare*, "to look." An expectation of who will turn up is not only an expectation of how they will look but also a looking for or a looking out for. An expectation can be hopeful and directive. If you expect such-and-such to turn up, and they turn up, an expectation has been met.

Diversity can also involve a "looking out for." A typical statement in a job advertisement for public sector organizations is "women and ethnic minorities encouraged to apply," although this mode of address is increasingly changing to a tagline such as "xxx is an equal opportunities employer," or even "xxx promotes diversity." I suspect, however, that the tagline preserves the implication of the address it replaces, conveying without naming the minority subject. The logic exercised here is one of "welcoming," premised on a distinction between the institution as host and the potential employer as guest. To be made welcome by an explicit act of address works to reveal what is implicit: that those who are already given a place are *the ones who are welcoming* rather than welcomed, the ones who are in the structural position of hosts.

The logic often used when diversity is institutionalized could be described in terms of "conditional hospitality" (Derrida 2000: 73; Rosello

2001): the other (the stranger, foreigner) is welcomed with conditions or on condition.[17] Rauna Johanna Kuokkanen describes how the academy "presents itself as a welcoming host but not without conditions" (2007: 131). When diversity becomes a form of hospitality, perhaps the organization is the host who receives as guests those who embody diversity. Whiteness is produced as host, as that which is already in place or at home. To be welcomed is to be positioned as the one who is not at home. Conditional hospitality is when you are welcomed on condition that you give something back in return. The multicultural nation functions this way: the nation offers hospitality and even love to would-be citizens as long as they return this hospitality by integrating, or by identifying with the nation (see Ahmed 2004: 133–34). People of color in white organizations are treated as guests, temporary residents in someone else's home. People of color are welcomed *on condition* they return that hospitality by integrating into a common organizational culture, or by "being" diverse, and allowing institutions to celebrate their diversity.

I am speaking of whiteness at a seminar. Someone in the audience says, "But you are a professor," as if to say when people of color become professors then the whiteness of the world recedes.[18] If only we had the power we are imagined to possess, if only our proximity could be such a force. If only our arrival could be an undoing. I was appointed to teach "the race course," I reply. I am the only person of color employed on a full-time permanent basis in the department. I hesitate. It becomes too personal. The argument is too hard to sustain when your body is so exposed, when you feel so noticeable. I stop and do not complete my response.

When our appointments and promotions are taken up as signs of organizational commitment to equality and diversity, we are in trouble. Any success is read as a sign of an overcoming of institutional whiteness. "Look, you're here!" "Look, look!" Our talk about whiteness is read as a form of stubbornness, paranoia, or even melancholia as if we are holding onto something (whiteness) that our arrival shows has already gone. Our talk about whiteness is read as a sign of ingratitude, of failing to be grateful for the hospitality we have received by virtue of our arrival. This very structural position of being the guest, or the stranger, the one who receives hospitality, allows an act of inclusion to maintain the form of exclusion.

Institutional Racism

Institutional whiteness can be reproduced through the logic of diversity. To recognize the institutionality of whiteness remains an important goal of antiracist work, as does the recognition of institutional racism. We need to keep alive the question of why institutionality is something that needs to be recognized. We also need to ask what is being recognized in such recognition.

The struggle to recognize institutional racism can be understood as part of a wider struggle to recognize that all forms of power, inequality, and domination are systematic rather than individual. The critique of the psychologizing of racism made by antiracist scholars and activists over generations is thus part of the struggle to recognize institutional racism (see Hesse 2004). In other words, racism should not be seen as about individuals with bad attitudes (the "bad apple model"), not because such individuals do not exist (they do) but because such a way of thinking underestimates the scope and scale of racism, thus leaving us without an account of how racism *gets reproduced*. The argument can be made in even stronger terms: the very identification of racism *with* individuals becomes a technology for the reproduction of racism *of* institutions. So eliminating the racist individual would preserve the racism of the institution in part by creating an illusion that we are eliminating racism. Institutions can "keep their racism" by eliminating those whom they identify as racists.

The definition of institutional racism that is widely accepted in the United Kingdom is offered in the Macpherson Report (1999) into racism within the police force, the product of an inquiry into how the police handled the murder of a black male teenager, Stephen Lawrence. That the police handling of the murder became the occasion for the recognition of institutional racism is crucial: the report argues that how the police responded to the murder was not simply a product of racist attitudes held by individual police but was the result of racism within the police force *as such*. To quote from the report, institutional racism amounts to "the collective failure of an organization to provide an appropriate and professional service to people because of their colour, culture, or ethnic origin. It can be seen or detected in processes, attitudes and behaviour which amount to discrimination through unwitting prejudice, ignorance, thoughtlessness and racist stereotyping which disadvantage minority ethnic people" (1999: 28; see Solomos 1999).

A politics of recognition is also about definition: if we recognize something such as racism, we also offer a definition of that which we recognize. In this sense, recognition produces rather than simply finds its object; recognition delineates the boundaries of what it recognizes as given. In this report, the definition of an institution as racist involves recognition of the collective rather than individual nature of racism. But it might also foreclose what is meant by "collective" by finding evidence of that collectivity only in what institutions fail to do. In other words, the report defines institutional racism in such a way that racism is *not seen* as an ongoing series of actions that shape institutions, in the sense of the norms that get reproduced or posited over time. We might want to consider racism as a form of doing or even a field of positive action, rather than a form of inaction. For example, we might wish to examine how institutions become white through the positing of some bodies rather than others as the subjects of the institution (for whom and by whom the institution is shaped). Racism would not be evident in what we fail to do but in what we have already done, whereby this "we" is an effect of the doing. The recognition of institutional racism within the Macpherson Report reproduces the whiteness of institutions by seeing racism simply as the failure "to provide" for nonwhite others because of their difference.

We might notice how a psychological language creeps into the definition: "processes, attitudes and behaviour which amount to discrimination through unwitting prejudice, ignorance, thoughtlessness and racist stereotyping." In a way, the institution becomes recognized as racist only through being posited as *like an individual*, as someone who *suffers* from prejudice and who can be treated, so that he or she can act better toward racial others. If the institution becomes an individual, then the institution can also *take the place of individuals*: the institution is the bad person, rather than this person or that person. In other words, the transformation of the collective into an individual (a collective without individuals) might allow individual actors to refuse responsibility for collective forms of racism. Les Back observes, "There is something in the blanket assertions of institutional racism that is somehow comforting for its speakers" (2004: 4).

We can be comforted by blankets; they provide us with a cover. Back (2004) and Shona Hunter (forthcoming) focus on the problem of the use of the adjective "unwitting." Even if "unwitting" is used to make sense of how racism often bypasses individual consciousness and intentionality (by thinking about whiteness as a habit formation), the language of unwitting can also allow individuals to refuse responsibility for racism. Back suggests that "the unwitting notion of racism somehow abrogates responsibility like a racist playground spat 'I didn't mean anything by it' " (2004: 4). In the case of higher education, I suspect that the risks of disidentification are particularly high: disidentification from racism can take place via disidentification from "the institutional." It is not only that individuals can respond by saying "I didn't mean anything by it," but they also might not see themselves as involved "in it" at all. This refusal might take place given that individuals already tend to disidentify from institutions: if the institution is the racist subject, then tolerant and liberal academics can easily imagine that they are not. The recognition of institutional racism can become a technology of reproduction of the racism of individuals.

Solutions to problems can create new problems. There is more to say about the consequences of institutional racism becoming an "institutional admission." I am uneasy about what it means for a subject or institution to admit to racism. If racism is shaped by actions that are not seen by those who are its beneficiaries, what does it mean for those beneficiaries to see it? We could suppose that the definition restricts racism to what we can see: it claims that racism "can be seen or detected" in certain forms of behavior. I suggest the declaration might work by claiming to see racism (in what the institution fails to do) *and* by maintaining the definition of racism as unseeing. If racism is defined as unwitting and collective prejudice, then the claim to be racist by being able to see racism in this or that form of practice is also a claim not to be racist in the same way. The paradoxes of admitting to one's own racism are clear: saying "we are racist" becomes a claim to have overcome the conditions (unseen racism) that require the speech act in the first place. We say "we are or have been racist," and insofar as we are witting about racism (and racists are unwitting), then we show "we are not racist," or at least not racist *in the same way*.

We are witnessing some of the paradoxes that follow when institutional racism becomes part of institutional language. Indeed, I argue that the recognition of institutional racism can easily be translated into a form of *institutional therapy culture*—where the institution becomes the sick person who can be helped by receiving the appropriate treatment. When institutions recognize institutional racism, it is as if they are making a confession. The institution, "having confessed" to racism, might be understood as on the road to recovery. A recovery from racism can even be a way of "recovering" racism, as if admitting to racism is a way of getting over it.[19] Admission implies "getting over it," or even "being over it." I develop this argument further by thinking through how diversity offers a language of reparation in chapter 5.

The problems of recovery narratives are evident if you consider comments made by Trevor Phillips on institutional racism on January 19, 2009, during an interview with the BBC to mark the tenth anniversary of the Macpherson Report. Phillips said: "The Stephen Lawrence Inquiry was a great shock to the system. It shook people out of their complacency and meant that we had new laws and a new attitude and that meant for example that the police have changed their behaviour quite dramatically. Nothing's perfect, there is still a lot of work to do, but we are in a different place than we were before."[20] The recognition of institutional racism becomes shock therapy, leading to the adoption of new attitudes and new behavior. The institutions are "shocked" out of racism, "shaken" out of complacency. Phillips offers what we could call a before-and-after narrative: the very recognition of institutional racism offered in the report means that we are no longer in that place it described; we are in a new place. In other words, the institution in being shocked into recognizing its racism is no longer racist. For Phillips, "the we" of the police slides immediately into "the we" of the nation: "We are in a new situation. Britain is a modern diverse country. Britain is the best place to live in Europe if you're not white." The "shock" of recognizing institutional racism is what allows us to recover from racism.

Note also how the recognition of institutional racism is converted into an expression of pride: diversity pride as national pride (a "modern diverse country" that is "the best place to live in Europe if you are not white"). In an essay on multiculturalism published in 2008, Trevor Phillips suggests that diversity is indeed a national attribute, such that when racism occurs the nation is acting "out of character." As he describes: "Historically we are diverse, open-minded, and anti-racist. But every now and again we forget our true character." When diversity becomes a view of the nation, racism not only recedes but becomes understood as a distortion of the truth (it does not express our truth).

In this narrative, racism is projected onto strangers; racists are estranged from national character (if we are racist, then we are unlike ourselves). Racism also becomes understood as accidental (as if every now and then, it just happens) as well as being anachronistic, a sign of a time that is no longer, as that which plays no part in contemporary British experience or even as that which was never British. In the BBC interview about the police and racism, Phillips suggested that most people in Britain are not racist because they "wouldn't have a problem" having a person with a different ethnicity as their neighbor. Thus, he said, "the blanket accusation 'institutional racism' no longer quite helps us to understand what is going on." For Phillips, any racism within an institution is explained as not really "going on," even when it is ongoing: "In many of our institutions, there are still old-fashioned attitudes that don't really catch up with where modern Britain is at and how British people today feel. That's the next task that we've got to tackle." In this description, racism becomes what is "old-fashioned" *as if it lingers only insofar as institutions are not expressing what is in fashion.* Institutional racism becomes what is out of fashion, no longer a description of where we are or where we want to be. We learn from this: if we recognize the institutional nature of racism, this recognition is not a solution. Institutionality can simply be redefined such that it no longer refers to the processes it was introduced to describe.

I have spoken of "institutional racism" primarily in terms of what an institution might recognize. The language of institutional racism can become part of institutional language without being offered as a form of recognition. One diversity practitioner I interviewed in the United Kingdom mentioned that the phrase "institutional racism" was adopted in her organization's race equality policy. She spoke of getting the term into the policy as an achievement:

> I think that it's very useful that the university formally signs itself up to the Macpherson definition of institutional racism.
>
> Does it define itself as institutionally racist?
>
> We don't say that, we just say the university supports that definition. And a definition of a racist incident, those definitions are there. So in that sense they are useful that they are available where there is a difficult situation.

If the organization "supports the definition," then the definition can give support in situations of organizational trouble. The use of the definition within the university's own documents allows practitioners to have a reference point when dealing with racism in particular situations. In other words, the inclusion of the definitions allows the phrase "institutional racism" to be adopted in "difficult situations" when racism comes up.

This was the only interview in which "institutional racism" was brought up. At one level, this is not surprising: even to name racism is to describe a series of actions that the organization is not allowed to permit. To bring up racism is to bring up the issue of compliance and even suggest a failure to comply. This means that the term "institutional racism" brings up as well as describes a difficulty. Perhaps the unease with this term persists *despite* this culture of institutional admission, such that it is not a term exercised with much consistency in institutional self-description or in the descriptions of practitioners.

Researching diversity is attending to what does and does not come up in accounts of institutional life. It means showing *how* institutions matter. My task in the following chapters is to consider what the institutionalization of diversity means for those employed as diversity workers (*doing diversity*) or those whose arrival is coded as a sign of diversity, such as people of color (*being diversity*). What does it mean to have a body that provides an institution with diversity? I have begun with the question of what it means to institutionalize diversity. My aim has been to show that institutions should not be treated as the social actors. Institutions provide a frame in which things happen (or don't happen). To understand how "what happens" happens, we actually need to narrow (rather than widen) the frame: to think about words, texts, objects, and bodies, to follow them around, to explore what they do and do not do, when they are put into action.

The previous chapter explored how practitioners experience institutions as resistant to their work, even though they are employed by those institutions to "do diversity." This resistance is often described through the metaphor of the brick wall. Diversity work can be all the more frustrating because the frustrations are difficult to explain; diversity workers encounter obstacles that are often not visible to other staff with whom they work. Frustration is by no means the only way practitioners experience institutionality, but the repetition of accounts of frustration might point to how diversity work can take the form of repeated encounters with what does not, and seemingly will not, move.

Yet at the same time, diversity as a term seems ubiquitous. As Nirmal Puwar notes, "The language of diversity is today embraced as a holy mantra across different sites. We are told that diversity is good for us. It makes for an enriched multicultural society" (2004: 1). The language of diversity certainly appears in official statements (from mission statements to equality policy statements, in brochures, as taglines) and as a repertoire of images (collages of smiling faces of different colors), which are easily recognizable *as* images of diversity. "Diversity" can be used as an adjective, as a way of describing the organization, a quality, or an attribute of an organization. The language of diversity can also be used normatively, as an expression of the priorities, values, or commitments of an organization. The descriptive and normative uses of diversity are not unrelated. As Gavan Titley and Alana Lentin suggest, diversity's "apparent descriptiveness is central to its normative character: diversity implies a value-based project of transformation towards the irreducible and irrevocable" (2008: 11). After all, descriptions are not neutral: describing an organization as being diverse also indicates the values of that organization (even if it is not self-evident what the value of diversity refers to, as I show in due course). My aim in this chapter is to explore what might in the first instance appear to be a paradox between, on the one hand, the routine uses of the language of diversity by institutions and, on the other, the experience of many practitioners of an institutional resistance to diversity becoming routine. We can turn the paradox into a question: how does the institutional will to diversity[1] relate to the institutional wall? Or more simply: how does will become wall?

To answer these questions, we need an account of how the word "diversity" arrives, how diversity becomes part of routine description. The term "diversity" has been understood as a replacement term, taking the place of earlier terms such as "equal opportunities" or "antiracism."[2] We cannot simply explain these changes of vocabulary in terms of internal developments within the equalities sector. There is a great deal of suspicion within this sector that the term "diversity" is an import. It is even talked about as a foreign term. In particular, critics suggest that the increasing use of the language of diversity reflects the spread of a U.S. managerial discourse (Kandola and Fullerton 1994; Deem and Ozga 1997; Kirton and Greene 2000; Benschop 2001; Lorbiecki 2001; Blackmore and Sachs 2003). The use of "diversity" within universities has been treated as a symptom of what academics have called the "corporatization of the university," as we can note from a title of a chapter in Mike Hill's (2004) book on whiteness: "the multiversity diversity."

The shift to the language of diversity could thus be understood in market terms; diversity has a commercial value and can be used as a way not only of marketing the university but of making the university into a marketplace. Others have called this the "Benetton model" of diversity, in which diversity becomes an aesthetic style or a way of "rebranding" an organization (Lury 2000: 147; Titley and Lentin 2008).[3] More specifically, and perhaps given the widespread use of "business case" arguments for diversity within public and private sector organizations, "diversity" has been identified as a management term. Diversity becomes something to be managed and valued as a human resource. Scholars have suggested that the managerial focus on diversity works to individuate differences and conceal the continuation of systematic inequalities within universities. For Deem and Ozga, the word "diversity" invokes difference but does not necessarily evoke commitment to action or redistributive justice (1997: 33). What is problematic about diversity, by implication, is that it can be "cut off" from the programs that seek to challenge inequalities within organizations and might even take the place of such programs in defining the social mission of universities. For Benschop, the word does not make the right kind of appeal, because it does not appeal so powerfully to "our sense of social justice" (2001: 1166). For these scholars, among others, the institutional preference for the term "diversity" is a sign of the lack of commitment to change and might even allow organizations such as universities to conceal the operation of systematic inequalities. As Himani Bannerji argues, the language of diversity might have efficacy as a "coping mechanism for dealing with an actually conflicting heterogeneity" (2000: 37). Diversity could be understood as one of the techniques by which liberal multiculturalism manages differences by managing its more "troublesome constituents" (Fleras 2011: 121).[4] Diversity can thus function as a containment strategy.

My discussion of the languages of diversity is indebted to these important critiques. Not only do they provide a political horizon for my discussion, but many of the practitioners I interviewed share this horizon: they are aware of (and in some cases suspicious about) the institutional appeal of the language of diversity. Rather than focusing on how the language of diversity arrives into educational organizations, I want to discuss how the languages of diversity are mobilized in various ways by different actors within them. My aim is to give a sense of the complex and multiple ways those involved in diversity work actually work (or in some cases don't work) with the term "diversity."

Official Diversity

"Official diversity" refers not just to the use of diversity by officials but also to how diversity acquires the status of official description. In this section I consider diversity as an "institutional speech act," drawing on John Austin's book *How to Do Things with Words* (1975). Austin's title is evocative— suggesting not only that words have the potential to do things but also that there are instructions to be followed; we can acquire the know-how that might enable us to exercise this potentiality (in the form of the "how to"). Austin appears to de-limit the potentiality of words by suggesting that some utterances do things and others do not. He distinguishes between descriptive or constative utterances, which report on something, and performative utterances, which do something (though, as we shall see, this distinction does not hold). A descriptive utterance reports on something, which might be true or false. In contrast, a performative utterance does not report something: "it indicates that the issuing of the utterance is the performing of an action" (Austin 1975: 6). If constative statements can be true or false, performative statements, Austin suggests, are happy or unhappy; they can succeed or fail depending on the circumstances of their utterance (for example, an apology would be unhappy if the speaker was insincere, or if a person who declared x did not have the authority to make the declaration).

Austin's discussion is restricted to specific kinds of speech acts, those that take the form of the first-person singular. I want to expand the terms of his analysis by considering what I call "institutional speech acts." An institutional speech act would typically take the form of the first-person plural. Even though it might be spoken by an individual, such as a vice chancellor, it would be an institutional speech act if that person is speaking for or even as the institution. An institutional speech might make claims *about* an institution, as well as on *behalf* of an institution. Such speech acts might involve naming: the institution is named, and in being given a name, it is also given attributes, qualities, and even character. Institutional speech acts, in making claims about the institution (for instance, by describing the institution as having certain qualities, such as being diverse), might also point toward future action (by committing an institution to a course of action). They might say "the university regrets," or simply "we regret." They might also say "the university is diverse" or just "we are diverse." If the former case seems to indicate an attitude or feeling, what does the latter case say or do?

At first glance, it would seem that the speech act "we are diverse" is a constative utterance. The "business" of the statement is to describe "some state of affairs" (Austin 1975: 1). Diversity utterances would thus be verifiable statements; they could be measured in terms of their truth value. The utility of equal opportunities data can be understood at least partly in terms of how data can be used to test the validity of diversity as a constative utterance. For example, data is used to demonstrate whether staff or students come from diverse backgrounds. In one conversation during an equal opportunities meeting, we talked about how data could be used to show "how white" the university was. In other words, we wanted the data to challenge the use of diversity as a description. One practitioner I interviewed used data to expose that the university at which she was employed was failing its "strong ethos" of being a diversity-led institution to make clear that "it actually can't afford not to move into a leadership role in those areas." In other words, data is used as a technology for exposing the failure of the university to live up to its use of diversity as self-description: "Yeah, yeah, it's embarrassing when it goes up." Data becomes a technology for exposing the gap between official descriptions of diversity and what the organization is doing.[5] In chapter 4, I explore the significance of this gap between "saying" and "doing" for how we can understand institutional power.

The speech act "we are diverse," however, does not simply take the form of a constative utterance, partly because it is unclear what the word "diversity" is describing. This lack of clarity might not be specific to diversity but may reveal the very trouble with description. Austin shows how constative utterances are not straightforward: "Once we realise that what we have to study is *not* the sentence but the issuing of the utterance in a speech-situation, there can hardly be any longer a possibility of not seeing that stating is performing an act" (1975: 139).[6] Even to state something can be doing something, for example, a statement can be an affirmation: it can affirm the existence of what is stated. What a statement is doing will be dependent on the situation in which it is made. In different situations the same words will have a different force. As a result, it is impossible to distinguish between utterances *at the level of the sentence*. If we do things with words (*by* or *in* saying something), then what those words do depends on the circumstances in which they are said. For Austin, given his concern with first-person singular utterances, circumstances are restricted to what he calls the "speech-situation." In the case of institutional speech acts, the institution is not only the subject and object of the sentence (insofar as the one who is speaking is speaking for or as the institution as well as about it) but also the situation in which the speech act takes place. The taking up of an utterance (what allows it to be happy or unhappy) would depend not only on other actors (who might or might be not the addressee) but also on the institutional culture, on how words that are spoken then circulate, and whether or how an institution is modified by the utterance.

I suggest that the performative aspects of what are apparently descriptive utterances are more explicable if we focus on the institution. What is created by the description of the university as diverse might be the very idea of a university as being diverse, which as an idea then circulates within the community that is being described. The "diverse university" becomes a shared object, if others within the university repeat the description; the repetition of the utterance gives it force. We could think of process in terms of the generation of a public. Michael Warner argues that a public exists *"by virtue of being addressed"* (2002: 67, emphasis in original). To address a public is to generate a public that can be addressed. The circularity of this logic, Warner suggests, is essential to the phenomenon of the public. Diversity becomes a public by virtue of being given as an address. The vice chancellor who speaks of diversity is in turn "citing" a convention of speaking.[7] The circular logic of an address is the basis of diversity as a circulating system. The circulation of the word "diversity" creates the very idea of "the diverse institution," and in turn, this idea gives the word "diversity" its circulatibility.

It is important to note that even if diversity acquires currency, it is not, as I suggested earlier, ubiquitous. The word "diversity" appears as if it is everywhere, but that appearance might be part of what it is doing. Actually, the word "diversity" is far from everywhere. Even a cursory glance at typical university mission statements confirms this: certainly some universities refer explicitly to diversity in the opening preambles of statements, but many do not. Diversity usually appears under the specific heading of equality or as a heading in its own right. I offer a reflection on the status of equality policies as documents in the following chapter. What interests me here is the implied relation between an overall mission statement and the equality statement.

For example, one university has the following as the opening sentence of its mission: "The mission of the [xxx] is to contribute to society through the pursuit of education, learning, and research at the highest international levels of excellence." The opening sentence of its equality statement is: "The [xxx] is committed in its pursuit of academic excellence to equality of opportunity and to a pro-active and inclusive approach to equality, which supports and encourages all under-represented groups, promotes an inclusive culture, and values diversity." Here the relation between the university mission and the diversity mission is explicit: diversity becomes one means for pursuing its prior end of excellence; diversity becomes a technology for this pursuit. So "in its" pursuit of excellence, the university values diversity. I return to the relationship between diversity and excellence in the next chapter. What I want to note here is how in official language, the word "diversity" derives its value from what is already valued. Diversity is incorporated as an official term insofar as it is made consistent with the organization's goals. I have already noted how putting the word "diversity" into circulation becomes a key aim of diversity work. But the incorporation of diversity into description can also pose a problem for diversity workers. The use of diversity as an official description *can be* a way of maintaining rather than transforming existing organizational values.

When diversity becomes a routine description, what is reproduced can be the routine of this description. Statements like "we are diverse" or "we embrace diversity" might simply be what organizations say because that is what organizations are saying. We might call this the "lip service" model of diversity. Diversity becomes a convention, or a conventional way of speaking about the university. Diversity becomes a ritualized or polite speech. Austin argues that such forms of speech have "nothing to do with the performative" (1975: 81). I suggest that official uses of diversity might be performative in a conventional sense: they bring about the convention of speaking in this way. When it becomes a convention to speak about the organization as diverse, then the speech act maintains a convention.

When diversity becomes a conventional form of speech, what is being named as diverse becomes less significant than the name "diversity." In one meeting in Australia that I attended, a practitioner talked about how diversity was being used to refer to flora and fauna. Institutional diversity becomes eco diversity. This mobility of the word "diversity" means that it is unclear what diversity is doing, even when it is understood as a convention of speech. Diversity might be more easily incorporated into official speech because it can be used as a description or affirmation of anything. A vice chancellor, as part of an address to the Universities U.K. Annual Conference, said: "This brings me to the matter of diversity. Our universities make a broad contribution to the world. These contributions are made by a diversity of institutions." Here, diversity becomes a value of a sector: the sector is diverse because institutions are diverse in the sense that they differ from each other. Diversity becomes movable as a quality (of the sector, of the institution, of the people in the institution, and so on). The mobility of the word might have something to do with the ease with which it can be incorporated into official language.

However diversity is used, it seems to be used as a way of accruing value, as what adds value to something. Perhaps diversity creates something by adding value. A director of personnel said to me: "And we have a very diverse student body, don't we? Our student body is the body that is extremely diverse. It comes from so many different countries and things." We learn from this description how diversity can become an attribute, which is how a singular body is created (if students come from diverse countries, then they can be apprehended and thus treated *as* a diverse body). Diversity in being attributed creates a certain kind of body. Interestingly, as a technique of attribution, diversity can become a container: allowing the presentation of a body as unified in its diversity.

Diversity thus involves the aesthetic realm of appearance, as well as the moral realm of value. It creates a body that can be seen and valued as a diverse body. Official descriptions are part of an aesthetic and moral order: *an appearance of valuing*. Perhaps the significance of official description lies with the officials: diversity might matter less in terms of the content of the speech act and more in terms of who is speaking or the authority of who is speaking. Many diversity practitioners spoke of the value of diversity being spoken about by officials, whether or not those officials were committed to diversity: "People know that if the vice chancellor isn't saying the right things then they don't have to, either." Diversity becomes about "saying the right things," such that the official speech creates a cultural requirement about what can and cannot be said. When the official speaks the language of diversity, then others must also speak that language. To value diversity would mean: to make diversity the right way to speak.

Once diversity is the right way to speak, it accrues value. One practitioner notes: "If the vice president is saying it then it stops it being a bad word then, doesn't it?" A key task of the diversity worker is to get the word "diversity" spoken by the right people, so that the word can move down the organization. Or as another practitioner describes: "if they are saying it's important, then people further down the chain, who are actually going to be doing the work, because let's face it, it's never going to be the vice chancellor and the pro vice chancellor actually doing the work on equality issues, they are just going to be telling someone else to do it. People further down just hear that message of 'yes, this is important,' and the people higher up think this is important. I think it's better if they do understand it as well, but for me the most important thing is for the leadership to be saying it's important." When those who *are* important say diversity *is* important, diversity can *acquire* importance.

If those with authority speak of diversity, then an institutional culture is generated around the word. In circulating, words create lines and pathways in their trail. Once a pathway is created, we tend to follow its trail.[8] When officials give diversity value or use diversity to describe the values of the institution, it gives the term somewhere to go: "When the senior leadership is in tune, is keyed into a certain set of issues . . . that filters down the line and people get to know about it, it gets discussed, they don't value it, people down the line don't value it, or if they do, it doesn't translate into organizational culture because there's nowhere for it to go." When words such as "diversity" get repeated by officials, becoming official words, they acquire a life; they have further to go. What is being achieved by the mobility of these terms remains another question.

The Diversity Word

Talking with practitioners about the language of diversity enabled me to understand how words have institutional lives. Because diversity work can mean working against an institutional defense system, diversity work often involves becoming self-conscious about words to find ones that can "get through." Words become tools or means of doing something.[9] To work *with* words is to work *through* their associations: words can be more and less affective depending on their associations. Thinking about associations is what allows us to interrogate the circumstances of speaking about diversity or in the language of diversity beyond the restricted idea of a speech situation: when words are near other words, this is a sign of their saturation and thus of their past associations. A history of affect is that which does not need to be revealed to be affective. Proximities not only exist between words but, as I will show, suggest an intimate relation between words and bodies.

Almost all the practitioners I spoke to use the language of diversity. My opening set of questions in the interviews was simply to ask about the word itself: why do they use this word, how do they use this word, and what does this word mean to them? Some practitioners suggest that they use the term "diversity" because it is the term in use. The appeal of the term might point to a circularity or loop: we use diversity because it is being used; it is being used because we use it. It is important to note that this circularity is not specific to diversity but describes the slippery phenomena of what we might simply call linguistic fashion: words come in and out of use by being used or not being used. Institutional knowledge can be defined as knowledge of fashion: knowing which words are most popular is about how one can be affectively aligned with others. One practitioner observes: "I would say that the term 'diversity' is just used now because it's more popular. You know it's in the press, so why would we have equal opportunities when we can just say it's diversity?" We can "just say it's diversity" if diversity is "just used now." When words are popular—measured in terms of what is "in the press"—they become available and useful.

Part of this appeal of diversity seems to be about newness. Using a newer word allows you to be aligned with the value system of the institution given that "newness" is often what is given value. "Diversity" as a newer word is a buzzword: what we can hear might be the sound of its busy-ness. Potentially, then, the buzz of diversity might be how it cancels out other noise, such as the noise of racism (for a discussion of racism as noise, see chapter 5).

The story of diversity's arrival is thus also a story of recession, of how other terms have lost their appeal, becoming old, tired, and dated:

> I think it [equity] became a tired term because it was thrown around a lot and I think . . . well I don't know . . . because our title is equity and social justice, somebody the other day was saying to me "oh there's equity fatigue, people are sick of the word equity." . . . oh well okay we've gone through equal opportunity, affirmative action—they are sick of equity—now what do we call ourselves?! They are sick of it because we have to keep saying it because they are not doing it [laughs].

The tiredness or even "sickness" with the old terms is here a symptom of a certain institutional reluctance: you have to repeat the terms because they are not doing it; they are not doing it because you are repeating them. The implication of the arguments about equity fatigue is that in using less tired words, practitioners might themselves be energized or perceived as more energetic: "those terms had got tired and I think that there's a bit of 'if one thing gets tired, looks like you've got tired as well.'" If you can become tired by your association with tired words, then the word "diversity" offers a way of appearing or even being less tired. This practitioner goes on to say: "you're put in a position where you have to say these things because nobody else will say them. People don't listen to you because you're the one who's saying it." You keep saying it because they are not saying it. The tiredness is part of the loop of repetition: you use the terms more and more because they are not working, and they are not working because you use them more and more. For this practitioner, diversity offers a way out of the loop of repetition. But it does not necessarily resolve the problem of the loop. The implication of this argument is that certain words get heavy or acquire baggage from their use: they get weighed down by their associations. The weightiness that words acquire means that the more they circulate, the less they can do. "Diversity" as a lighter word can thus do more. Of course, it is possible that diversity will also become tired through repetition: as one practitioner described: "They're not tired of it yet, I think it's a term that they think 'oh yeah diversity.' Diversity they can cope with." Coping with diversity might be conditional; they are not tired of it *yet*.[10]

My interviews with diversity workers taught me about the relationship between words and bodies, how certain words stick to certain bodies, such that bodies in turn can become stuck. As one practitioner described: "You know, you go through that in these sorts of jobs where you go to say something and you can just see people going 'oh here she goes.' " We both laughed, each recognizing that the other recognized that scene. That scene, so familiar: I could even see the eyes rolling. The familiarity was partly from my own experience in Women's Studies, of being "the feminist" at the table. But it was more than that. In *The Promise of Happiness* (2010), I wrote about the figure of the feminist killjoy, reflecting on my experiences as a feminist daughter at the family table. Around the table the family gathers, as if we are securing more than our place. Someone says something you find problematic. You respond, quietly, perhaps. You might be speaking quietly, or you might be getting wound up, recognizing with frustration that you are being wound up by someone who is winding you up. However she speaks, the one who speaks as a feminist is usually heard as causing the argument. *Another dinner ruined.* Institutions also have tables around which bodies gather. Some are at home in these gatherings more than others. The diversity practitioner, rather like the feminist killjoy, is heard as an obstacle to the conversational space before she even says anything. She poses a problem because she keeps exposing a problem. *Another meeting ruined.*

The tiredness of the terms is thus an institutional tiredness—it is the resistance to hearing the words that slows them down. If the institution has ears, then they are blocked: the words do not get through. A strategy is what practitioners develop as a means of getting through. One practitioner suggests that diversity work for strategic reasons should be disassociated from earlier forms of equality work:

> This office two and a half years ago, which was when I started here, had being the office of gender equity. It had focused primarily on staff, women's issues in the staffing area, and a bit to do with improving access for women into nontraditional areas of study and postgraduate studies but primarily being a staff activity. They had done some really important work and I certainly don't mean in any way to minimize or denigrate my predecessor, but I think to be totally frank that it had become a bit dated and it had actually begun to alienate and become marginalized from the business of the university.

"Equity work" is understood here as dated and as alienated from the core business of the university, as out-of-time and out-of-kilter. The appeal of diversity might not simply be that it is a new word but that it shares an emphasis on the new: for example, by sharing the emphasis on the university as a form of business, in which the new becomes a core value or form of capital. The word "diversity" is more in tune with the languages employed to redescribe what universities are doing. Institutional language can be thought of as a tuning system or as requiring attunement: if being incorporated by an institution requires that you are in tune, then being out of tune is to get in the way of its tune. What is out of tune is overheard; it sounds abrasive. Diversity offers practitioners a way of sounding "in tune" and thus "in place" by *not* sounding abrasive.

We can note also how "the equality office" is evoked as a physical body that becomes an alien body within the body of the institution. The task of the diversity practitioner is thus to create a new body. This practitioner claims a home within the university by disassociating herself from the historic work of the office. The disassociation is made for pragmatic reasons, rather than out of an ideological conviction. She describes: "We felt that people are just so jaded from hearing about women and sexual harassment." To avoid jading people, you have to avoid using certain kinds of language. We could thus describe diversity as an avoidance technique: a way of avoiding being avoided. As this practitioner further develops: "I've had people say to me, you know, they thought they were the feminazis in the equity office and so there was a significant amount of resistance and people just weren't included, they weren't seen to be anything other than peripheral. Generally the office was not engaged with the university community in a really good way." During this interview, I was struck by the willingness to repeat stereotypes of what feminist and equity work actually involved (violent stereotypes of that work *as* violence) to create a space for a different kind of work. There is no doubt an agreement in the repetition: an agreement with the judgment that feminist and equity work didn't work because they were too extreme. Rather than challenging the judgment, the strategy is to generate a different kind of image. If *that* is what they are thought to be, then you have to modify the thought by creating a new image. The diversity officer can "take up the place at the table" by not speaking in a problematic language or a language of problems. Modifying the equity office's image means challenging methods that had been previously used.

This practitioner suggests that the resistance to the equity office meant not only that equity work was not included as institutional work but that others within the wider university community were not being included by the equity office. Rather than this problem being an institutional problem, it becomes defined here as a problem with the equity office. One aim becomes to redefine the relationship between diversity work and institutional work in more positive terms. As she describes further: "If I start off by saying 'I'm here to change your values,' I suspect that that's not a terribly helpful way to develop a collaborative working relationship." The shift from the language of equality to the language of diversity becomes linked to a shift from a confrontational to a collaborative working model, to sharing rather than enforcing values. "Diversity" as a term might allow practitioners to work "with" rather than "against" an institution. Diversity work becomes realigned by being aligned with the institution.

It is important for me to note here that the identification with the institution and its core values might only be an impression. This practitioner actually described her role to me as being that of a "counterhegemonic worker." She redefines the relationship between the equity office and the institution to create an illusion of working with the institution, or being in line with the institution, to enable her to work more effectively against institutional norms and values. The alignment of diversity with institutionality in other words is maintained only *at the level of appearance*. It is possible then to use the terms of an organization as a way of disidentifying from its norms.

Diversity appeals are often made because diversity seems appealing: it is more consistent with a collaborative style. If the word "diversity" is understood as less confronting, then using the language of diversity can be a way of avoiding confrontation. Diversity is more easily incorporated by the institution than other words such as "equality," which seem to evoke some sort of politics of critique or complaint about institutions and those who are already employed by them. Diversity becomes identified as a more inclusive language *because* it does not have a necessary relation to changing organizational values. Indeed, diversity's inclusivity might be here because it is *not* associated with the inclusion of minorities (the language of "minorities" is stickier and associated with certain kinds of social critique). I wonder partly whether the apparent inclusivity of diversity is as much a desire as a description, given the ease with which, as Nirmal Puwar has pointed out, in policy discourse, diversity still tends to be associated with those who "look different" (2004: 1; see also chapter 1). Perhaps the promise of diversity is that it can be both attached to those bodies that "look different" and detached from those bodies as a sign of inclusion (if they are included by diversity, then we are all included). The promise of diversity could then be described as a problem: the sign of inclusion makes the signs of exclusion disappear.

The appeal of the term "diversity" for some diversity workers is practical: if the word is less threatening, then it can be a way of getting through people's defenses. As one practitioner describes, "I think it's really difficult: to use a term that's not acceptable is not to be able to do anything. In a way you need to use a term that's not going to make people feel threatened if you're going to try and work with them." Diversity replaces other more "unacceptable" terms that can make people feel threatened. I explore in the final chapter of this book how embodying diversity can mean being perceived as threatening no matter what you say or do. Suffice to say here that the word has less negative affective value than other words, which explains why it is repeated and acquires mobility. As another practitioner describes, "You've got to get the right stuff happening in the right terminology going so that makes that a little bit easier because it's not a scary word." As I discuss in due course, the fact that diversity is not a scary word is part of the problem: if it is detached from scary issues, such as power and inequality, it is harder for diversity to do anything in its travels.

What happens when the words we use allow us to pass over the reasons we use them? What happens when words become comfortable? As one practitioner suggests, "I can see the value of diversity, but I don't think it replaces equality of opportunity. I think they are two different things that are closely interrelated and that sometimes when people talk about diversity it's a more comfortable word to hide behind than thinking really hard about how you do actually achieve equality of opportunity." The comfort of diversity is here explicitly defined as a form of hiding, a way of not having to think hard thoughts. The comfort of the word "diversity" in turn might allow people to feel more comfortable within the institution. We might consider here Gloria Anzaldúa's powerful critique of how diversity can be "treated as a superficial over-lay that does not disrupt any comfort zones" (Anzaldúa and Keating 2009: 205). If the zone of diversity is one of comfort, then diversity might provide a cushion, both softening the edge of critique and allowing institutions to be reinhabited as softer spaces.

It is precisely because diversity has less negative connotations, providing a cushion, that diversity, at least for some practitioners, is a starting point, a way of getting through people's defenses. As one practitioner describes, "So you can start to engage those people because we've got to find ways of doing it so they are not defensive and they are the ones that have to do the work. If we can find a way of getting them to participate in the conversation without—and I don't mean just to protect their poor little egos, I'm running around that—but we've got to find an in. Otherwise I just sit there and I look at these white guys, middle-class, middle-aged, successful men in front of me who don't give a stuff what you are talking about, they don't give a shit because they are already here—the people who haven't made it here just didn't have what it took, and that's their attitude. So I need to find ways of getting to those people." Diversity is an "in" and a "to," a way of getting *in* by getting *to* certain people, those who would otherwise not be concerned with diversity given their own history of arrival (a history that can convert into a way of occupying space as the comfort of being "already there"). The language of diversity might be what enables practitioners to get people to the table. Once they are comfortable, perhaps you can aim to unseat them by addressing more uncomfortable issues.

The circulation of diversity certainly allows it to accumulate positive affective value. I commented earlier that the differences between the speech acts "we regret" and "we are diverse" is that the former seems to indicate a feeling or attitude. Perhaps this difference is not so clear-cut: the statement "we are diverse" could also be read as a feeling statement, in which the "we" that speaks or is spoken is the one who can deliver the affective promise of diversity. We could think of the speech act as what I have called a "hopeful performative" (see Ahmed 2010: 200). Borrowing from the promissory logic of positive psychology (when subjects repeat happy words to talk themselves into being happy), diversity as a speech act might be understood as generating its own promise, *as if we can catch the positivity of diversity from repeating the word.*

Diversity becomes a positive tool for action because of its status as a positive term. We can reflect on the significance of positivity as an organizational value. In the following chapter I consider diversity in relation to the ideas of good practice. Here I focus on how practitioners think about the positivity of the term. In some cases, the positivity of diversity is associated with its status as a politics of incentives or rewards: diversity is a kind of "yes" politics that encourages people to do something, rather than a "no" politics that aims to prevent people from doing something. As one practitioner describes:

And it's a bit like using the legislation as a banner to say "you've got to do as you're told" and about the policing role. And you know the saying, you get a lot more with a teaspoon of honey than a teaspoon of vinegar. And I think it's about, and people are staunch advocates for women might say, well, you're taking the easy option. But I don't see going in and saying to people, "you've broken the law" and laying the law down on the table—that's not going to change their attitude. We've got to make people change their attitudes, and by being inclusive and by trying to do it in a fashion that people will accept, we're going to get further than by going and saying "these are the rules and regulations and if you don't abide by them you get the sack."

The association of diversity with honey is partly created here by what diversity as a politics refuses: it is not about policing or "laying down the law"; it does not threaten people. For this practitioner, because diversity is not threatening, it is more likely to change attitudes. Diversity accrues positive value by being separated from a certain style of doing politics that would involve "laying down the law."

The idea that diversity takes us beyond legislation was widely articulated by practitioners. Diversity becomes positive as it provides a motive for action that is not based on compliance. It is proactive, rather than reactive. As one practitioner puts it,

I think for me with equality, as I said there is some legal framework and I think [it is] sometimes overemphasized. There's a tension really because you need to make people aware of the legality, but you want to go beyond that, don't you? You don't want it to be about compliance, so for me, I actually think diversity is actually a far more positive word than equality, so for me it's about celebration. Whereas equality feels a bit more about oh, you know, meeting legal requirements almost, I don't know that is just personal.

Diversity as a mode of celebration hence takes us beyond compliance and a culture of legality. As another practitioner describes,

I think people are genuinely worried about it because there is so much recent legislation and change and you know high-profile cases where things have gone wrong. People are genuinely worried, and I think what we're trying to get across is that the business case for this in itself is worth recognizing, it's a good thing to do in its own right. But at the same time, recognizing that we do have legal responsibilities, that we have to do certain things, so it's a balance between kind of the carrot and the stick almost, really. And I think on occasions I would say some other colleagues have gone too far with the stick rather than the carrot and that people don't always respond well to that.

This practitioner does not suggest that we need to replace equality with diversity, or the stick with the carrot, but that we need to find a balance between them. The implication is that diversity as a carrot might generate a better set of responses. Again, note the evocation of the history of equality work as having "gone too far with the stick." Does diversity "stick" because it is not associated with sticks? What follows the thought of diversity as honey or as a carrot? It certainly associates diversity with desire: as something that individuals and institutions might want to do, to have, and to be.

Diversity as a "feel good" politics is clearly evident in the cultural enrichment discourse of diversity, which one practitioner described as "the Thai food stall" model. Diversity can be celebrated, consumed, and eaten—as that which can be taken into the body of the university, as well as the bodies of individuals. Indeed, diversity might even be a way of "eating the other" to borrow bell hooks's (1992) evocative description. Diversity evokes the pleasures of consumption. The bodies of others, by adding spice and color, "liven up the dull dish that is mainstream white culture" (hooks 1992: 21). Take, for example, the poster "Enjoy Diversity" (see figure 3). Diversity is imagined here as an arrangement of colorful sweets. Does diversity involve not only the aestheticization of color but the demand that those of color be sweet? As Sirma Bilge has pointed out, one of the slogans used in this campaign was "Racists neither have courage nor taste."[11] The enjoyment of diversity is narrated as that which can take us beyond racism, which in turn is reduced to poor or bad taste. Those who enjoy diversity have good taste. But if diversity is digestible difference, then other forms of difference become indigestible, as that which the

Figure 3. Diversity becomes colorful sweets, as that which can be eaten and enjoyed. THE ENJOY DIVERSITY! POSTER IS FROM UNITED AGAINST RACISM: HTTP://WWW.UNITEDAGAINSTRACISM.ORG.

organizational body cannot stomach.[12] The sweetening of diversity (as sugar, as honey) might thus be a means of establishing the limits of what an organization can take in.

Most practitioners I spoke to formally and informally were very conscious of the positivity of the term "diversity" and what is at stake in its institutional appeal. For some, its positivity is what makes diversity a useful tool for getting things done, whatever those things might be. But for others, the positivity of the term is the problem. As one practitioner describes:

So now we'll talk about diversity and that means everybody's different but equal and it's all nice and cuddly and we can feel good about it and feel like we've solved it, when actually we're nowhere near solving it and we need to, I think, have that, well diversity as a concept fits in much better with the university's idea of what it's doing about being the great benefactor. I have consistently ignored it, in fact I have business cards that I've had printed out that say equality manager and the thing that's going on my door says equality manager and some of the committees use it and I've just kind of ignored the fact that they do because I think it is a really unhelpful concept, it's such a cop-out, it just kind of allows people to get away with thinking "oh everybody's different," and really kind of ignoring barriers which are oppressing, because if you look at everybody as an individual then you can take away the fact that there is institutional racism, sexism, disability-ism, etc., within the university.

For this practitioner, the very talk about diversity allows individuals to feel good, creating the impression that we have "solved it." Diversity thus participates in the creation of an illusion of equality, fitting in with the university's social mission: the idea the university has of itself as doing good ("the great benefactor"). Diversity can allow organizations to retain their good idea of themselves. It also creates the individual as the proper object: if diversity is what individuals have *as* individuals, then it gives permission to those working within institutions to turn away from ongoing realities of institutional inequality. This practitioner felt so strongly about the cop-out of diversity that she had taken the word "diversity" off her business cards even though she was employed as an equality and diversity manager. She refuses to identify with this term and thus refuses to give up on other terms, such as "equality." Other practitioners also expressed skepticism about the appeal of diversity as a form of institutional happiness:

> Diversity obscures the issues. . . . Diversity is like a big shiny red apple, right, and it all looks wonderful, but if you actually cut into that apple there's a rotten core in there and you know that it's actually all rotting away and it's not actually being addressed. It all looks wonderful, but

the inequalities aren't being addressed. Diversity to me is a promotional exercise, there are some benefits to it, but they are that it's a fashionable term at the moment so it can start to engage people and they want to know more. You get companies like Ford and all these private organizations that are really into, you know, diversity in a big way, so that in itself can influence others by what other organizations are doing, so I think, well, I just have a fear that it doesn't address the reality of institutional cultures. Okay, it might work to change the culture slightly but not by much.

Diversity might be promoted because it allows the university to promote itself, creating a surface or illusion of happiness. We could call this simply the "happy diversity" model, in which "diversity talk" becomes "happy talk," as Joyce M. Bell and Douglas Hartmann (2007) describe.[13] Diversity provides a positive, shiny image of the organization that allows inequalities to be concealed and thus reproduced. When listening to this practitioner, I was very much reminded of Betty Friedan's critique of the image of the happy housewife, whose "beaming smile" hides an infection (1965: 19–20; see Ahmed 2010: 50–51). The smile of diversity stops a "rotten core" from surfacing. This practitioner suggests that diversity is a way of not addressing institutional cultures, or perhaps addressing them only "slightly," which implies that a slight address can be a way not to address. We can return to my earlier comments about official diversity: diversity is what gets spoken about, creating an idea of the university as diverse. The creation of an idea of the university *as* diverse might modify the idea of the university slightly. Indeed, a slight modification of the idea of the university might be a way of protecting what goes on by obscuring what is ongoing.

If, for some practitioners, the positivity of the term "diversity" makes it useful as a way of getting people to the table, then for others the positivity is a problem because it allows the reasons you might want people at your table to be obscured. We could describe the difference as one of strategy. In both cases, the positivity of the word "diversity" is crucial to a decision about what words to use and how to use them.

Diversity Strategies

Words are used strategically when they become the means to achieving an end. For some practitioners, the word "diversity" is a means to an end; it is a way of getting through institutional and individual defenses. The choices made by practitioners are, of course, more than choices about words. Practitioners also have to make cases: for example, for justifying the need to make procedural changes in the organization or conduct of committees; to get the resources to support a diversity project (such as staff training); to undertake research on organization and equality, including what I described in the previous chapter as "perception data." A case is how an argument is presented for something.

Some diversity workers, in making such cases, use the languages that are typically used by the audience they are addressing. In other words, they understand their language choices to be determined by the addressee. Of course, any such determination involves an act of reading: practitioners not only listen to the words used by those to whom they are speaking, they also make their own judgments about what different audiences can hear. As one practitioner describes: "It's whatever works, if a person can only hear that case—give them their language what they can hear and other people you talk to . . . some people it's compassion, sometimes it's pragmatic, sometimes it's fear, sometimes it's . . . it's whatever is going to be the appropriate handle for the type of person." Diversity work here is about working out what works for whom: it involves not just reading institutional character, as I suggested in the previous chapter, but also reading individual character, working out what is "the appropriate handle" to reach different types of people. This process takes time; it often involves trying different words out until you find the right one for the right person. As this practitioner further describes, "Use one, one time, use another one the next time and a different one the next time. Keep utilizing different sorts of language until you can hit on the right one with the right people." You keep using different languages at different times, until you hit the right one: the right one is whatever term works for the audience with whom you are working.

Some practitioners speak of making cases as a form of translation: you translate your diversity case into the kind of case that is most likely to get uptake, as we can note from the following quote:

Depending on the audience that I'm working with, I make my pitch at different levels. I mean I am a complete whore when it comes to using any means that I can to get the stuff on the agenda to get things happening. I don't care. So if I have to mount the argument about productive diversity because we can't afford to lose people of talent and they need to be provided with opportunity to engage with the university so that we can maximize our bottom line, if you like, I'll use that argument, because the end effect is the same. If I'm in a situation where people are kind of anti the feminist thing but they are pro-internationalism, I don't care, I will talk to them about the issues around globalization and internationalism and the need for enhancing understanding of people of difference. I will use those discussions, I will use those terms, because those are the terms that they understand. Because I know that if we can get a situation where people are starting to put in inclusive curricula and using people of color in their references and bringing knowledges from other areas in the world because they think they are doing it because it's going to enhance their international reputation and be useful for their international graduate outcomes for their students, the things that will happen is that they will open up their space for every minority group. So I really don't care. I will use whatever the lever is that I think is going to get some progress happening because you can build on that. If you can start momentum it will grow. It's getting the momentum happening in the first place.

This practitioner identified her mandate as "enabling cultural change" and defines her project in terms of outcomes, "end effects," or "things happening." She is willing to use whatever language works, to make arguments in the terms that enable "momentum." Evident in this willingness to use the words that work is a kind of indifference (not caring, using whatever). No words, in other words, are too compromising, if they are the words that work (you can be a "whore" with language, saying whatever, doing whatever). It is important for me to note that this practitioner is the same one who describes herself as a counterhegemonic worker. If a relationship to language is defined in purely instrumental terms, it can actually create a space from which to disidentify from the words being employed. There is a detachment from the words themselves, as they become simply and only a means for doing things. A political question becomes the extent to which we can separate ourselves from the words we use. I would regard this question as an open empirical question, one that is always worth asking ourselves, as we work "on" as well as "in" institutions. If we do things with words, then words can also do things to us. We don't always know what they will do.

After this particular interview, I began to think about diversity strategies in terms of "switching." Diversity workers switch between different languages, as different languages can switch different buttons on (an "institutional switch" is what allows something to get turned on). What is interesting to note here is how apparently contradictory logics can be used simultaneously: in other words, the business model and the social justice model can be used together, or there is a switching between them, which depends on a judgment about which works when and for whom. This switching involves attaching the word "diversity" to other words, by mobilizing different kinds of vocabularies. Practitioners work with the term "diversity," by attaching it to the other words that are already valued by the different constituencies with which they work.

Data also becomes an important resource for diversity workers as an institutional switch. As this same practitioner describes, "It was not about, oh, we should do it because it gives us a warm and fuzzy feeling. It was about these are our performance indicators, this is the reason why, these are the reporting requirements that we have, and this is what we should be doing and here's the data to support that." Data becomes a crucial technology also in the sense that it aids the production of the competent self. Data is assumed to be "hard," a form of evidence whose "truth" is detached from an emotional orientation to the world ("a warm and fuzzy feeling"). Such a performance is, of course, strategic: to be heard, diversity officers cannot afford to be seen as soft, as such a perception would allow diversity itself to be seen as soft, and hence as having less value for the organization. The diversity officer comes to embody the value of diversity by *appearing to inhabit the values of the university*. By appearing "like them," the diversity worker is no longer seen as the stranger but as a native, one who is at home within the culture of the university.[14] The professionalization of diversity and equality work thus involves the production of a new kind of body for the diversity worker. The shininess of diversity might be about not only the promise of new words but also of new bodies.

Diversity workers tend to employ the terms that are already valued by those with whom they are working, as well as by the institutions in which they are working. An alignment with institutions is produced not simply by using the word "diversity" but by putting this word near the other words that institutions regularly employ. Diversity is made more appealing by associating with the ideal image the university has of itself, that is, by what it already imagines as its primary mission or its core values. As I pointed out in chapter 1, this makes diversity practitioners very good readers of what we can call institutional character.

In some cases, the word "diversity" is already exercised within how organizations are marketed. One practitioner says of her institution, "Diversity is part of its ethos; it would even market itself that way." Another practitioner describes her university as one that "tends to pride itself on its equity credentials." However, she also suggests that "sometimes they are not acted on as well as they should be." Having diversity or equality credentials does not necessarily mean you do anything. Or, as another practitioner puts it: "So people see us as being an equity university, but that doesn't mean that we actually do anything, so we don't actually have a lot of programs in place, we don't actually have strategies in place to recruit students from low socioeconomic backgrounds like most universities have to because we don't have to do anything." To be seen as "being diverse" can be a way of "not doing diversity," because the organization says it "is it," or that it already "does it," which means that it sees there is nothing left to do.

In other cases, practitioners work to associate the word "diversity" with the core missions of the university because these missions are *not* expressed in these terms. One practitioner, for example, suggests that she can embrace the positive languages of diversity because they fit more easily with the university as a "global university." As she describes:

> Diversity was something we wanted to embrace. We felt diversity had positive connotations. This being a global university, obviously we have to be good diversity people or we might as well shoot ourselves in the foot, marketing-wise. "Equity" was also a word we were quite happy about. We didn't want equal opportunity, we felt that that word had had its day and while I hear my colleagues yesterday sometimes defending those things, we share a view about not trying to fight that sort of stuff too hard. So we identify what we think is a winner and go with that. We didn't want "equal opportunity" or "affirmative action" or any words that I thought were dead in the water and also I personally think, I've done a bit of PR, and I think you are much better off with new terms.

"Being global" is thus associated with being good diversity people. You "become good diversity people" because that is what being a global university requires. Marketing is a way of thinking about the languages that organizations use to describe themselves to others in which the terms of description are the terms of value. As this same practitioner describes: "Being financially successful as a global university is being able to deal with (for the want of a better word) variety of people, so if you are going to go global you have to be able to engage with global citizens, some of them are like us and some of them aren't." The term "diversity" is consistent with the idea of the university as "being global." Importantly, diversity becomes a means by which certain others, those who are "global citizens," can be addressed: if diversity is about a variety of people, then that variety takes some forms and not others. Perhaps those who are not "like us" become those who do not speak the language of diversity.

The discourse of global citizenship is indeed useful: it associates diversity work with the skills of translating across cultures. The figure of the global citizen could be usefully related to that of the global nomad, those who in moving across national boundaries and translating between differences can feel more at home in the world. The founding member of

Global Nomads International, Norma McCaig, suggests that "in an era where global vision is imperative, when skills in intercultural communications, linguistic ability, mediation, diplomacy, and management of diversity are critical, global nomads are better equipped" (1996: 100).[15] Diversity can become a form of equipment, a set of skills that extends the global reach of individual subjects.

We can certainly note how diversity becomes an elite technology or a technology for elites. Homi Bhabha has argued that multinationals can affirm their "commitment to 'diversity'" insofar as diversity is associated with elites, in other words, insofar as "the demography of diversity consists largely of educated economic migrants—computer engineers, medical technicians and entrepreneurs, rather than refugees, political exiles or the poor" (2004: xiv). Diversity can be a way of doing advantage, or becoming more advantaged, rather than challenging disadvantage. Perhaps "diversity" is a successful term because it can more easily be associated with commercial and professional success. The ease with which diversity circulates suggests it can accumulate commercial as well as affective value. However, this is *not* to say that diversity work only works in this way.

Diversity in Conversation

In this chapter so far I have focused on how practitioners use the languages of diversity and on the strategies and tactics they develop "to get through" individual and institutional defenses. It is important to note that conversations are not just framed in instrumental terms, as a means of doing something, but are also understood as a space in which diversity work happens. Diversity practitioners have to find a way of participating in ordinary conversations about what the organization is about. As one practitioner observes, "There are conversations going around that are currently asking the question 'what are our values, who are we as a university, are we doing all the things that we said we do in our mission statement, etc.'" She pointed out that through conversations she realized that although "equity is in the mission statement," it was not in the "series of cascading documents that went into greater and greater detail and complexity." Conversations are important not simply because they keep the question of the organization's mission alive but because they reveal how that mission does and does not get translated. Talking about diversity within the ongoing conversations "about" what the university is "about" becomes crucial to embedding equality and diversity within these cascading documents.

I arrived to the research presuming that the emptiness of diversity was a sign of its *lack* of political value and utility. But the political efficacy of this word was related by some practitioners to its emptiness: "because I think diversity it's a word that nobody actually knows what it means, equity has some basis in being fair, people can understand that even if they misunderstand it, but if you want to start talking about diversity, I find that people say 'well what do you mean by diversity?' and so you have people who are talking about valuing diversity and people who are talking about counting people who look different . . . maybe because it's still not a tied-down concept." The absence of an agreed-on meaning for diversity can mean that it can be defined in quite different ways. We should note that some of these definitions seem quite problematic even if they are familiar ("counting people who look different"). The aim of diversity work would not be to resolve the problematic but to include it as part of the conversation. The experience of diversity would refer us back to the diversity of experience. Or, as another practitioner based in an Australian university describes, "I think with diversity, it just conjures up a variety of anything and everything that you are doing. You have to consider it from all angles. You can't just consider issues from a middle-class Anglo-Saxon environment. It just doesn't work anymore. It's just not that. You know, that's not the real world anymore. So diversity is such a good word to make you think of all the different elements that go into whatever it is you are trying to do." Diversity can be a conjuring trick: it can mean a variety of "anything and everything." If this variety can be conjured by diversity, then it challenges a world that refuses variety, a world that considers issues only from a singular viewpoint. Although conjuring variety might seem to separate diversity from something particular, this variety is a refusal of the generalization from a particular (the middle-class Anglo-Saxon environment). The very lack of referentiality becomes a certain starting point for a critique of how some viewpoints are given a referential function.

Diversity is regularly referred to as a "good" word precisely because it can be used in diverse ways, or even because it does not have a referent: "We certainly wouldn't be opposed to changing our name again at some point in the future if we thought that was going to benefit our tasks and our goals. We haven't come across any better words, and although I said that we wanted social justice to be a stronger part of the way that we were recognized, personally I wouldn't put it in the title. Diversity has actually been a very good word for us because we have been able to throw all sorts of things under that heading." Diversity is a good word for some practitioners because different kinds of institutional actions can be included under its name. We might note the use of the verb "to throw." Diversity is understood as an empty container; we can throw more things into a container if it is empty. If diversity can mean anything, then practitioners can define it in ways that enable them to do the work they want to do. Of course, it remains possible that diversity will be defined (officially, or by other actors within organizations) in ways that compromise what practitioners want to do with it. If practitioners can throw "all sorts of things under that heading," they also have to engage with other people about the term and how they make use of it.

Some practitioners, however, suggest that their task is to encourage others within the institution to use diversity in the right way. One practitioner suggests, "I would say in a general sense it's very easy for terms to lose their meaning; as they become more widespread they can become shortcuts for issues if you like. And so it's important that terms like 'diversity' are put in their rightful context." Even if diversity workers cannot determine the contexts in which diversity circulates, they can aim to give it the right context when and where it does come up. We might think of this process as a politics of reattachment: practitioners aim to reattach diversity to the meanings it may lose on or in its travels. If the success of diversity is partly that it becomes detached from histories of struggle over inequality, then the success of diversity work might require reattaching the word to those same histories.

In my own experience of writing a race equality policy (which I refer to in more detail in the next chapter), I was struck by the importance of conversation, even if the outcome of the conversation was the document (which seems at one level to suggest that the point of conversation lies elsewhere). We talked among ourselves as a group of staff who had all arrived at the meetings and into the institution in very different ways. We also had very different relationships to the words we eventually used in our document. To some extent, our conversations affected what words passed into the document: we included the word "diversity," but we were careful to put it near other words, including "equality," "whiteness," and "racism." The conversation did not lead us to adopt an official definition of any of these words. What mattered was the creation of a space in which we could talk about the words themselves. The words became lines of connection between those of us who had been given the responsibility of translation.

I have no interest in idealizing such conversations. And, yet, I think they matter because they show that not deciding in advance about the meaning and value of diversity can allow diversity to be shared as a question. All speech acts are shaped by the ordinary terms of their use. To speak is to be involved in a community of speakers; it is to follow rules or be shaped by conventions, which allow subjects to convey meanings not simply by what is said but by deploying the pointers that allow you to do things or get things done. If diversity is a pointer, then it is a way of directing or being directed. You have to learn as well as follow its point. A community can take shape through the circulation of diversity. Diversity does not refer us to something (a shared object that exists outside of speech) or even necessarily create something that can be shared. But in being spoken, and repeated in different contexts, a world takes shape around diversity. To speak the language of diversity is to participate in the creation of a world.

Equality and Performance Culture 3

In the previous chapter I discussed my experience as a member of a working group that was established to write our university's race equality policy. I suggested that the conversations we had in this group were instructive and should not be treated only as a means of generating the policy document. The document does not need to be framed as the point of the conversation, even if the imperative to write the document provided the starting point.

Nevertheless, I did learn from what happened to the document. Writing the policy coincided with the arrival of a new vice chancellor. He set up some meetings with members of the university that took the form of an official address. The meetings were certainly a performance, and the performance was of a style of leadership—a way of constituting a singular body in relation to the collective body of the university, as the subject and object of an address.

I was surprised at one of these meetings when the vice chancellor, with a letter in his hand, referred to the race equality policy we had written. It turned out that the letter was from the Equality Challenge Unit (ECU).[1] With an extravagant smile, and waving the letter in front of us (somehow the phys-icality of this gesture mattered), he talked about the content of the letter, which took the form of a congratulation (or which he gave the form of a congratulation), informing the university that it had been given the "top rank" for its race equality policy. "We are good at race equality," he said, with a beaming smile, pointing to the letter. It was a feel-good moment, but those of us who wrote the document did not feel so good. What is at stake in this performance of good feeling? *A document that documents the inequality of the university becomes usable as a measure of good performance.*

Thinking about the theater of this moment led me to question the con-sequences of race equality becoming part of what I call simply "perfor-mance culture." I use this term to refer to what was diagnosed by the phi-losopher Jean-François Lyotard as the performativity of a system.[2] In *The Postmodern Condition: A Report on Knowledge*, Lyotard observes the changes in how higher education legitimizes itself: "The question (overt or implied) now asked by the professionalist student, the State, or institutions of higher education is no longer 'Is it true?' but 'What use is it?'" (1984: 51). The criterion of utility is expanded to include saleability and efficiency. Lyotard suggests that the shift in the criteria for judging knowledge can also be understood as a shift in the relation between higher education and the social system. He argues: "The desired goal becomes the optimal contribu-tion of higher education to the best performativity of the social system" (1984: 48). A good policy becomes that which in advancing the perfor-mance of an institution also increases its contribution to the social system.

Lyotard's diagnosis could be described as prophetic. The shift to an efficiency model has involved a cultural and technical shift: the introduc-tion of a set of disciplinary technologies for judging the efficiency and accountability of educational organizations. Michael Power (1994) has de-scribed this shift as "the audit explosion." The arrival of audit systems into higher education involves adopting self-regulatory mechanisms from the private sector, in particular from finance, by the public sector. A per-formance culture is at once "a disciplinary system of judgments, classi-fications and targets" (Ball 1998: 190). We must note as well that perfor-mance culture *is* institutional culture. Institutional performance involves an increasing self-consciousness about how to perform well in these systems, by generating the right kinds of procedures, methods, and materials, where rightness is determined as the fulfillment of the requirements of a system (which henceforth gradually loses its exteriority).[3] Performance culture thus also involves performances in a theatrical sense: as Jill Blackmore and Judyth Sachs suggest, for an institution to perform well is "being seen to perform" (2007: 108). Doing well involves generating *the right kinds of appearance*.

This chapter explores how equality work in the United Kingdom, partly as a result of legislative changes I detailed in the introduction, has become embedded within performance culture. It is important for me to state that in noting how equality becomes embedded within performance culture, I am *not* dismissing the new equality regime as a symptom of the extension of performance culture. The history of equalities legislation might indeed remind us that the development of state mechanisms for ensuring the accountability of public institutions has progressive as well as disciplinary ends. At the same time, when equality becomes another performance indicator, it cannot be treated as outside the disciplinary regimes, whose ends might not be consistent with equality understood as a social aim or aspiration. Equality can be treated as an institutional performance and as contributing to the optimal performance of an institution. What are the political implications of this shift? What does it mean to be good at equality or diversity, or for equality or diversity to be a measure of the good? How do practitioners think about these questions?

Documenting Diversity

Any system of measurement requires units of measurement. In this section I explore how documents come to provide such measurements. Documents are not simply objects; they are means of doing or not doing something. Annelise Riles suggests that documents are the "paradigmatic artefacts of modern knowledge practices" (2006: 2), while Lindsay Prior considers documents as "fields, frames and networks of action" (2003: 2). We can ask what documents do by considering how they circulate within organizations, creating vertical and horizontal lines of communication. To ask what documents are doing, we need to follow them around.

Documents are clearly forms of writing. But they might also take form in specific ways when they have a routine function of measurement, that is, when the task or aim of the document is "to document" an organization in some way. One of the most significant impacts of the equalities legislation from the Race Relations Amendment Act of 2000 (RRAA) onward is how these laws have generated documents. Each new act required public bodies to write a new policy document. The most recent Equalities Act of 2010 also requires the writing of a new document or, to be more precise, the creation of a new document by merging all the previous documents (Single Equality Scheme, SES). These acts were important not simply in terms of how they expressed a change of public duty but also in the very practical impact they have had on the nature of equality and diversity work. No wonder many of my interviewees in the United Kingdom reported what has become known as "document fatigue." Many practitioners expressed a sense of exhaustion with writing documents, a sense that "writing documents" is the only work they have time to do. As one interviewee describes, "You end up doing the document rather than doing the doing." The implication of this description is that while doing the document is doing something, it is also a way of not doing something: you do the document *rather than* "doing the doing," where this other sense of doing would require doing something more than the document.

Most of my interviews in the United Kingdom took place in 2004 and 2005, in a period after the RRAA when practitioners were writing gender and disability equality policies. My questions were directed in such a way as to give practitioners an opportunity to reflect on their experience of writing or being involved in writing the race equality policy. However, I did complete a further interview in 2009 (see the introduction), as well as have a number of informal conversations with practitioners, during the period when practitioners were preparing or being asked to prepare the SES. In this interview, we discussed the cumulative effect of having to write new documents in response to each new scheme:

> Once it became you go to write this scheme by this and that scheme by the other, then you just end up spending more and more time writing schemes, and so you end up on a computer in a room rather than going out and talking to people. You feel more detached. And I have a prob-

lem with that because I think it is about contact, and if you write things in isolation you get detached and your policies won't work. They might give legal guidelines but they are not workable in your institution. It is all a paper exercise. And I just feel that I have been pushed more and more back to writing these policies and I never even get to explain to people what they are meant to be doing about them, you just can't do any more in the time available.

When diversity work becomes a matter of writing documents, it can participate in the separation of diversity work from institutional work: writing documents can mean not having time to participate in the kinds of conversations discussed in the previous chapter. Documents are paper: if diversity work becomes paper work, then practitioners can end up feeling as if it is "all a paper exercise." The more you spend time on or with paper, the less time you have to do things with that paper, to "explain to people" what you are doing. The detachment of the diversity worker (physically expressed in the isolation of working on the computer) becomes an institutional detachment.

When the document becomes a fetish, the diversity worker also becomes detached. Rather than participate in fetishizing these documents, we need to reflect on the circumstances of their production. Returning to the RRAA, it is worth noting that the act names specific duties under the general duty to promote race equality. For further and higher educational institutions, the specific duties are described as, first, preparing a written statement, and second, maintaining a copy of it. Both the writing and maintenance of the document become legal duties.

If the law requires the writing, then the written documents in turn often refer to the law in their opening preambles. This is a typical example: "Recent legislation aimed at promoting race equality and eliminating race discrimination, has placed positive duties on public bodies including the Higher Education Institutions. To meet these statutory responsibilities, the University through Court has established a formal Race Equality Policy applicable to all staff and students, and has approved a comprehensive Implementation Plan to meet the objectives of the Policy. Both the Policy and the Implementation Plan are available at this Web-site." This document is written in the language of compliance. If the law requires the document, the document incorporates the law as a term of its existence.

The law is also an occasion of action. Many practitioners describe the importance of the legislation as a "kick start." One interviewee comments: "Within higher education it only really started with the RRAA legislation when everybody's kicked up the backside. At the first conference—you should have been here, it was great. You know it was total panic that the world was going to end." We learn from this panic. The idea of having a duty toward race equality is anticipated as the theft of a certain world. I realized during my interviews that panic can be useful.

Practitioners report how much of the energy in this initial stage was directed toward finding someone to write the document. So the first duty was not so much to write but *to find the writer*. The document is not the starting point, even if the legislation seems to start from this point. How were these documents written? Many universities either appointed a new race equality officer, whose primary duty was to write the document, extended the duties of an equal opportunities officer already in place, or gave responsibility for writing the document to a member of human resources. For those appointed as race equality officers, documents were written in situations of extreme pressure. One practitioner spoke of the situation she found herself in: "The initial policy, I basically had to kick-start and get done quite quickly, because I was appointed in February 2002 and we had to have something in place." Or as another describes, "I think the real push was the Race Relations Amendment Act. I think they realized that they were not going to do it without somebody to really direct the work and coordinate the work. It was just me originally, and then I said I really need an assistant." The feeling that the response to the act was "just me" was articulated widely by both my interviewees and those I spoke to at diversity conferences. The push to act from the law is what brings a "just me" into place.

Appointing someone to write the equality policy becomes part of the fulfilment of the equality duty: this is how an appointment can function as a form of compliance, as I discussed in chapter 1. It is important to note that the location of the diversity practitioner as the policy writer also makes a difference to where the document goes. If the policy is written by someone who is viewed as lower down in the organization's hierarchy, then the document might be less taken up. Many practitioners spoke of how the documents, even when they are signed by vice chancellors, are not authored and thus authorized by them. As one interviewee describes, "But I suspect that most race equality policies, like ours, are not written by the vice chancellor, and he does not have any idea what's in them and they're written by somebody much further down the line. In our case I think it was probably written by the PA [personal assistant] to the director of human resources because that was the only person who had time to write it, and I suspect, looking at ours, and looking at those from other universities that she just copied somebody else's." The signature does not mean that the document is signed up to; leaders and managers often do not know about the content of the documents to which they lend the form of their signatures. Who actually writes the document can be understood as an expression of the commitment it does or does not embody. Indeed, the possibility that a document is a copy of another document is structural; race equality documents are forms that can be replicated. To write a race equality policy can thus be to write a form that can be copied. To write a race equality policy can be to copy a form.

Race equality policies as documents are part of an "inter-documental" university: some documents are copies of other documents. Not only that: documents are supposed to exist within a family of documents, with each one referring to others. Documents can also acquire authority as derivative of other documents: "There is a statement at the beginning of the charter, which says this text is from various other university documents and it's a way of bringing together statements of principle in a way in which people can use. So in a sense it is a derivative document." This self-referential world can be hard to map. Reading one document can mean being led to another.

If documents are derivative, then their authority can be referred and thus deferred. At the same time, unless documents refer to each other, they do not participate in the documentary world of the institution. As another practitioner describes: "I remember the debate that there was to dovetail this new policy with other existing policies. So I think there is always a balance to be had that in what sense you have a standalone document which makes some statements and with more difficulty how you get around the second path to keeping everything up to date. And things start to unravel and I think that can be really difficult." Doing documents can be an undoing: you have to keep updating them, if they are not to stand alone, but if you have to keep updating them, then it is hard to keep up with the task: "things unravel."

The proliferation of documents produces a certain kind of affective relation to the documents themselves. Practitioners spoke with a sense of caution about whether the documents, even if they are what practitioners are doing, are themselves doing anything. There is a kind of tiredness around them: as one practitioner suggests with reference to mission statements: "I think you can get mission statement fatigue, can't you? You reach a point where people just think oh you're just churning out another mission statement and it doesn't mean anything." The diversity worker becomes a document machine, one that churns documents out.

The point of the document can be to have a document you can point to. Many practitioners suggest that the documents are not themselves the point; what matters are the groups that are created in the process of writing them. One practitioner suggests that what was useful about writing the document was "the networks it helped set up." When only one person writes the document, it loses its point by becoming the point. Joyce Hill, the former director of the ECU, which oversees equality issues in higher education, describes the problems with the practice of the equality or diversity officer being asked to write the policy:

> The institutions that have come nearest to [having a working group] actually do better on average, do better race equality policies and action plans and implementation than those who tell the registrar to sit down and write a policy. Or even the poor old equality officer who should "take it away and write it please" because that actually leaves it really in one person's brain and tends to make it as it were the specialist activity of somebody when it absolutely is not and can't be because ultimately it's the responsibility of one and all.

How documents are written affects how they might be taken up. If the document becomes the responsibility of an individual within the organization, then that organization can authorize the document, give it a signature, and refuse responsibility for it at the same time. This is not to say that having a working group or network in place simply avoids this problem. In my own experience as a member of a race equality group with the responsibility of writing a document for the university, there was a sense of shared ownership of the document within the group. We were able to talk about what it meant to write the policy, as well as what the policy should be about. However, this did not mean it was any easier for the document to be shared beyond the terms of its authorship. Such groups can easily be constituted *as if they are individuals* with sole responsibility for the document. I pointed out in the introduction that I was one of only two academic staff in the group, and we were both of color. Given that we were working at a very white organization, it was quite transparent that "how" the group was constituted replicated some of the problems we were trying to address. The uneven distribution of responsibility for equality can become a mechanism for reproducing inequality.

We can also think about the relationship between the emergence of groups within the organization and the policy. In one conversation I had with two people from a personnel department (the director of personnel and a diversity officer), the confusion surrounding the process itself became noticeable.

> DIRECTOR: The truth of the matter is, I did it myself, because I deal with most cross-divisional issues. Then the group that helped, it was invented after that, wasn't it?
>
> DIVERSITY OFFICER: Yes, it was.
>
> DIRECTOR: And the race equality officer, she amended it, didn't she?
>
> DIVERSITY OFFICER: She updated it last October.
>
> DIRECTOR: And it must have been signed off by the race equality working group that we had. And when was that group set up? Was it as a response to the act or did it preexist the act?
>
> DIVERSITY OFFICER: It was set up in October 2002.

DIRECTOR: It was set up when we knew the act was coming. When was the Race Equality Act [RRAA]?

DIVERSITY OFFICER: 2000, but I don't think that it was until May 2002 that the policies were due in as it were. That's right.

DIRECTOR: So we must have set it up on or around we were due to put the policy in.

It is interesting that the director, who said he wrote the policy—"the truth of the matter is, I did it myself"—kept asking the diversity officer to clarify the timing, process, and mechanisms that were put in place. As part of this conversation about what happened, a number of actors are named: the writer (the director of personnel), the amender or updater (the race equality officer), and the signer (the race equality working group). This conversation shows us how the formation of such a group is inseparable from the response to the act: it is set up "on or around" when the policy came in. The fuzziness of recall is important. If it becomes hard to separate the group from the policy, then it becomes easy for the group to stand in for the policy.

Who writes the documents is crucial to what they do, even if the signs of authorship are not transparent within the documents. But writing does not simply create documents—it also keeps them going. Documents are often described as "living documents" (Hunter 2008), and part of their point is that they are continually updated and rewritten. I recall in one meeting we had with other project teams for the Centre for Excellence in Leadership, the director kept talking about the living document, as if we had a responsibility and duty to keep it going by caring for it and nourishing it. Rewriting is not simply what "keeps the document going" but can also involve people in the life of the document (whether or not they want to be involved). If documents are not the starting point, they are also not the end point. We can consider where these documents go once they have been written. One practitioner described the importance of consultation as a process of sharing ownership:

Right, first stage I wrote it. . . . My first port of call was the Black Minority Employers [BME] Network, who agreed to act as my reference group. Then I did draft one which went to the vice chancellor. Draft two went out for wide consultation, including sending it to some community groups, student union organizations, all staff by electronic bulletin, city council, the local PCT, posting it on the website and sending it to the Equality Challenge Unit. Then changes were made and draft three went back to the BME Network, who further made changes and it then went to the equality and diversity committee, and then following their approval it's now going to the board.

The document is passed around. Each passing is the occasion for redrafting such that it not only acquires new forms but becomes a new form. This practitioner did not make explicit the extent to which the groups were involved in redrafting the document. But the link between consultation and redrafting is widely documented. As another practitioner describes:

> Well, yes, I did write it, but there was a lot of involvement of other people, so I would say that everything that was in it was from a forum and it wasn't really just my ideas, it came from a group of people. One person wrote it in the end. It was good because of the involvement and engagement of people and people taking responsibility for it and then keeping those people involved, even up to now to make sure that they are progressing and that there is usable action, and then there was consultation after that with various committees and trade unions, and so on. I think there were about four drafts written, so in that way I didn't write it and go here you are, it was more of a working document, through that whole time.

A working document is one that multiple actors work over. To work over a document is to become involved in its political life. The body of the document becomes part of the body of the institution.

Consultation becomes an organizational ideal: it suggests an organization is being responsive and has an open ear. As one practitioner describes: "Consultation is an important part of the work; it's very important to have quite a reasonably broad working group who work on the policy as well, advice can also be sought from the Equality Challenge Unit and the CRE, but it is important that the race equality policy and action plan go out for consultation as well so that people have an opportunity to comment on the consultation, on the race equality policy and action plan." Here, consultation is about giving others an opportunity to comment on the document. But if the document goes out for consultation, it does not necessarily mean people's comments will be included in the redrafting. One of the risks of consultation is that it can legitimize the document as collective without necessarily being collective. When consultation becomes a routine, it does not mean organizations actually use it to change what they are doing (you can receive feedback without engaging with the feedback you receive). In other words, organizations can consult in order to say they have consulted. Consultation can thus be a technology of inclusion: you include "the others" in the legitimizing or authenticating of the document *whether or not* their views are actually included.

Some practitioners describe consultation as a problem rather than solution. One interviewee describes how we live in "a culture of consultation" in which people feel overconsulted: "We've just finished setting up our website, which has an electronic registration facility, so really as much as we can do. What we have discovered, and this was about one of the first things that came through at this stage without actually having engaged in consultation with these groups yet, is that a lot of people don't want to consult because they're perfectly happy with the way things are and many of the external groups are suffering from consultation phobia, because everybody wants to talk to them about it." Perhaps consultation phobia belongs in the same affective horizon as equity fatigue. There is a sense of tiredness with a process when it does not seem to do anything, which is partly how the process does not do anything. The assumption that people don't want to be consulted because they are "happy with the way things are" allows the status quo to be justified. If a culture of consultation can generate a fatigue with consultation, then it can preserve an idea of institutional happiness.

Consultation is often thought of as a mode of communication. It involves a very particular line of address: between those who consult and those who are consulted. A document becomes a line of address. There are of course other ways of communicating with documents. The ECU emphasizes the importance of communication to what documents can do. As they describe:

It is important to look at how you're going to be publicizing and publishing the race equality policy and action plan. It's not enough to really just put it on the website and hope for the best, you know, just put it on the institution's website, you need to raise awareness of it. A lot of institutions are doing things like producing summary leaflets of their race equality policies that they are including in freshers packs [starter packs for new students] so people are aware of what the institution's stance is on race equality as a whole and they have a signpost because it tells them how they can get copies of the race equality policy and action plan.

Publishing the document is about raising awareness. Creating a culture of awareness is described in terms of publishing strategies, repackaging the document into more usable forms. Can redrafting be thought of as repackaging? As one practitioner described to me:

The previous one was printed off and a hard copy attached to every member of staff's pay slip, it was promoted widely in the student resource pack, posted on the website, posted on staffnet, etc. We had quite a lot of coverage in [xxx], which is our staff newsletter, we've also left it at reception areas and sent it to local organizations, etc. Oh, and it was included in the staff handbook. But since we've changed and we're now becoming a much more e-friendly university, as I think is virtually everywhere else, the staff handbook is now in electronic format only, we now have e-bulletin, which is good because you can put links into it, but it's now getting so long that you have to put something snappy in the title. When this one is approved and the new action plan is drawn up, that will be promoted widely in [the] e-bulletin and we'll leave hard copies around, we probably won't have copies printed, although I'm not sure, that'll depend on the budget, but we'll certainly produce something nice.

Repackaging can be thought of as creating friendly documents. The appeal of such documents might be similar to the appeal of the word "diversity," discussed in the previous chapter. Friendly documents might accumulate value through their circulation, but that circulation might depend on not challenging anything. They can communicate (in the sense of being sent out, and even in the sense of reaching their destination) because as a form of communication they have been emptied out of any difficult content. If circulatability relies on friendliness, then documents might even be passed around *more* when they are doing *less*. More challenging documents are more likely to get stuck.

For other practitioners, the key is to make the document accessible. One way of reviewing the impact of policies is through their accessibility:

> One key aspect that was looked at during the implementation review was the accessibility of documentation. So, for example, it's a simple test there of whether a prospective staff member or student or current staff member or student would be able to understand where the institution was at with regards to race equality work. Would he or she have to plough through tons of documentation just to get a basic idea, or is it something that is easily accessible? If, for example, someone needs to be more aware of a particular procedure under the race equality policy, is it easy for them to access that information? So, for example, there [are] tests like that during the implementation review that the consultants were asked to look for, and obviously the more information you have, the more an institution might need to consider how accessible that is to someone who wants to just know what the institutions do in the area of race equality.

To make documents accessible is to remove "tons of documentation," so that any prospective staff member can find information about what the organization is doing. Indeed, creating an ability to find information about what the organization is doing becomes part of what the organization is doing.

Some practitioners are skeptical about the emphasis on communication and accessibility. One suggests: "I'm inclined to be quite skeptical about whether they are used at all. You've got a document and you put it on the Web, you do some advertising about it when it goes on, so people are aware of it . . . but the idea that it's banded around and pawed over I think that would be naive." Or as another describes, "It gets put into everything; it's in every contract of employment now; it's on everybody's

Internet sites; it's on every student bit of paper they get given; it's on every college bit of paper; it's all over the place, you can't get away from it. Does anyone read it? I wouldn't know, I wouldn't have thought so." The more a document circulates, we might assume, the more it will do. But the circulation of the document can become *what it is doing*. Diversity work becomes moving documents around. If the movement becomes the action, or even the aim, then moving the document might be what stops us from seeing what documents are not doing. If the success of the document is presumed to reside in how much it is passed around, this success might "work" by concealing the failure of that document to do anything.[4]

The document is the paper in the trail. Passing around the document creates a trail. If passing the document is the point of the document, then the point can be simply *to create a trail*. It is interesting to note that the circulation of documents involves changing hands: it is not simply that universities put them on the website, or disseminate them by reproducing them as glossy "user-friendly" leaflets. Many include race equality policies in the packs new staff receive when they are first appointed. When I arrived at my new institution in 2004, not only was I given a pack that included the college's race equality policy, but the personnel officer took the policy out of the pack and said, "I am required to show you this under the terms of the Race Relations Amendment Act." The officer pointed to the document by pointing out that she was required to do so under the terms of the law. Such an utterance places the circulation of documents "under the law" and makes the gift of the document a way of being subject to the law. So it is not simply that documents change hands but that they also get directed in specific ways by how we speak about them, which in turn affects what they do.

Equality and Audit

A race equality policy has a documentary aim: to make accessible in the form of a written statement the key priorities of an organization regarding race equality and to provide an action plan. The documents also come to be treated as units of measurement, allowing an assessment of whether an organization is fulfilling its duty to promote equality. The generation of documents could thus be described in terms of the bureaucratization of diversity (Mirza 2009). Under the equality regimes, diversity and equality become auditable.

It is important to note here that equality within the higher education sector is not audited in the United Kingdom in a strict sense. Although universities as public bodies have a duty to promote equality, there is no proper mechanism for ensuring their compliance. There are no external auditors for equality that are comparable with the Quality Assurance Agency for Higher Education (QAA), for example. The QAA states on its website that "the primary responsibility for academic standards and quality in UK higher education rests with individual universities and colleges, each of which is independent and self-governing." But then it suggests that the "QAA checks how well they meet their responsibilities, identifying good practice and making recommendations for improvement."[5] There is no such external body that has this kind of "checking role" for equality in higher education.[6] The ECU, for example, has a primary mission to support and promote rather than regulate equality work in the higher education sector.[7] How, then, can it make sense to discuss equality as becoming auditable?

In the period after the RRAA, the ECU took on the role of auditor in a limited way: they inspected all the race equality policies and produced a ranking of the initial policies. They also entered into communication with each university or college, initially by sending out letters. Such a letter from the ECU about my former university receiving the highest rank generated the feel-good performance that I referred to in the opening of this chapter. Although they did not produce a league table on diversity and equality performances, the ECU did publish a list of thirty-four higher education institutions (HEIS) that were given an "exemplar" ranking. This process of ranking is one way of addressing the consequences of equality being treated as auditable, even if equality is not audited in a strict sense.

The question of audit elicited strong feelings among those I spoke to. Practitioners offered different, even opposing views on what it would mean for equality to be audited. Some suggested that auditing equality would be a good thing, as universities only take seriously those activities that are subject to audit. As one practitioner describes, "I think it would be useful in the higher education sector because it wouldn't have been done, just thinking about how they could operate and how they've been lagging behind, it was the push; you know you had to do it." Audit becomes here "a push," perhaps even "the stick," which would compel action, as a compulsion that energizes or creates an institutional drive or institutional will.[8] As another practitioner indicates: "Every institution has to produce something with an action plan and I think that's useful. But the weakness of the system is that no one monitors whether you do anything. If there was someone external who came in and checked, I think that would mean it was taken more seriously." The suggestion here is that diversity and equality are not sufficiently embedded into audit culture. The implication is that commitment would only come with checks.

Other practitioners suggested that introducing more-rigorous compliance procedures would not work given that audit culture tends to generate a consciousness of audit. As a director of personnel explains:

> An audit can establish if we have gone through processes, it can't really determine whether we are altering culture here. It can perhaps show whether we are reaching various targets, say, you know, the same teacher of leadership staff who come from various backgrounds over time. But the trouble is when dealing with audit you tend always to respond in terms of process: we have done this report; we have got a plan out and all that sort of stuff. And I could see that you could get a rough idea if universities were putting effort into diversity by doing that, but the trouble is that in universities we have an audit-aware culture in administrations. And so people are practiced at how to show auditors that processes are being gone through.

Showing process is not the same thing as having a process. If diversity and equality were audited, then universities would be able to show they have gone through the right processes, whatever processes they actually have in place. In other words, if you can become good at audit by producing auditable documents, then the universities who "did well" on race equality would simply be the ones that were good at creating auditable systems. Michael Power argues that audit culture is about "making things auditable" (1994: 18). Or, as Cris Shore and Susan Wright describe in their excellent account of audit in higher education, "The result has been the invention of a host of 'auditable structures' and paper trails to demonstrate 'evidence of system' to visiting inspectors" (2000: 72). The suggestion here is that institutions create "evidence of system" for the auditors, rather than supply evidence of the systems in place. If equality is audited, then organizations can create evidence of equality systems that are *not* actually the ones in place. The documents would then be "fabrications" of the institution (Ball 2004: 148).

What are the effects of measuring race equality documents *as* indicators of institutional performance on race equality? I have already mentioned my own experiences of writing such a document. I noted how a document that documents the inequalities within a university became usable as a measure of equality. Being judged to have written an exemplary race equality policy is quickly translated into being good at race equality. Such a translation works to conceal the very inequalities the documents were written to reveal. The existence of the document is taken as evidence that the institutional world it documents (racism, inequality, injustice) has been overcome. The creation of equality systems can thus conceal the inequalities that make such systems necessary in the first place.

We must persist with the question of what is being measured when we measure such documents. I asked this question to one diversity practitioner, who answered, "We are good at writing documents." I replied, without thinking, "Well yes, one wonders," and we both laughed. We wonder whether what is being measured is the level of institutional competence in producing documents. Institutions are able to translate their writing competence into an equality competence. As this practitioner further described:

> I was very aware that it was not very difficult [for] me and some of the other people to write a wonderful aspirational document. I think we all have great writing skills and we can just do that, because we are good at it, that's what we are expert at. And there comes with that awareness a real anxiety that the writing becomes an end in itself, the reality is being borne out by, say, for example, we were commended on our policies and when the ECU reviewed our implementation plans last year there

were a number of quite serious criticisms about time slippages, about the fact that we were not reaching out into the mainstream and the issues had not really permeated the institution and the money imple-ment[ed] in certain specific areas. And it was not that there was hos-tility; it was much more of this kind of marshmallow feeling.

This is a fascinating statement about the politics of documentation. The practitioner describes her skill and expertise in writing a "wonderful aspi-rational document," although this is not necessarily the kind of document that was written. Being good at writing documents is a competency that is also an obstacle for diversity work, because it means that the university gets judged as doing well because of the document. This very judgment about the document blocks action, producing a kind of "marshmallow feeling," a feeling that we are doing enough, or doing well enough, or even that there is nothing left to do.

Many practitioners and academics have expressed concerns that writ-ing documents or having good policies becomes a substitute for action: as one of my interviewees puts it, "Too much time can be spent on actually writing policies and action plans and I suppose it can detract from just getting stuck in." Or to refer to a quote I cited earlier: "You end up doing the document rather than doing the doing." The very orientation toward writing documents can block action insofar as the document gets taken up as evidence that we have "done it." As another practitioner describes, "Well, I think in terms of the policies, people's views are 'well, we've got them now so that's done, it's finished.' I think actually, *I'm not sure if that's even worse than having nothing*, that idea in people's heads that we've done race, when we very clearly haven't done race." The idea that the docu-ment is doing something can allow the institution to block recognition of the work that there is to do. So the idea that the document "does race" means that people can think that race has been "done." As another practi-tioner describes very powerfully:

I think the university has written them because it had to, and now thinks it has finished all that it needed to do, it has implemented the Race Relations Amendment Act and it's got a race equality policy and it's probably very nicely written, but I think it's slightly lying to the outside world about what the university does about race and what it thinks about it, you know here's our nice policy now. Also, to a lesser degree I think, it is lying to potential students and staff because I think they're probably intelligent enough to read between the lines, but I think it's also slightly lying to ourselves and saying "oh we're nice and we're good at this and we try so hard to be accessible," and that's really not the truth, and we really do need to face up to the situation that the university is in. I don't think it's any worse than any other university or any other public sector body, I think they're probably all in a similar position, where we're just kind of not admitting that we have problems with equality and *it's really bloody obvious if you look round, but actually just saying that is hard.*

The document becomes not only a form of compliance but of conceal-ment, a way of presenting the university as being "good at this" despite not being "good at this" in ways that are apparent if you look around (an obviousness that is probably more obvious to diversity workers than many others given that institutional habits can protect those who inhabit institu-tions from seeing what is around). Returning to my argument from chap-ter 1, diversity becomes a form of image management: diversity work creates a new image of the organization as being diverse. It might be image management—or perception management—that allows an organi-zation to be judged as "good at equality." Just as changing the perception of an organization from being white to diverse can be a way of reproduc-ing whiteness, so, too, being judged as good at equality can be a way of reproducing inequalities.

However, not all institutions did well in this initial ranking. My impres-sion from talking to practitioners about this process was that negative judgments were more useful. This was certainly the view of the ecu. As Joyce Hill described:

I think it affected different institutions in different ways. Some it gave them confidence to kind of forge ahead, others thought, right, well that's that done then and didn't really do anything much about it subsequently. The real galvanizing effect was on the ones that were in the bottom half of the list and although that produced, of course, naturally, some questions and queries and grumbles and some people, you know, questioned whether they'd been looked at fairly and all the rest of it. Inevitably that'll happen, but it had a huge impact on getting people, shaking people out of either a negative or a complacent view.

Indeed, the value of an auditable system might be the utility of negative judgment that organizations will take equality more seriously when it poses a risk to their reputation. When reputation is risked by doing badly on equality, organizations are forced out of complacency. A diversity officer from the ECU concurred: "Feedback we got two weeks ago was that those institutions that were labeled as exemplary are worse off. And those that got the bottom rating in the paper exercise have been more proactive in the implementation of action plan. So for them it's not just been a paper exercise, they've embedded or aimed to embed it as part of their work." "Doing badly" leads to equality becoming more than a paper trail. The experience of the process was that of the threat to reputation, which is how the process becomes more than paper work.

This view, that being shown to have done badly has more value than being shown to have done well, was expressed by a number of my interviewees. As one practitioner reflected at length:

> For us the ranking acted as a kind of impetus to do more but to recognize that although we weren't in the bottom two we were going to be hauled back in within six months or whenever it was to resubmit that we would need to make the policy more robust and do further work. So I think for us it acted as a spur really. We came at the bottom of the pile on race. The reason was because it was a paper exercise and it was interesting and in a way I was not disappointed that we were at the bottom [of] the pile because it turned 'round in terms of senior management's role. We really do this well and we do that well and how come? So we had a lot of engagement from management who would normally have avoided it. So that was interesting for me, and then the second time we submitted it and it was still a paper exercise and the feedback we got was that we were developing appropriately, but required significant improvement. . . . So it's really interesting how you can start off negative and become positive.

Here, coming at the "bottom of the pile" is described as a spur to action. I am interested in how paper becomes a pile in this description. The pile of papers is the pile of universities. Those at the bottom of the pile are those for whom the paper was its own exercise. To come at the top of the pile, by implication, is to make the policy more than its paper. Yet at the same time, as we have seen, coming at the top of the pile can mean that senior management is not engaged in the process; the top of the pile would refer to those whose paper work is in the right order. For this practitioner, the utility of doing badly is partly how it interpellated management: doing badly threatens the organization's reputation. One wonders whether to be at the bottom of the pile of papers is how the paper comes to matter.

However, the effects of doing badly are not uniform. In one unusual case, a university ended up swapping its race equality document that had been written by multiple actors from within the institution with a policy written by an external consultancy:

> Later on the ECU reviewed all the policies and they said that ours didn't meet the requirements. It led to a whole stack of unpleasant exchanges between [xxx] and the Equality Challenge Unit and the Equality Challenge Unit came off worst. Not least of which, because of the policy that we had had, and many other of the local universities had also used and now were equally wrong. So for [xxx] to play the game, they didn't write the policy we now have, but gave it out to an external consultancy and said you tick the boxes for the ECU because frankly at that point, senior managers in the organization would have just stopped.

This is an extraordinary account of what is at stake when equality becomes auditable. This university had written an equality statement in advance of the act that did not follow the recommendations about how to fill in the form. Their submission did not meet the requirements. The hostility that follows not doing what is required is resolved by the university submitting a second policy, which was written by an external group. Such a policy can only be generic; it is written to meet the requirements by those who are not involved in the organization. So to meet the requirements, the university submits a document that is even more detached from what it is actually doing. They are then judged to have met the requirements. The implication here is that "doing well" and "doing badly" are judgments made in relation to a system, measuring the extent to which a document is consistent with the system. The criterion of consistency thus encourages the separation of the document from the institution being documented.

When diversity becomes ticking the boxes, then organizations know how to fulfill the requirements. As Michael Power argues, one of the big problems with audit culture is this tendency to produce comfort rather than critique (1997: 124–26). To succeed at equality becomes an aim that allows organizations to keep doing what they are doing. Even when organizations fail to generate auditable documents, it does not necessarily inspire organizational self-critique. It can lead to a narrowing of the gap between the letter of the organization (the document) and the letter of the law.

Good Practice

I have considered what is at stake when equality becomes treated as auditable, asking what judgments of "doing well" or "doing badly" are judging. I have also suggested that these judgments measure the extent to which the documents submitted by organizations are consistent with a genre. Equality competence can thus be a measure of an institutional competence in fulfilling a set of technical requirements. I want to consider what it means to think of equality as a good performance, whereby the value of equality derives from how it promotes the "good" of the institution.

Race equality documents are passed around as a form of compliance. Yet it is worth noting here that the new equalities legislation is often referred to as having a "positive spirit" that moves us beyond compliance. One of the primary ways of expressing the move beyond compliance is the idea of "good practice." As Joyce Hill suggests:

> The word that we are very wary of is the word "compliance" and really as a group we have more or less vetoed its use haven't we, tacitly at least. We'd far rather talk about meeting the requirements of or fulfilling the requirements of something. Because compliance does sound very much like a kind of minimalist tick box approach, look over your

shoulder, see whether you can be done for not doing something as it were. Whereas our approach is very much yes, of course, to meet the requirements of the legislation that's the very least one can do, but to do that in a spirit of understanding what the legislation is really there for and to tackle the what it is really there for and not just what it actually, literally says. So that you move into fulfillment, I feel, rather than compliance. So you move into the area of good practice and set standards which are in the good practice zone rather than the compliance zone. Although you set up your good practice zone in such a way that it embraces the compliance, wouldn't you say that's our general kind of tack? And consequently I think the word "compliance" is then an unhelpful word to use because it's the sort of minimalist cop-out phrase.

We can reflect on the distinction made here between meeting the requirements and fulfilling the requirements. To fulfill the requirements would move us beyond compliance, as a "minimalist cop-out phrase." By implication, the cop-out of compliance does comply with the law "as the very least one can do" and might even meet its requirements. The law then does make possible a "tick box approach," even if the spirit of the law takes us beyond such an approach. I would even describe the tick box as a specter behind this law: the tick box is what we want to avoid in interpreting the legislation, yet it is also what the legislation puts in place. Moving beyond compliance becomes a matter of compliance, but one that takes us into a different zone, described by Joyce Hill as the "good practice" zone.

The positive duty to race equality becomes associated with being good at race equality: going beyond the tick box is a better institutional performance. Yet "good practice" is clearly a term used within a tick box approach, insofar as "doing well" is presumed to be something that can be measured, distributed, and shared. An anecdotal example mentioned by one of my interviewees was of a university that had as its target that 100 percent of its staff be diversity trained; it then put diversity training online so it could meet this target. Having met the target, online diversity training becomes good practice.

Good practice and the tick box can thus be seen as operating in the same zone rather than different zones: after all, both are implicated in what Jill Blackmore and Judyth Sachs describe as "the performative university": "one that focuses on measurable and marketable consumer satisfaction" (2003: 141). Although "good practice" is defined as "going beyond compliance," I argue that good practice has become an institutional routine. Not only has it become routine to talk about good practice but good practice is how equality and diversity become embedded within institutional routines. Good practice becomes a set of practices that enable an organization "to look good." I explore in chapter 5 how the desire for good practice can involve turning away from ongoing signs of racism and inequality. Suffice to say here that good practice can be a mode of attention: a way of sharing practices that are not about exploring the problems with organizational culture but about "solutions." One of the problems with good practice is the assumption that to offer solutions requires not focusing on the problems. The solution can thus become a means of negating the signs of a problem.

We can draw here on Pushkala Prasad and Albert J. Mills's (1997) important critique of diversity within organizations. In the introduction to *Managing the Organizational Melting Pot: Dilemmas of Workplace Diversity*, they focus on how "workplace diversity" is increasingly commodified, "becoming trendy consumer items marketed in the form of executive seminars, T-shirts and mugs, museum exhibits and workplace training modules" (17). In particular, they suggest that diversity becomes a kind of showcase, "a setting that facilitates the most advantageous arrangement and display of certain objects" (8). Diversity becomes a matter of rearranging things, so that an organization can appear *in the best way*.

I would argue that "good practice" can be a showcase, a way of repackaging and rearranging the organization, so that it puts on its best display. An example of this process of display can be taken from the ECU toolkit on communications, "Good Talking: The HE Communicators Equality and Diversity Toolkit." One of their examples of good practice — here defined in terms of "good talking" — is the case of a university that has "produced institutional equality and diversity gifts and novelties that are in great demand" (2004: 8). For equality and diversity gifts and novelties to become a sign of good practice is clear evidence of how they are being repackaged. Equality and diversity become properties of objects that are passed around. An organization can even get a tick for its novelties.

When equality and diversity become performance indicators, they present the "best view" of the organization. It is thus not surprising to note the increasing proximity between equality, diversity, and excellence. Bill Readings, in *The University in Ruins*, offers a genealogy of what he calls "the university of excellence." He suggests that excellence becomes generalizable as a value precisely because it is empty of content: "Excellence is clearly a purely internal unit of value that effectively brackets all questions of reference and function, thus creating an internal market" (1996: 27). Excellence is the way a system can reflect back on itself. In passing, Readings notes how the word "diversity" as a "watchword" (as a word that can be understood as both rallying cry and slogan) can be "tolerated without threatening the unit of the system" (1996: 32). I want to suggest that diversity and excellence can operate as terms that are emptied of meaning or content in part as they point to each other. In pointing to each other, the empty place of one word can be filled by the other.

Diversity thus becomes a technology of excellence. Some of the practitioners I interviewed worked at universities that received the initial rank of exemplar, which also included use of the word "excellent." Joyce Hill said she was uncomfortable with the use of the word "excellent": "I think that excellent is too absolute a thing at that very early stage of the process, the first implementation date, and I think it's too absolute for a situation in which however well you are doing it, you're learning how to do it. I'm afraid that the funding council rather thought that having excellent was a good idea because it would be nice if there were some that got a label called excellent. But I had my reservations at the time and I still have my reservations about that." We can learn from the decision of the funding council. They want to use "excellent" because "it would be nice" if some were to receive such a judgment. The very association of equality with excellence becomes a nicety, not only as a way of distinguishing between organizations with the social field but as a way of rewarding the most deserving for their performance.

When equality is measured, it can be used as a measure of how well an organization is doing. Take the case of the ECU's ranking of HEIS. A number of universities make reference to their ranking as excellent in the subsequent race equality reports. For instance, one university referred to this rank in their 2005 annual report. The vice chancellor states: "We aim for excellence in everything we do, and our approach to race equality should be just as professional and rigorous as all our other activities. Working to remove any real or perceived barriers which might deter people of the highest quality from applying . . . is very much part of our mission to maintain and develop our position as a world-class university." When an organization's race equality document is ranked as exemplar, then that rank is incorporated into its self-description as world class. When equality policies are ranked excellent, organizational pride can take the form of equality and diversity pride.

In one interview with a practitioner who worked at an elite university, we talked about the incorporation of the ECU ranks. She suggested that "excellence is what we do, that has to be what we do, what else do we do round here, you know. . . . And we got exemplary status, and we were put on their website as one to copy because I mean, in a way it's very obvious what you should do." Those policies that are ranked as excellent become models, contributing to the increasingly generic nature of the policies themselves. In this particular interview, diversity is described as consistency with excellence. The practitioner suggested her university "does diversity" because "people really care about excellence," which means "they really get hacked off when somebody second rate is appointed to anything and they don't care what they look like." Diversity becomes what the university does *because* they care about excellence; as a world-class institution, it can afford not to care what people look like. Diversity can even take the form of an indifference to difference. Note as well how the language of diversity is exercised as the language of merit.

As I suggested in the previous chapter, some practitioners actively challenge the social perception of diversity as a confrontational form of politics. To be associated with excellence becomes another technique to challenge these "negative" associations. As this practitioner describes, "You want to be associated with excellence right? Excellence, you don't want to be attached to the dead hand of the '70s. It's like Arthur Scargill[9] you know, do you want to be Arthur Scargill or do you want to be Bill Gates you know, who do you want to be? I'd rather be Bill Gates, that's my view." We probably could have no better representation of the starkness of a political choice: two key figures, one associated with elites and global capitalism, the other with political struggle against power and campaigns for justice for workers; one associated with life and futurity, the other with the past and death ("the dead hand of the '70s"). Excellence offers an active identification with futurity and the market; it becomes a promissory discourse, *as that which offers a greater return.*

The association of diversity with excellence thus performs a very particular kind of work. Diversity accrues life value by being aligned with organizational value. Another practitioner says, "Our aim in the diversity project is to help the organization to see how diversity will help meet the strategic plans. So how can diversity help make us top ten in 2010? What will thinking about diversity enable a head of a school that is already very successful be more successful? That would be my real aim and to live our vision for race, which is excellence through diversity." "Excellence through diversity" can become "just another means" to achieve excellence. It can become a way of promoting the organization *as* excellent. Diversity is imagined as how to make the already successful even more successful. When diversity becomes a value for the organization, it allows the accumulation of organizational value.

My argument here has been that in becoming embedded in performance culture, equality can participate in concealing inequalities. The organization presents itself as good at equality or as being diverse. However, the consequences of my argument are not that the new equality regimes are inherently problematic. As practitioners, we work with the limits of the law, which often means working by exposing the limits. It is worth noting that in the informal conversations I had with practitioners, in Australia and the United Kingdom, about the project, after the tape had been turned off, I relayed my own story of writing a race equality document that was then used as a feel-good moment. Most of the practitioners responded by nodding knowingly. There was certainly recognition of the institutional politics at stake in this performance of good feeling. But the sense I got from their responses was that this moment could be viewed not only as one of co-option but of opportunity. If organizations invest in diversity or equality, even as shiny veneers, we can "do things" with their investments.

Critiquing how equality and diversity become embedded within performance culture is *not* to suggest that we should not go through these motions. It is worth acknowledging that I am completing this book in 2010 after a change of government in the United Kingdom has ushered in an era of increasing conservatism. The idea of "the public university" is under attack (Couldry and McRobbie 2010). Unsurprisingly, we have also experienced a gradual but increasing withdrawal of public commitment to equality, which shows us the precarious as well as conditional nature of such commitment. In a period of extreme cuts to public spending, equality and diversity are being repositioned as what the nation cannot afford to have. One of the arguments made against equality by representatives of the new conservative government is that it has become just another bureaucratic procedure. For example, Theresa May, the minister for women and equality in the current Conservative and Liberal Democratic Coalition Cabinet (as well as home secretary) has indicated a desire to drop the "socioeconomic" duty from the Equality Act as it "would have been just another bureaucratic box to be ticked."[10] My analysis in this chapter shows how May is right to describe the new equality regime as box ticking. But if there is a right, there is also a wrong. The wrong can be heard in the dismissal of the "just another." We learn from how easily a critique of performance culture can be transformed into caricature that there is still a purpose to ticking boxes. If equality can be a way of "going through the motions," these motions give the institution a direction; the motions themselves direct attention. If documents are how we "spend time," then documents involve as well as become resources. The next chapter considers how "going through the motions" can be related (or not) to the question of institutional commitment.

A common expression that comes up in the diversity world is "hearts and minds." At formal and informal meetings and workshops I attended, this phrase was used regularly to describe what diversity workers need to "get into." This expression indicates that although diversity might be appealing at a surface level (the "shiny veneer of diversity"), it does not necessarily mean it has been incorporated as a value by individuals. "Hearts and minds" often stands for a sense of commitment that is missing. Hearts and minds is not simply a reference to the individual: the aim of diversity work is also to *get into* the institution, which as I pointed out in chapter 1, is often psychologized or given interiority, as if it has a heart and mind of its own. For diversity workers to reach the heart and mind of an institution would mean becoming an institutional insider; it would mean that diversity becomes part of how the institution feels and thinks.

If "hearts and minds" can stand for a sense of commitment that is missing, then commitment is offered as a way we can get beyond the tick box approach to diversity discussed in the previous chapter. A tick box approach is when institutions can "show" that they are following procedures but are not really "behind" them (showing can be a way of *not* committing). Yet even if commitment is posed as an alternative to the paper trail of diversity, it remains elusive and difficult to define. In this chapter, I ask why commitment matters to diversity and equality work.

To make a commitment is to pledge to do something. Commitment used in this way would be close to its etymological root as a "sending out." We also use the term "commitment" to refer to a state of being bound to a course of action or to another person or persons. This chapter explores the relationship between commitment as a pledge that is sent out and commitment as a state of being bound. Previously, I considered how diversity becomes a matter of documents, which are written in order to be sent out. An institutional commitment might be readable in the documentation of a commitment (what I call simply "statements of commitment"). Statements of commitment are sent out and are institutional means of sending commitment out. But an institutional commitment would also refer to something more substantial: what an institution is behind or gets behind. This chapter explores what follows the structural possibility of divergence between the forms of commitment: how acts of commitment can be made in situations where commitment is not given in the sense of being bound.

Statements of Commitment

In the previous chapter I discussed how diversity work involves working with documents, with specific reference to the race equality policies written as a requirement of the Race Relations Amendment Act (2000; RRAA) in the United Kingdom. We could read these documents as statements of commitment to race equality: indeed, the language of commitment is often exercised in the first sentences of these documents. These documents seem to "commit" the institution to doing something. Or do they?

Let me quote from the opening paragraphs of two race equality policies:

> The Race Relations (Amendment) Act 2000 (RRAA 2000) places a requirement on a wide range of public authorities, including all Further

and Higher Education institutions, to promote race equality in a pro-active way through all their functions and to publish a Race Equality Policy. This Race Equality Policy has been published to inform all [xxx] staff and students and all other partners of our institutional commitment under the requirements of the RRAA 2000. [xxx] recognises that by embracing diversity it can achieve its ultimate goal to become a "world class University" and pursue excellence in research, teaching and clinical service.

[xxx] values its diverse community and is opposed to racism in all its forms. The [xxx] is committed to the fair and equal treatment of all individuals and aims to ensure that no-one in the [xxx] community is disadvantaged on the grounds of race, cultural background, ethnic or national origin or religious belief.

These are certainly interesting documents to read in terms of how they show the different ways universities can be imagined as a subject "with" a commitment "to" race equality. In the first document, the policy begins with law, framing institutional commitment in terms of compliance. The commitment, in other words, is named as a way of being subject to law. Commitment here sounds rather close to compliance. We commit insofar as we are required to do so. Commitment is literally "under" the law. We might note that an institutional commitment can be named without necessarily being a commitment to something in particular; *we are committed to whatever the law commits us to do.*

The second quote begins by valuing diversity and refers to racism as what the institution opposes. This statement *of* commitment can also constitute the university as subject *with* commitment to equality and anti-racism. This statement of commitment takes the form of a self-declaration, a declaration of principles that the institution already has. At the same time, the institution is brought into existence by the document as a subject with principles.

How we read these statements of commitment does matter. If the statement of commitment is read as bringing about what it names, then it could participate in the creation of the idea of the university as being antiracist. Such an idea could participate in the concealment of racism within the university. Declaring a commitment to opposing racism could even function as a form of institutional pride: antiracism, as a speech act, might then accumulate value for the organization, *as a sign of its own commitment*. We need to question what follows from this use of commitment as a mode of subject constitution. What do such commitments do? I have already explored the paradoxes that follow when the language of institutional racism becomes part of institutional language. Statements of commitment to antiracism can also have paradoxical effects. A commitment to antiracism in referring to racism as what an institution is "against" could even be used to block the recognition of racism within institutions. In the next chapter I consider how statements of commitment (to equality and diversity) can be used *in* or even *as* an institutional response to racism, often taking the form of an assertion disguised as a question: "how can we be racist if we are committed to equality and diversity?"

When reading these documents as commitments, it becomes evident that commitments are not simply doing what they are saying. Statements of commitment can thus be understood as opaque: it is not clear what they are doing if they are not doing what they are saying. A commitment does not necessarily commit the institution to anything or to doing anything. Statements of commitment (as part of a series of "making commitments") can be understood as "non-performatives."[1] What do I mean by this? We need to return to the meaning of the term "performative." As I pointed out in chapter 2, a performative utterance for Austin (at least provisionally) refers to a particular class of speech. An utterance is performative when it does what it says: "the issuing of the utterance is the performing of an action" (1975: 6). Conditions have to be in place to allow such words to act or, in Austin's terms, to allow performatives to be "happy." The action of the performative is not in the words, or if it is "in" the words, it is "in" them only insofar as the words are in the right place to secure the effect that they name (they are uttered by the right person, to the right people, in a way that takes the right form). Given this, as Judith Butler argues, "Performativity must be understood not as a singular or deliberate 'act,' but, rather, as the reiterative and citational practice by which discourse *produces the effects that it names*" (1993: 2; emphasis added).

I want to introduce here a concept of "the non-performative" as a way of rethinking the relationship between names and effects. I am not suggesting that the non-performative is a particular class of speech acts. In a way, I introduce the concept of non-performative for performative effect (I want to do something by naming certain kinds of practices as non-performatives).[2] Non-performatives describes the "reiterative and citational practice by which discourse" *does not produce* "the effects that it names" (Butler 1993: 2). In the world of the non-performative, to name is not to bring into effect. For Austin, failed performatives are unhappy: they do not act because the conditions required for the action to succeed are not in place (for example, if the person who apologizes is insincere, then the apology would be unhappy). In my model of the non-performative, the failure of the speech act to do what it says is not a failure of intent or even circumstance, *but is actually what the speech act is doing.* Such speech acts are taken up *as if* they are performatives (as if they have brought about the effects they name), such that the names come to stand in for the effects. As a result, naming can be a way of not bringing something into effect.

If statements of commitment do not do what they say, then to analyze what they do, we need to follow them around. When asking practitioners about the process of writing race equality policies, I asked specifically about statements of commitment. What do they (or do they) commit the university to do? In the following exchange between myself and three interviewees from the personnel department of a university, we can hear the hesitation that follows such a question.

QUESTION: Do you feel that the statement itself commits the university to something?

RESPONDER 1: I would say yes but don't know why.

RESPONDER 2: Yes, it does, but my angle, I suppose, is that you have to have reminders, examples, arguments all the time.

RESPONDER 3: And I think it's a good working document that people can take with them.

RESPONDER 1: But people don't like being told to read it.

RESPONDER 3: Yes, they don't like it.

RESPONDER 1: We don't like being told we have to tick these boxes.

RESPONDER 3: It is true, but it exists and I think it's a reference document and people will go back and read it if they wanted to find out something. But people don't want to be told to read it.

If we took statements of commitment as performatives, we would say that they commit you to something. But such performativity is far from taken for granted by practitioners. The first response is that the statement of commitment does "commit," but for unknown reasons. This uncertainty is telling, suggesting that commitment is in some way mysterious or, as I described earlier, opaque. Commitment needs to be explained, even when a commitment has been made. The commitment does not follow the letter of the document. If it is not obvious whether "commitment" does what it says, then it is not obvious why it says what it does, even when commitment is spoken or written as an explicit verb.

The second response also offers a yes, but a qualified one: the statement of commitment does "commit," but it has to be supplemented by other forms of institutional pressure (reminders, examples, and so on). In other words, the commitment is not given by the document but depends on the work generated around the document. It is interesting that the next intervention begins with a further qualifier "but": "but people don't like to be told to read it." If the statement of commitment does not necessarily commit the university to doing anything, practitioners have to keep up pressure on the commitment. But this pressure can mean that documents do not work. This is a telling pressure for diversity workers: you have to put pressure on documents because they do not work, and the pressure on documents is what makes them not work. The compulsion to read the document means that it loses rather than gains currency. If people are required to read it, then they "don't like it."

The following utterance moves from "they don't like it" to "we don't like being told to tick boxes." The implication here is that even commitment can become a tick in the box. As I pointed out in my introduction to this chapter, the concept of commitment is highly valued in the diversity world insofar as commitment seems to move us beyond the tick box approach to diversity, in which institutions go through or along with a process but are not behind it. A tick is a check mark that says yes. A tick box approach is when an action is completed to indicate yes. If commitment can become a tick in the box, it suggests that institutions can make commitments without being behind them. Even a commitment can involve going through the motions. As a result, "being behind" can become an institutional performance: a statement of commitment might create *an illusion of the behind*.

The final utterance redescribes the statement of commitment as a "reference document" that people can use. This document then exists insofar as people refer back to it, as something that can help them do things. Such documents by implication can only work if they are not obligatory: if people do not have to use them, they might work. What this sequence of utterances shows is not only how statements of commitment are not perceived as commitments in and of themselves but how this lack of commitment in the document, which means that we have to work on them to make them work, is what makes them less likely to generate commitment in others.

Statements of commitment can thus be described as non-performatives: they do not bring into effect that which they name. A commitment might even be named *not to bring it into effect*. However, it does not follow that commitments do not do anything. We can explore how practitioners *assume* this non-performativity as a way of doing something. I asked another practitioner why such statements of commitment are useful:

Oh that's hard. I think you cannot not have them, if you don't have them, well, to me as a practitioner it's a starting point. Again it's whether that gets fitted into practice. Commitments can't come without other actions. So the commitment to me is about what the institution believes in and what it intends to do—it can't stand alone, it has to come with how you're actually going to do it. I think if they were not there then, well, I refer to them quite a lot as well, you know, if you're trying to, let's say there's an issue that's come up and somebody is not, maybe there's an issue and perhaps they're racist in what they bring up in their practice or something like that and it's good to refer back to these documents, but actually you're an employee of the university and the university has made a statement about this. So in terms of watching other members of staff and in my own experience, I have used it for that.

The sentence "commitments can't come without other actions" is instructive. It suggests that commitment is an action, but one that does not act on its own but depends on other actions: we might call these "follow-up" actions. For a commitment to do something, you must do something "with it." In other words, commitment might be a technology that can be used or deployed within institutional settings. The statement of commitment is also described as a "reference point," something you can use in a situation when challenging how others act within the institution. In particular, you can use a statement of commitment to show that an individual action is inconsistent with the statement. In other words, even if the statement of commitment does not commit the institution to something, it can allow practitioners to support their claims for or against specific actions committed by individuals within the institution. A statement of commitment can thus function as a supporting device.

Practitioners use statements of commitment as devices insofar as they do not describe what is being done. I asked another interviewee about this mechanism: "So you actually quote the document itself, that's interesting, and does it work?"

> It does not work on its own, no, but it is one way of seeing things, people will argue and argue, but when you say it's about what the university wants you to adhere to because this is what it believes in, then you can't really go against that as an employee, can you? Nobody can challenge that.

Although a statement of commitment can block action by constructing the university or organization as "already committed" or behind race equality, they can also be used to support other actions within specific settings. Practitioners use such statements to challenge people, by showing they are "out of line" with the direction of the organization, even if this line is itself imaginary. Statements of commitment can thus be called on in tricky situations: "the fact of having the document there, it's useful in the sense that you are meeting leader obligations and it's useful in tricky situations that you can use it to the foundation, you can use it to explicate the principles that the university is meant to be acting upon, so it's not unuseful." To describe these documents as "not unuseful" is of course not the same as describing them as useful: perhaps the claim here is that the documents can be useful. The potential utility of the statement is that it generates a set of principles that the university is "meant to be acting upon." It thus allows practitioners to indicate when specific actions are inconsistent with the principles the university is meant to be acting upon. If there is in some sense a lie in the commitment (because the university does not have the principles the statement gives a commitment to), then it can be a useful lie. By producing the university as if it were a subject with such principles, the documents then become usable as they allow practitioners to make members of the university, as well as "the university" itself as an imagined entity, subject to those principles.

We now have a new critical lens with which to reinterpret the status of what I called "official description" in chapter 2. The ease or easiness in which diversity becomes description shows how diversity can be a way of not doing anything: if we take saying diversity *as if* it is doing diversity, then saying diversity can be a way of not doing diversity. We might supplement Austin's title with the following: *How Not to Do Things with Words*. We need to refuse to read such commitments as performatives, as if they bring into effect that which they name. That is not to say that commitments do not matter, or that they do not do any work. They do "do work." Indeed, this non-performativity is what makes statements of commitment usable as tools. Practitioners can use commitments because they fail to describe what is ongoing or going on within organizations. If organizations are saying what they are doing, *then you can show they are not doing what they are saying.*

Committees and Commitment

Commitments are not in the words alone. When commitments do become action points, those actions often aim to show how the words are not acted upon. I want to develop this argument by thinking about how commitment can be structured or distributed. It is worth noting that the term "committee" derives from "commitment." A committee structure is certainly how an organization makes decisions about its commitments or decides who decides about commitments. A decision can take the form of a decision about who will decide. Those of us who spend time in committees know these "decisions about decisions" too well. How many times have you been in a committee when the decision is to pass the decision on to another committee! The passing of x between committees is a structure of deferral as well as referral.

Committees could be described as an institutional habit, to return to my argument from chapter 1. We all know that being in a committee involves signing up to a certain way of doing things, however much organizations might vary (variation is often in degrees of formality and informality). A committee can also be an expectation of who does what, as an expectation of what as well as who turns up. My first experience of university committees was being assumed to be the student representative each time I turned up. If to be a member of a committee is to be given a place at the table, it does not mean anyone can simply take up that place. Some more than others are given a place at the table, just as some more than others are at home in the body of an institution.

A committee is also a conversational space. It offers an official space for conversation, although this does not mean that all these conversations are official. The informal conversations that take place before the official start of the committee can be framing devices. Casual conversations that happen in official spaces are those that do not refer to the official agenda: these might include conversations about lives, or conversations about institutions that take the form of gossip. If institutions bracket such conversations as a break from institutional life, or as only permissible during breaks, then what is bracketed is filled with institutional life: everyone knows such talk saturates official spaces.

We need to attend to the effects of this saturation. I talked informally with a diversity practitioner. She told me of an occasion when she arrived at a meeting of the diversity and equality committee and the senior staff (who were all white men of a certain age) were talking about what they used to eat at Cambridge for breakfast (a conversation, she said, about bananas), a casual conversation about a shared history of consumption that is at once an institutional history. This conversation was a way of taking up space; it allowed these individuals to *occupy* the official space of the meeting.[3] The practitioner described her realization of this occupation: "I realized how far away they were from my world." When we reflect on diversity, we are reflecting on the creation of worlds that give residence to some and not others. Institutional habits refer not only to what an institution does or tends to do but also how certain people become habituated within institutions—how they come to occupy spaces that have already been given to them.

Diversity work is occupational: the aim of embedding diversity and equality requires occupying committees that structure the flow of matter in organizations as I showed in chapter 1. To embed diversity into institutions would mean making diversity part of the routine of a committee. We discussed the need to make diversity a routine in our race equality working group. One of our agreed aims was that we should get every committee within the organization to discuss the implications of their decisions for diversity and equality. The view of the group was that it was important that the university's diversity and equality committee was not the only committee in which diversity and equality were being addressed. We wanted the committees to be technologies for distributing commitment to diversity. This aim of making diversity into a standing item for committees is widely shared. As one practitioner describes, "I mean there are some committees that have diversity as a standing item so it's always discussed." Of course, to have diversity as a standing item does not guarantee whether or how it will be discussed.

If committees are distributors of commitment, then they are key spaces in which diversity work happens. For many practitioners, organizing diversity and equality committees is central to their job description. Certainly this kind of committee work can become the object of diversity work in problematic ways. One practitioner in an informal conversation said that she felt that preparing for committees (getting the papers ready, sending them out, writing up minutes, and so on) was all she had time to do. In a follow-up formal interview, she suggested that the institutional focus on "getting through" the equality and diversity committee was actually a way it suspended rather than enacted its commitment to equality and diversity. As she described: "They wanted to meet just before the committee to see if there were 'any elephant traps.' That's a quote. All the concern was how to get through the committee, without it being controversial. There was never a meeting afterwards on action points or follow-up or anything." When the equality committee becomes a routine, it can provide a means of avoiding action as well as difficulties. To avoid a trap can be to avoid the situations in which you might be required to amend what is being done. Institutions can "do committees" as a way of *not* being committed, of not following through.

This practitioner also spoke to me about what appeared to be an institutional success story: a decision was made and agreed on by the university's equality and diversity committee that all internal members of appointment panels for academics should have had diversity training. This decision could be described as good practice. It was made properly by the committee that was authorized to make the decision (the equality and diversity committee), which included members of the senior management team (SMT). The minutes were then sent to council for approval, which alone has authority to make the recommendation into policy. The story:

> When I was first here there was a policy that you had to have three people on every panel who had been trained. But then there was a decision early on when I was here, that it should be everybody, all panel members, at least internal people. They took that decision at the equality and diversity committee which several members of SMT were present at. But then the director of human resources found out about it and decided we didn't have the resources to support it, and it went to council with that taken out and council were told that they were happy to have just three members, only a person on council who was an external member of the diversity committee went ballistic—and I am not kidding, went ballistic—and said the minutes did not reflect what had happened in the meeting because the minutes said the decision was different to what actually happened (and I did not take the minutes, by the way). And so they had to take it through and reverse it. And the council decision was that all people should be trained. And despite that

I have then sat in meetings where they have just continued saying that it has to be just three people on the panel. And I said but no council changed their view and I can give you the minutes, and they just look at me as if I am saying something really stupid, this went on for ages, even though the council minutes definitely said all panel members should be trained. And to be honest, sometimes you just give up.

It is useful to note how easily a committee decision can be bypassed by an individual if he or she claims authority by exercising authority. Even though the committee with the authority to make this decision has made it, the director of human resources unmakes the decision by taking any reference to it out of the minutes. The decision made by the committee is thus not referenced in the minutes. In this case, it happens that an external member of the council is also a member of the equality and diversity committee and notices the gap between the decision of the committee and the minutes. An individual actor takes the decision out of the document, and an individual actor put it back in. We can note from this example the importance of not assuming that a committee that is given authority to distribute commitment is the primary actor: committees (and their commitments) can easily be bypassed because the documents they produce are written by individuals whose interests do not always coincide with the committee. Even if those who are members of the committee have the opportunity to amend the minutes, it does not guarantee that the minutes will simply document the decision made by the committee (the documentation of any decision involves its own decisions).

We also learn from this example how a commitment can be made fully, passing through an organization in the proper way, through the right channels, without changing what happens in the day-to-day running of the organization. The policy has been made and authorized, and should have force, but individuals within the organization act as if it has not been made. If people act as if a commitment has not been made, then it has not been made. The practitioner who points out that the policy has been authorized is not heard, or if she is heard (referring back to an earlier discussion, we can imagine eyes rolling as if to say "oh here she goes"), she is heard in a way that blocks any hearing of what she is saying. For an institutional commitment to be made, individuals have to agree that it has been made: it is thus possible that institutions can make commitments without those commitments becoming given.

Even if practitioners can make committees make commitments, those commitments can lack force; they do not override the commitments that have already been made. The past is experienced as a momentum that overrides what a committee decides in the present. This momentum was described by one of my interviewees as "institutional indifference or sort of frigidity or frozenness about equality issues." The words "frigid" and "frozen" convey a sense of coldness as well as hardness in the institutional relationship to equality. The organization can be committed to a new policy without anything happening. Indeed, a new commitment defined as a policy can even be a way of keeping an old commitment in place.

A policy, even when it has been adopted by committees, can thus be treated as a stranger, as if it comes from outside the institution. This estrangement can happen even if that policy has been agreed to by the highest committee, the one with the most authority to decide, the committee that stands above all over committees. A policy decision when made by the right people in the right place using the right words can still not be recognized by those within an institution as a commitment. In such cases, commitments must be understood as non-performatives: as not bringing into effect what they name. The very appearance of bringing something into effect can be a way of conserving the past, of keeping hold of what has apparently been given up. As another practitioner describes, "You can put all policies in place and put all the training in place and assume it will all happen and it has not happened."

We could describe this situation in terms of the gap between what an institution makes a commitment to and what it is already committed to. Time becomes a crucial matter here. A commitment is a pledge of future resources. Indeed, performative speech acts are often addressed to the future ("I will," "I do"), which is how they bring something about. As Judith Butler (1993) and Jacques Derrida (1988) have noted, this futurity depends on the past: a performative acquires force only through citation and repetition. A non-performative speaks to a gap between the past and future tense. The speech act is a commitment that points to the future it brings about ("we will henceforth have *all* internal members of appointment panels be diversity trained"), but the past that accumulates overrides this futurity, as what the institution is committed to, by sheer force of habit. Perhaps a commitment can be made precisely because the weight of the past will not allow that "yes" to acquire the force needed to bring something about. A "yes" might even be utterable when it does not have any force, or a "yes" can be more easily uttered *if it is emptied of force*. In other words, it might be easier for an institution or individuals within an institution to say "yes" if there is nothing behind it.

Commitments can be sent out because there is nothing behind them. How do institutions become committed to something in the stronger sense of being behind or bound? To answer this question, we need to address the relationship between commitment and institutional habits. The embodied nature of habit—we can think of this as bodily habituation—suggests habit is how we become behind an action. The phenomenologist Maurice Merleau-Ponty offers a description of a body-at-work defined in terms of its situation:

> My body appears to me as an attitude directed towards a certain existing or possible task. And indeed its spatiality is not, like that of external objects or like that of "spatial sensations," a *spatiality of position*, but *spatiality of situation*. If I stand in front of my desk and lean on it with both hands, only my hands are stressed and the whole of the body trails behind them like the tail of a comet. It is not that I am unaware of the whereabouts of my shoulder or back, but these are simply swallowed up in the position of my hands, and my whole posture can be read so to speak in the pressure they exert on the table. (2002: 115)

Here, the directedness of the body toward an action involves an orientation of the body toward certain things. To have an end in sight (a purpose that is also a task or goal) makes some objects and not others come into view (the desk is near to hand for the writer whose purpose is writing). A body would be "habitual" when it performs actions repeatedly, such that the performance becomes second nature. When it performs such actions, the body *does not command attention*, apart from at the "surface," where it "encounters" an external object, such as the hands that lean on the desk or table that feel the "stress" of the action. The body is habitual insofar as it "trails behind" in the performing of an action: it is not an obstacle to the completion of an action; it is not "stressed" by what is being encountered. For Merleau-Ponty, the habitual body does not get in the way of an action: it is *behind the action*. What trails behind might also be what accumulates force. Think of when you are committed to action, such as a stroke in tennis. If your body is already behind the stroke, you cannot pull back from it. A commitment is about how a body is directed such that it cannot pull back from an action. The action is "being completed" without the need for a decision, and a decision cannot intervene in its completion.

An institutional body can be thought of as a habitual body: a body that in doing some things has certain ends in view, which is what gives it a behind. An institutional commitment is thus how the organization has already acted such that it is committed to a series of actions. This "already" can be experienced as momentum. As I discussed earlier, if organizations have plumbing, then diversity practitioners have to work out where things get stuck. Thinking about commitment gives us a new language to describe what gets stuck. It is not simply somewhere in the organization that things get stuck. Stuckness is an expression of what an institution has already committed to.

I want to relate this discussion of institutional habits to "institutional will." We often refer to institutional will—or perhaps more commonly, "political will"—as that which is necessary to bring something about. When used in this way, institutional will operates in the future tense: what an institution is willing to do, where willing requires some exertion of energy or effort. Indeed, we might say that we need an institutional will in those political situations where something additional has to be invested: in other words, an institutional will is needed to transform a situation in order not to reproduce what would habitually be produced. When used in this way, an institutional will would be required to break an institutional habit.

I suggest instead that an institutional habit could be understood as a continuation of will. In offering what might seem a counterintuitive argument,[4] I draw on the philosopher Hegel. For Hegel, habit and will are continuous. He suggests that human beings "stand upright" as an act of will that has been converted into habit: "a human being stands upright has become a habit acquired through his own will" ([1827–28] 2007: 156–57). A habit is thus a "continuation" of willing, "it is a continuous will that I stand but I no longer need to will standing as such" (157). A habit is *a continuation of willing what no longer needs to be willed.* I think this formulation is especially useful for rethinking the category of "institutional will." A habit is how an institution keeps willing something without having to make something an object of will. Returning to the foregoing example, we might note that individual actors can tussle over the object of will (in the minutes, out of the minutes) without changing the form: the institutional will is willing that is continuous with what has already been willed; an institutional will is that which does not need to be made into an object of will.

An institutional will can thus survive individual acts of volition if those acts are inconsistent with what is being willed. In chapter 2, I asked how the institutional will to diversity relates to the experience of the institution as wall, which I reposed as a simple question: how does the will become a wall? We can now understand how the wall itself could be described as will: *the wall then would be an expression of what the institution is willing to bring about.*[5] Referring back to Hegel's terms, a wall could be described as an "institutional standing." There is "a continuous will that [it] stand but [it] no longer need[s] to will standing as such."

The will is made out of sediment: what has settled and accumulated over time. No individual actor needs to make this wall into an object of will.[6] No individual has to block an action that is not continuous with what has already been willed. In the example, we might note that the director of human resources did not need to take the decision out of the minutes for the decision not to bring something into effect. We come up against the wall when a decision is made that is discontinuous with the institutional will. Perhaps the wall is will insofar as it embodies what an institution is *not* willing to bring about. The wall is an institutional "no" that does not need to become the subject of an utterance. The gap between the signs of will (the yes or will to diversity) and institutional will (the no or the wall to diversity) is noticeable only when one attempts to cross a limit.

Individuals and Commitment

Thinking of the continuity between will and habit offers another lens through which to address commitment. A symbolic commitment does not necessarily represent an institutional commitment and can even be given "given" its absence. I return to the question of the committee as a commitment distributor. Although many practitioners talked to me about the importance of committees, they are also self-conscious that the decisions of committees, including those that lead to official policies, cannot be treated as institutional commitments. A committee structure can participate in creating the illusion of a commitment, such that what passes through the body of an organization is not necessarily what the organization is behind.

Individual commitment comes up as an important supplement to institutional work precisely given how easily institutional commitment can be made without becoming given. One practitioner reflects: "The vision, you know everyone looks at the vision and tries to hang whatever they do onto the vision, because that's the training and that's what you're supposed to do, so you always refer back to it. If it's not there, that commitment, then it really is lost because no committee, or policies, or what have you are not going to go anywhere." Without "that commitment" or "vision," a decision or a policy made by a committee will simply not get anywhere.

We can see how the opacity or elusiveness of commitment (the "that" that you are supposed to do) becomes part of the dilemma. Commitment becomes powerful as a discourse in part by describing something that seems either absent or present, an intangible thing that is given tangible qualities in institutional talk, as that which enables or prevents change, as that which allows a flow or determines a blockage. A central difficulty for diversity workers is described here: it becomes difficult if the success or failure of institutional work appears to be caused by such an obscure phenomenon. I explore in this section how individual actors become important as "commitment carriers," which offers a less obscure way for dealing with the same phenomena.

Practitioners often speak of the importance of committed individuals to enabling an institutional commitment: "There's an awful lot of time needed so you have to have people who are committed, otherwise it's just not going to happen." Those who are committed, who are willing to give time to diversity, are typically described as "diversity champions." The story of institutional diversity is often narrated as a story of diversity champions. One of the reasons some practitioners prefer the term "diversity" is that as a positive term, it is more likely to be championed: "I like diversity because having diverse people means you are more likely to end up with champions, but not everyone's going to be a champion, people have different interests and different focuses and different strengths." In my own workplace, I was an equal opportunity representative for my department and I attended a committee with other representatives. A decision was made to rename us "diversity champions" because this name was seen as more positive, proactive, and enabling.

A diversity champion is not simply a name given to someone who has an official role. A diversity champion is regularly described by practitioners as having a genuine commitment to diversity and thus being willing to speak up and stand up on behalf of certain policies. Many of my interviewees talked pragmatically about the importance of who does this standing up: it is important that diversity champions are senior and credible people within the organization, people whose views will be taken seriously. One practitioner describes, "So what you need are champions who may be different in each unit of your business, as it were. It's to do with, if that person says I think diversity and equality is actually extremely important, it has a credibility that you don't get from me because those peers are going to say, well, this guy is no soft touch, they are very clever, they have great judgment, they don't waste their time on stuff that is not important, I will take this seriously." If diversity is devalued as soft, as I noted in chapter 2, then diversity work can aim to harden diversity, by finding champions who are not viewed as a "soft touch."

Diversity championship is also a discourse of leadership.[7] It becomes essential that leaders become diversity champions: "One of our priorities, of course, is to institutionalize the equity university values that are championed and we are lucky to have them continue to be championed by quite senior people in the management here." Note "champion" is used here as a verb: diversity is institutionalized when "senior people" champion diversity. The commitment of leadership is necessary for values to become embedded within organizations: "I think that if you have lots of nice policies and programs in place but if you have no commitment from senior management, they will gradually whittle away through underresourcing and lip service." The commitment of senior management is necessary for policy to be translated into action—to go beyond lip service, when organizations are saying as a way of not doing.

Some practitioners spoke about this commitment as a kind of hap, accident, or chance (we *happened* to appoint a leader who *happened* to be committed to diversity). The key is to transform this hap into a structure: "If we looked at every institution, we might say well it is accidental (whether you have a commitment), but it might be that it's accidental at the start, but then as your reputation grows and the fact that you're doing it, it becomes part of senior management thinking. It then stops being accidental and people are actually being chosen for their commitment." Diversity work could be described as resistance to the casualization of the commitment to diversity.

In telling successful stories of diversity, practitioners often allude to the personal commitment of their vice chancellors: "I mean, I think certainly the vice chancellor himself is personally committed to the whole equality and diversity agenda. I think that's a genuine commitment. Obviously with things being as they are, occasionally that agenda can get driven down the list of priorities. But I think it is increasingly seen as integral to everything that we do. That's easy to say, but I think increasingly people are recognizing that's a reality we have to face now. So I would say it is taken seriously and the office itself is well thought of, well regarded by staff and students." If the commitment of organizational leaders is (unsurprisingly) understood as crucial to the success of diversity work, it is narrated as a means to an end. The point of this commitment is that it must be distributed to others; it does not stay within an individual:

> Now, one of the things that probably helps in terms of trying to embed all of the work and university issues is that currently, and this is never forever, we have a vice chancellor who is extremely knowledgeable and

is a driving force in ensuring that equity issues for our students and staff are confronted so, while I have got that clear I feel really comfortable in confronting head-on a range of equity issues either for staff and I'm sure the PVC [pro vice chancellor] does for students. Without that influence and without that determination and specific knowledge and drive at that level my position might look, even on paper it might be the same, but in reality it might be different . . . that commitment spreads.

The difference made by a committed leadership is not then a difference you can necessarily see on paper. But it makes a significant difference to how diversity practitioners experience the institution.

If commitment is located in the body of a leader, it is also something that must spread to others through forms of influence, promotion, and drive. The commitment of leadership is thus often described as a starting point: "Having committed leadership, you could not achieve equality and diversity without leadership and without leaders who are at the top levels of the organization. How can you create change? How can you change the culture of the mainstream? Who is it that's actually influencing those areas? It is people from the top, the deans, the vice principals, and if you can get them it's about the hearts and minds of them. If you can start the change with them then it can follow into the institution. I think that's your starting point." You start with the commitment of leadership because this commitment is more likely to affect a sense in commitment in others.

It was noteworthy that some practitioners spoke explicitly about how to get commitment to spread from the top to the bottom of the organization by setting up champion groups at lower ranks who are more in touch with the "grassroots" networks:

We have an equality and diversity committee who tend to be made up of middle to senior managers, deans, directors, associate deans, etc., who are very able, and by and large they're there because they have an understanding of the issues but they don't have the spare capacity and the grassroots knowledge, the sort of networking at grassroots level to champion things like consultations and feedback and going round and asking people "did you know this training was available?" So, I'm looking at setting up a network, an equality champions group, involving people of lower ranking if you want to use that language who have an undying commitment to equality and diversity. They may even use it as a cv builder, I don't care, but they're more in touch with all the networks. I do think it's important that they have some way of feeding in to the dean or director, because otherwise they will just become a toothless tiger. I am hoping that as this is developed along with the new structure it will be embedded from the outset.

Networks come to matter as ways of distributing commitment, or even as distributors of commitment, as the "lifeblood" of the organizational body. Networks thus feed the organization; they are also what give the leadership of the organization its bite.

Other practitioners talked to me about the importance of having champions "in the middle" of the organization: "There is lots of enthusiasm from the bottom up. I think people in middle management don't get a sense of either the vision or the practical operational sense that they can do to implement vision." This practitioner located a gap between the enthusiasm of the bottom and the visionary statements of the top. Things seem to get stuck in this gap. Behind the hopeful narrative of individual commitment "spreading" is thus a more anxious one: the location of commitment in the bodies of individuals can be a way that commitment does *not* spread. A common theme within my interviews was *how to translate individual commitment into collective commitment*. If the point of translation is to close the gap between individual and institutional commitment, then it also exposes a gap. One practitioner, for example, talks about how her university's dependence on what she calls "equity champions" sustains the vulnerability of diversity as a framework for action: "I think one of the major problems over the years has been that we have relied very heavily on equity champions throughout the university and in an environment where universities are increasingly becoming very funding conscious, those equity champions are still doing their work, but it has slipped on their list of priorities because they legitimately have other very real worries, such as the financial survival of the university." The reliance on individuals who champion diversity and equity is here identified as a source of weakness, insofar as the values of equity and diversity are embodied by such people rather than by the university. As these people come and go, or as their priorities change, so too diversity and equality "come and go." The commitment of champions can be how the university itself appears to be committed: the university cannot commit to diversity insofar as such champions "do this work." The university might even appropriate their commitment "as its own." At the same time, without such champions, it is widely believed that there would be no commitment at all: the university only *has* commitment to the extent those within it *are* committed.

Even when organizations have committed to diversity in the form of policies that are authorized and passed through the right committees, committed individuals remain key to making things happen. Yet the commitment of individuals can also be a means for organizations not to distribute commitment. Many comments by diversity practitioners pointed to this paradox: they remain dependent on the ongoing work of committed individuals even when diversity and equity have been embedded within the strategic missions and operational procedures of the organization. This is why the work of diversity seems never ending: even when universities allocate resources to diversity and equity initiatives, that allocation seems to depend on individual persistence and individuals who keep saying that diversity counts after it has, as it were, been counted. The expenditure of time, energy, and labor of diversity champions is necessary, even if it also reproduces hierarchies within the university through the uneven distribution of commitment. The depletion of resources is partly manifest in the depletion in the energies and capacities of overcommitted individuals and units. If diversity and equity work is less valued by organizations than other kinds of work, then the commitment of some staff to diversity might reproduce their place as "beneath" other staff within the hierarchies of organizations.

One of the central debates around mainstreaming diversity and equity can be rearticulated in terms of the politics of commitment.[8] For example, one practitioner spoke of an attempt made by senior management to cut the equality and diversity committee. She describes: "They're always trying to cut down on committees. So they tried to cut the equality and diversity committee because 'we didn't need it,' because 'we are pretty good at equality and diversity,' and then you point out that if you didn't have that you would have to have some other mechanism, and then I took it a stage further and asked what are the other committees are doing, and have they got it as part of their remit, and they all just looked at me, and I thought this is pathetic, you can't even be bothered to find out what the others are doing, because I don't know, but I don't think very much." The explicit justification for cutting the equality and diversity committee is that all committees should be doing this work. But they are not. The idea that equality and diversity should be mainstream becomes an implicit argument that it is *already* mainstream when it is not. This practitioner went on to describe how she got her SMT to change its decision: "There was one institution that got rid of their equality and diversity committee because they decided to make the senior management team into the committee. That's what they did. I did propose that here, and that was when they decided to keep the committee." Keeping the equality and diversity committee then becomes a way that the SMT can avoid the labor of commitment.

In another of my interviews, having an autonomous unit was identified as a problem, insofar as it allows other actors within the university not to take responsibility for diversity and equity initiatives: "I think some of them [senior managers] will be aghast that they are responsible for doing anything . . . you know, 'I thought the equity and diversity unit did that' and that's one of the big problems when you have a very strong equity and diversity unit, then 'oh, well, that's their job.' " In other words, having an equity unit can allow the refusal of a more collective sense of responsibility: if the unit does diversity, then it might follow that others within the organization do not have to do it. The distribution of responsibility for diversity, what we could call the "organization of commitment," is uneven or even involves some "having" this responsibility so that others not only do not have to "have it" but can actually *give it up*.

At the same time, the project of "integrating diversity" by not having a diversity unit, which works on the principle that "everyone" should be responsible for diversity, does not seem to work. I would speculate that "everyone" translates quickly into "no one": unless responsibility is given to someone, it is both refused and diffused within the organization. By implication, working on diversity and equity requires an acceptance of the uneven distribution of commitment, rather than a fantasy that "everyone" can share responsibility. Of course, this issue remains complicated. On one hand, to depend on the uneven distribution of commitment is to repeat that unevenness (to allow diversity to be "given" to some units or bodies and not others), whereas on the other hand, to act "as if" diversity is a shared responsibility both conceals the unevenness and diffuses any commitment.

In one university involved in this study, a decision was made to disband the equal opportunities unit and relocate this work within human resources. The decision was justified as part of the project of integrating or mainstreaming diversity. The following conversation describes the history of the disbanding of the unit:

> INTERVIEWEE: Yes, well, that's another story, too. The university did have an equal opportunity unit, which had, let me see, about three or four staff. The university decided to disband the equal opportunity unit. The director's position was made redundant. One of the staff members went into a more student-focused area, and one of the other main staff members came to us as an equity and diversity consultant and she was very knowledgeable in what she did, very enthusiastic, would motivate people, she's a great trainer. But she left us in September 2002.
>
> INTERVIEWER: That's a while back.
>
> INTERVIEWEE: Yes, so what happened, I took on, one of her main roles was being the support or project officer for the gender equity and diversity committee, which is a committee of the vice chancellor and it has senior staff on it. So I took on that role, and then I seemed to get other little bits and pieces of her role, even though some of the other HR managers were also looking after some of the equity issues. So it was spread across.
>
> INTERVIEWER: So it was not officially handed over to you?
>
> INTERVIEWEE: No, no, because our general manager did not want me to be seen as the equity person. We did not want that, because what we were trying to do was share it across the board, because we were all feeling chock-a-block full of work anyway, that no one person had

the time to take it on in total, and we wanted to continue the efforts for mainstream equity and diversity across the university. That's why we did not want a central focus.

INTERVIEWER: So is that why there was no appointment made?

INTERVIEWEE: Yes, basically. I suppose in some respects it's worked. In other respects it has not worked, because we haven't been able to give as much attention as we would have liked to it.

The interviewee describes herself as the "caretaker" of diversity, even if she is not known within the institution as "the equity person." The project of mainstreaming is about spreading and sharing the responsibility for diversity, rather than giving it to someone. The general manager does not want one person to be "the equity person." But we can see that such an aim of sharing responsibility has not been fulfilled: the success of mainstreaming is limited by the lack of attention given to diversity and equity. If diversity is not someone's agenda, then it tends to fall off the agenda. As another practitioner describes, "If we were really successful, we'd do ourselves out of a job. That would be the aim, not to need a unit like this because the mainstreaming is so complete. When the HR director took up this mainstreaming (or should that be, became an advocate to mainstreaming) I think that was a dire day, because none of the universities are ready for that kind of concept where it's embedded in every HR policy and everything that everybody does, and it carries itself. Because none of the universities are at that stage, you just cannot get to all of the people." Here, mainstreaming, even as an ideal, becomes a problem in the sense that universities are not ready for it: to act *as if* mainstreaming is the case, because it *should be* the case, can be counterproductive because the conditions are not available in the present *to make it the case*.

Many practitioners expressed skepticism about the language of mainstreaming and how it can be used by senior managers to avoid giving support to diversity and equality work:

What does "mainstream" mean? You know does that mean it doesn't need people who are experts like us and everything's okay? That's not the case; we know that, particularly on race that's not the case. So you do need that element of support, but you do need a certain element of specialism and drivers and I think that's what we have tried to do between the different groups, have the drivers. . . . So it's not just us [diversity practitioners] that are doing it because in a way we are insignificant. We're the backbone to it, but you need the leaders and the decision makers to take responsibility in terms of mainstreaming, but they're not experts on it. So we have to act as the backbone to it. (Cited in Ahmed et al. 2006: 65)

Because diversity and race equality are not already mainstream—because everything is "not okay"—we need support, specialisms, and drivers. Practitioners or experts provide a backbone: giving support to the body of the organization. This comment shows the problems with how mainstreaming is taken up. When mainstreaming is taken up as if it describes what already exists, then mainstreaming is used by organizations to avoid appointing specialists in the area, or indeed to avoid giving diversity and equality the additional support that it needs. Another practitioner also alludes to the failure of mainstreaming:

We all say that in talking to each other in equal opportunities, we all say that that's what we have in our plans but whether they are actually put into practice is questionable. I have had a strategic action plan that we put together as a committee a year and a half ago, and one of the main themes about mainstreaming equality is that it has not succeeded because there has not been enough drive for us. It's got to be the people that are working at strategic level, so even though I'm there to advise and you're telling people how to do it, it's like saying you have a teaching and learning strategy and you have a group set up for that. I found out recently that there is nothing more than a passing reference to equality and diversity within that, so that to me is, is the message actually clearly getting through? (Cited in Ahmed et al. 2006: 65)

The argument here is not necessarily that mainstreaming should not be an organizational ideal. Rather, the point is that diversity and equality *are* not mainstream and that to treat them *as if* they are simply means the message will not get through. Without an institutional drive, you need those willing to be diversity drivers. Diversity and equality tend to fall off the agenda unless someone forces them onto the agenda, where that someone is usually the diversity or equality practitioner. Of course, as soon as something is forced on the agenda, then it is not mainstream. You do not have to force what is mainstream.[9] Mainstreaming thus fails to describe the kind of work that diversity work involves: having to push for, or drive forward, agendas that organizations are not behind.

Diversity workers often work with what is made but not given. You have to work around and with commitments, whether they are made on paper, by committees, or through individual bodies. Commitment is an interface between policy and action: if a commitment is made on paper, it does not necessarily commit unless you act on and with the paper. To generate institutional commitment means to make institutions "catch up" with what they say they do.[10] Diversity work plays what we could call a catch-up game, working in the gaps between what institutions say and what they do. Diversity workers thus work *with* as well as *in* the gap between words and deeds.

To work in the gap is to work for completion. Diversity and equality are not typically actions that are being completed. For such actions to be completed, if the university is not behind them, requires individuals to keep pushing for their completion. No wonder that diversity workers are often seen as pushy! Pushing is necessary when institutions are not behind what they send out. If "hearts and minds" stands for a sense of commitment that is missing, then diversity workers have to become what is missing: they become the "hearts and minds." Diversity workers in feeling and thinking *for* the institution aim to transform what the institution is *for*.

So far, this book has mainly drawn on the data collected as part of the research project I completed on diversity work, in particular from my interviews with diversity practitioners and my participation in various meetings and seminars on diversity. My aim has been to explore how the diversity world takes shape; how it comes to have certain habits, contours, rhythms, and orientations, without necessarily assuming that diversity is the only or best way of describing this world. If diversity is exercised as a vocabulary with a certain ease or easiness within the mission statements that give form to institutional priorities, then one of my key aims has been to explore some of the difficulties and dilemmas that practitioners experience in "doing diversity." Practitioners tend to inhabit this gap between what organizations say they do and what they "do do." As I explored in the previous chapter, strategies are often about closing the gap by making action catch up with rhetoric. If "closing the gap" describes strategy, then the diversity world is shaped by the failure of diversity to bring into existence the world it names. Or we could say a diversity world comes into existence in the failure to bring into effect what it names. Donna Haraway describes how "nothing comes without its world" (1997: 37).[1] The effort of this ethnography has been to track what does and does not "come with" the diversity world. A simple question, "What does diversity do?" has thus been not simply my starting point but a point I have kept returning to, in questions and conversations, in reflections and hesitations: in short, the question of what diversity is doing offers its own way of inhabiting the diversity world premised on an uncertainty about what is being done.

In this chapter, I step back from the world I inhabited as a researcher of the diversity world to think about how racism does or does not come up. In my interviews with practitioners, the word "racism" rarely entered the conversation: only in discussions of diversity training was racism mentioned at all, and then only in two instances. Of course, we might say that the word "racism" did not come up because I did not bring it up myself: the word "racism" was not in any of the questions I asked practitioners. But is it not surprising or at least interesting that talking about diversity— or even talking about race equality as a positive duty as we did in the United Kingdom–based interviews—did not bring up the question of racism? The realization that racism was not brought up in the main body of the interview (though as I consider in due course, it did come up off tape at the end of one interview, in a way that redirected my thinking) helped me think more about what it means and what it does for racism to be "brought up." Through the course of doing this research, I began to reflect about how speaking about racism becomes difficult *because* of how the equality and diversity world coheres; even practitioners who are aware of this difficulty can be silenced by it.

It is important for me to state at the outset that I am not suggesting that the equality and diversity world is the cause of the problems I am describing. Rather, I reflect on how the creation of diversity as a political solution can participate in making those who speak about racism the cause of the problem. Problems and solutions are very much part of the dilemma I account for in this chapter: if the emphasis on equality as a positive duty takes the form of finding practical solutions to problems, then it might be that the solutions are creating problems by concealing the problems in new ways. Recalling the tool kits discussed in the previous chapter, we might note that utility as an ideal can shape and restrict the form of what is available. I suggested in chapter 1 that solutions to problems can create new problems. I want to make a stronger argument here: solutions to problems are the problems given new form. In this chapter, I draw on some of my experiences as a person of color inhabiting the institutions of whiteness, my experiences of doing the project as part of a diversity team, as well as the wider political contexts of diversity and equality work in which racism "comes up."[2]

Diversity as Public Relations

We could describe diversity *as* a form of public relations. The Chartered Institute for Public Relations (CIPR) suggests that public relations include "the planned and sustained effort to establish and maintain good will and understanding between an organization and its publics."[3] Diversity could be considered a means by which organizations establish and maintain good will. Although public relations is described here as an ongoing work —"planned and sustained"—it is often what comes into force in a situation of crisis for an organization or, to extend the terms used in the definition of public relations, in situations of "bad will" or "ill will." If diversity might be how an organization establishes and maintains good will with its publics, then diversity also acquires utility in response to bad or ill will.

To argue that diversity is exercised as a form of public relations is to suggest that diversity is mobilized in response or as a response to a problem. The language of diversity is often exercised in institutional responses to reports of racism. I offer two examples of newspaper articles reporting on cases of racism in universities in the United Kingdom. The media is crucial to my argument as the interface between an organization and its publics. In both articles, spokespersons for the organization give an official response to an allegation of racism. The articles thus include what I call "institutional speech acts," where individuals speak for, as, or on behalf of the university by giving the university attributes in the form of value statements or commitments.

The first article, "Anxiety in the UK," reports on the experience of international students on a university campus (Pai 2005). Students had experienced racist attacks and, according to the report, were concerned about how the university had responded: "Students, particularly east Asian students, feel fearful of these attacks and are deeply concerned that something should be done. But, according to Jin, they have no proper channels of complaint and are worried that too much noise would have a negative effect on their status at college." The article shows the multiple ways that racism can affect the experiences of minority students: it can take the form of direct violence and harassment, as well as the threat of violence, and can also affect how students respond to this violence. The "anxiety in the UK" here is partly an anxiety that speaking about racism will have a negative impact on those who experience racism ("too much noise"). The anxiety is that to report racism will mean to be heard as noise.

There are indeed risks of speaking about racism. We learn from the responses of the college: "The spokeswoman said: 'This could not be further from the truth. The college prides itself on its levels of pastoral care.'" The response not only contradicts the students' claims ("nothing could be further from the truth") but also promotes or asserts the good will of the college. I am especially interested in how "pastoral care" creates an idea of the organization as "being caring." Pastoral care is tied to an organizational ideal as being good: we do not have a problem (with racism, with responding to those who experience racism?) *because we care for these students*. The response to a complaint about racism and how the college handles the complaint thus takes the form of an assertion of organizational pride. Note also the performative contradiction of saying in response to a claim that there are no proper channels of complaint that there *are* proper channels of complaint. The feedback to student anxiety that they will be heard as noise is to make them the noise, a sound that cancels out the happier buzz of diversity. The response to the complaint enacts the very problem that the complaint is about. The response "we don't have a problem," in other words, is a sign that there is a problem.

Organizational pride can take the form of diversity pride. Diversity as public relations can thus be mobilized in defense of an organization and its reputation. As the spokeswoman goes on to say: "We have many channels in operation to receive feedback from students. Standards of teaching in the college are frequently praised by students, and the college record demonstrates our high commitment to teaching and research." The moment of complaint becomes an occasion for promoting the value of the organization. Organizational pride thus prevents the message about racism from getting through. The speech act does exactly what it says that it does not do: it does not hear complaint by saying that it does hear complaint. If colleges have pride in their policies of pastoral care, then they fail to hear about racism. Returning to my argument in the previous chapter, we can note how commitments to antiracism can become performances of racism: as if to say "you are wrong to describe us as uncaring and racist because we are caring and committed to being antiracist." When antiracism provides a discourse of organizational pride, then racism is not recognized and is enacted in the mode of nonrecognition.

In a second article, "Anti-Racism Initiatives by Universities Are Failing to Have an Effect Off-Campus," we can also identify how organizational pride slides into diversity pride (Milton 2009). The article begins by reporting on Emma Thompson's comments in the press about the treatment of her adopted son at Exeter University: "She said Nick Griffin from the BNP would 'love it at Exeter because of the lack of racial diversity.' "[4] How does the university respond? According to the report, her comments were "vehemently disputed by the university." A staff member identified as the welfare officer responds: "Her comments were taken out of context and sensationalised by the media. We do a lot here to promote diversity both on campus and in the community. At Exeter we have just celebrated One World Week, which we tied in with Black History Month." The response to a challenge of diversity takes the form of a statement of how the university promotes diversity. Indeed, diversity as a form of good practice (One World Week, Black History Month) is used as evidence that there is not a problem with a lack of diversity.

In the same article, two other university representatives are cited: "Overt racism is not a problem on campus, but it can be a problem off campus," says the welfare officer. "We don't have a problem with racism here," says the head of communications for the university, "we take a much more holistic approach, working with the community. But we don't come at it as a way of tackling racism." Statements such as "we don't have a problem with racism" make those who report racism into the problem. Note also that the "holistic approach" of "working with the community" is explicitly linked to not coming at "it" as racism. Racism is not spoken about by those who speak for the university. When diversity is a viewing point, a way of picturing the organization, then racism is unseen.

Racism is heard as an accusation that threatens the organization's reputation as led by diversity. Racism is heard as potentially injurious to the organization. In other words, institutional racism becomes an institutional injury. As I discussed in chapter 1, the concept of institutional racism was introduced to show how racism is reproduced through institutions rather than simply coming from the individuals who inhabit them. But when institutional racism is addressed as an accusation, it becomes personalized, as if the institution is "the one" suffering a blow to its reputation. Those who speak about racism become the blow, the cause of injury.

The belief that there is not a problem with racism can take the form of a belief in the happiness of the organization. As one manager in further education describes:

> I won't sit in a room with you know a white senior management team that are going to sit there and say I think we have no problems with race within this college and I think we have no problems with ethnic diversity within this college because I don't see it, I think everybody is happy. I would say to them, well you need to go and talk to ethnic minorities and find out if they believe it or if I think that that's the case and if I don't think that's the case then, or the ethnic minority people don't think that's the case, their experience and their idea is more valid than actually what you're saying. (Cited in Ahmed et al. 2006: 84)

This description shows us how a claim that there is not a problem can exercise the language of happiness. A belief in happiness, that "everybody is happy," can allow management not to hear those who have a problem. Indeed, management might not talk to those who are likely to talk about such problems to keep their idea of happiness in place. The failure to talk to minority staff implies some level of awareness that those staff members will not share this perception of happiness. Preserving an idea of the institution as happy can involve an active turning away—or even keeping away—from those who might compromise this idea of happiness. To bring a problem to institutional attention can mean becoming the problem you bring—becoming what "gets in the way" of institutional happiness.

A commitment can be exercised to keep problems "out of the way." Completing a research project on diversity allowed me to witness first-hand how organizations respond to racism when they have already "committed" themselves to diversity by exercising their commitment as response. In one instance, the diversity officer for the Centre for Excellence in Leadership talks to a newspaper and uses the words "institutional racism." A newspaper report followed that quotes from the diversity officer about the existence of institutional racism within the further education sector. The director is "outraged" and sends off an email to all staff saying that "we would never accuse a college of institutional racism." I want to think about what is at stake in this "we would never." Institutional racism has already been identified within the sector. The implication is that even if institutional racism exists, we would *not* use the term "institutional racism" to describe its existence.

Racism becomes something bad that we can't even speak of, as if to describe x as racist is to damage or even hurt x. The organization becomes the subject of feeling, as the one who must be protected, as the one who is easily bruised or hurt. When racism becomes an institutional injury, it is imagined as an injury to whiteness. The claim "we would never" use the language of racism is a way of protecting whiteness from being hurt or damaged. *Diversity can be a method of protecting whiteness.* I would also point out that personalizing institutional racism creates a space for whiteness to be reasserted. The speech act "we would not accuse you of racism" can be translated into "I am not racist" insofar as the "I" that would not accuse the "you" has already identified with that you. To speak about racism would hurt not just the organization, reimagined as a subject with feelings, but also those subjects who identify with the organization. They would be hurt by what is heard as a charge, such that the charge becomes *about their hurt.* There is an implicit injunction not to speak about racism to protect whiteness from being hurt.

Speaking about racism is thus heard as an injury not to those who speak but to those who are spoken about. I want to use as another example a "racism controversy" in lesbian and gay politics. The "controversy" (there could be a discussion here about how critiques of racism are displaced by *becoming controversy*) relates to a chapter in *Out of Place: Interrogating Silences in Queerness/Raciality* (2005), a volume edited by Jin Haritaworn, Tamsila Tauqir, and Esra Erdem, titled "Gay Imperialism: Gender and Sexuality Discourse in the 'War on Terror.'" This chapter offered a critique of racism (in particular, Islamophobia) in gay politics, including as an example the work of Peter Tatchell and OutRage! The publishers received complaints about the chapter from Tatchell and his legal team. Tatchell described the chapter as "false and libelous." We can pause here and consider what the word "libelous" is doing in an act of description. Describing something as "libelous" is to evoke the specter of the law. A libelous text would not stand up to the weight of the law. Even to describe a book as libelous can be to threaten it with the law.[5]

Before a proper discussion about these complaints with the editors or authors, the publisher issued a formal apology to Tatchell, based on a set of counterassertions about Tatchell and OutRage! These included that he has never "claimed the role of liberator and expert of Gay Muslims"; "that he is not Islamaphobic"; "that neither he nor Outrage are racist"; "that they have not engaged in racial politics," and so on. As "counterassertions," these assertions counter what are assumed to be the "assertions" of the chapter. The apology effectively aligned the publisher with Tatchell, in such a way that the publisher simultaneously aligned itself against the authors of the chapter of the book they published. The decision not to reprint the book is now impossible to separate from the decision to apologize to Tatchell. As Aren Aizura (2009), Johanna Rothe (2009), and Umut Erel and Christian Klesse (2009) pointed out, the book has in effect been censored from existence. Furthermore, the censorship has been directed toward the critique of gay imperialism in particular. Note that censorship as a practice does not necessarily involve an individual actor who does the censoring (although it can). To censor is to delete what is objectionable. The objection to this chapter enabled the deletion of a book.

I had been wondering how I could respond to these events when I read the critical accounts of censorship offered by Aizura, Rothe, and Erel and Klesse. I was extremely grateful to them and others for writing about the politics of the apology and for making explicit how racism comes up as a mode of response to critiques of racism. There are huge risks in writing or speaking about racism. Even exercising the critical vocabulary of racism can generate a set of defenses, such that an exchange ends up being about the defenses rather than about racism (which is how such defenses are successful). I should also admit I experienced a sense of tiredness—we might call this political fatigue—as I witnessed these events unfold. The apology as a script seemed familiar: too familiar to be rehearsed, yet so familiar it sounded like a rehearsal. We can learn from how responses to critiques of racism sound like rehearsals. It is as if a script was written in advance, as if the very point of the script is to block the critique of racism from getting through.

When I read Tatchell's response to the critics, titled "Academics Smear Peter Tatchell,"[6] it became very clear that even the critiques of his response to the critique of racism were being blocked from getting through. Tatchell claims that many of his "detractors" were "spreading further smears." We probably think we know what it means to "spread smears." "To smear" originally meant to spread or daub with a sticky, greasy, or dirty substance, but it has come to mean "to stain or attempt to destroy a reputation." So these criticisms of the censorship of the chapter are read as attempts to destroy Tatchell's reputation, as a kind of "covering over" with dirt. In fact, the critiques that Tatchell refers to are hard to describe as smears.[7] They actually anticipate the defense that Tatchell made as they explore the problem of how the critique of racism offered in the original chapter had been displaced by being heard as accusatory, as a matter of individual reputation. Tatchell's response thus employs the exact discursive tactics challenged by the critiques by describing the critiques *as* accusations of censorship: "For defending myself against untrue accusations, I am now accused of 'censorship.' "[8] In fact, the critiques of the censorship of the chapter did not accuse Tatchell himself of censorship: in different but related ways, they argue that the book has been censored in part because of the decision by the publishers, which *as a decision* can be located within the problematic terrain examined by the original article.

Responses to critiques of racism take the form of counterassertion ("how can you accuse me of racism," "some of my best friends are black," etc.). These counterassertions might also offer an assertion of a given person's credentials. Counterassertions are often stronger than countering the original assertion in the form of a negative claim ("I *am not* racist"); they often make additional assertions in the form of a positive claim ("I *am* antiracist"). These responses fail to respond to the actual critique of racism *as they take the form of self-recognition* ("I don't recognize myself in the critique of racism"; "I recognize myself as an antiracist"). To respond to a critique requires not referring what is said or written back to oneself but engaging with what is being asserted. When self-reference happens too quickly (when someone responds by defending themselves against a critique by hearing that critique as an attack on their credentials), the opportunity for an engagement is immediately lost. We could describe the censorship of the critique of gay imperialism as the loss of an opportunity.

One difficulty is that responses to racism tend to exercise the figure of "the racist" as the one who can be charged and brought before the law. The very appearance of this figure is what allows a reduction of racism to an individual person who suffers from a false set of beliefs. The figure can do a great deal of work: it is relatively easy for someone to respond to a critique of racism by insisting or even showing *they are not that figure* (unless they are, say, a member of the BNP, and even then the new vocabularies of the BNP might allow someone to say something like "I am not racist, I just love this country"). The reduction of racism to the figure of "the racist" allows structural or institutional forms of racism to recede from view, by projecting racism onto a figure that is easily discarded (not only as someone who is "not me" but also as someone who is "not us," who does not represent a cultural or institutional norm).

Critiques of racism are heard as personal attacks on reputation (repeat: "how can you call me *that*?"), such that one of the biggest accusations you can make is the very accusation that you are accusing someone of racism. As Fiona Nicoll suggests, "The very idea of suggesting that someone might be racist has been elevated into a crime to rival (if not displace) racism itself" (2004: 20). The reduction of racism to an accusation is part of the displacement and thus reproduction of racism. *Indeed, one of the best ways you can deflect attention from racism is to hear racism as an accusation.*

When racism is heard as accusation, then public relations becomes an exercise: the response takes the form of a defense of individual or institutional reputation.

The language of diversity becomes easily mobilized as a defense of reputation (perhaps even a defense of whiteness). In Tatchell's own writings, there is a consistent representation of the LGBT movement as "diversity proud," as the very embodiment of diversity. In one article, "Malcolm X Was Bisexual. Get Over It," Tatchell contrasts LGBT History Month with Black History Month and suggests that the former shows solidarity with the latter by devoting "a whole section of its website to the lives of leading black LGBT people and links to the Black History month." He then observes, "Disappointingly, this solidarity is not reciprocated." Diversity becomes a means of constituting a "we" that is predicted on solidarity with others. Yet this solidarity becomes a mechanism of asserting the superiority of one form of politics over others.

I have suggested that diversity pride becomes a technology for reproducing whiteness: adding color to the white face of the organization *confirms the whiteness of that face.* Perhaps the very prodiversity orientation of LGBT Month shows us how the expressions of commitment to diversity can be mechanisms for reproducing whiteness. Black and minority ethnic groups might not want to express solidarity with diversity pride, because they would, in effect, be expressing solidarity with whiteness. In the U.S. context, Jane Ward has demonstrated very persuasively how the adoption of the language of diversity by mainstream gay politics can be a means of maintaining rather than challenging privilege. She asks: "Who gets edged out as diversity gets ushered in? Ironically the case studies reveal that working-class queer and queer people of color are often marginalized as organizational channels for managing and celebrating diversity are created" (2008: 16; see also Duggan 2003: 44).[9] The discourse of diversity is one of respectable differences—those forms of differences that can be incorporated into the national body. Diversity can thus be used not only to displace attention from material inequalities but also to aestheticize equality, such that only those who have the right kind of body can participate in its appeal.

We need strong critiques of how whiteness can operate under the sign of diversity in activist spaces, including LGBT spaces. We have these critiques behind us: I think especially of Audre Lorde's wonderful autobiography *Zami: A New Spelling of My Name* (1982), which explored some of the problematic consequences of white sexual minorities assuming an allegiance and alliance with sexual minorities who are also racial minorities. Lorde describes how a white lesbian friend "seemed to believe that as lesbians, we were all outsiders and all equal in our outsiderhood. 'We're all niggers,' she used to say, and I hated to hear her say it" (1982: 203). A claim to allegiance can operate as an identification that takes the place of the other by assuming we inhabit the same place.[10] Such identification with sexual outsiderness is at the same time a disidentification from whiteness (a not seeing whiteness) that keeps whiteness in place.

We need to keep making these critiques of how whiteness is reproduced by assuming anew solidarity across differences. If we can learn from these events, we can learn how hard it is to break through the seal of whiteness. As Aida Hurtado (1996) observes, whiteness can be a trickster, or just plain tricky: the responses to its exposure can enact what is being exposed. It is hard to get whiteness recognized by those whose political agency benefits from it not being recognized.

Being the Problem

Racism is treated as a breach in the happy image of diversity; racism is heard as an injury to the organization and its good will. To even use the word "racism" can mean to become the subject of ill will—to become what makes the organization ill, what compromises the health of the organizational body or what gets in the way of institutional happiness. Diversity can thus be mobilized in or as a response to the problem of racism. Describing the problem of racism can mean being treated as if you have created the problem, as if the very talk about divisions is what is divisive.

Black and critical race writers have shown us over generations how the experience of racism is the experience of being the problem. W. E. B. Du Bois taught us that the "real question" is "How does it feel to be a problem?" ([1903] 2003: 8). Du Bois is, of course, writing specifically of the experience of black folk in a country shaped by the historical presence of slavery. We need to attend to this specificity. At the same time, this sense of "being the problem" comes up again and again as a reference point for making sense of the senses of racism. Philomena Essed, for instance, explores how the discourse of discrimination makes those who experience discrimination (rather than those who perpetuate it) into the problem: "They not only have a problem, they also become a problem for others" (1996: 71). In making those who experience racism into the problem, racism does not become the problem (remember, "we don't have a problem with racism here"). To talk about racism is thus to be heard as making rather than exposing the problem: to talk about racism is to become the problem you pose.

Our experience of doing this research was certainly an experience of becoming the problem. I have suggested that diversity can work as a branding exercise, a way of reimaging the organization as "being diverse" through the inclusion of those who embody diversity. An inclusion can become a happy sign of the overcoming of exclusion. Diversity can be used as a technology of happiness: through diversity, the organization is represented happily as "getting along," as committed to equality and anti-racism. If your arrival is a sign of diversity, then your arrival can be incorporated as good practice. Bodies of color provide organizations with tools, ways of turning action points into outcomes. We become the tools in their kit. We are ticks in the boxes; we tick their boxes. As Heidi Mirza suggests, our bodies become targets.[11]

Our diversity team experienced the consequences of being a tick in the box. We embody diversity for the organization not only because our research project was on diversity but because we were legible as a sign of diversity (a team of many colors). The "yes" we embody became a demand for us to say "yes" in return or as return. We were continually reminded that we were the recipients of generous funding. We were indebted. The gift economy is powerful: a means of some asserting the power they have to give to others, which is at once a power to expect or demand a return. Diversity becomes debt.

We are at a meeting for the research projects. The director of the organization is present. We talk about our research, drawing on our interviews. They are all so interested. We are very committed to diversity, the director says. She talks about her personal commitment, over and over again. Sometimes the repetition of good sentiment feels oppressive. What are they trying to convince us of, I wonder? Enthusiasm can be oppressive, I learn. The occasion becomes about the enthusiasm of the white management. It becomes about their commitment to diversity. Commitment can even be a strictly monetary device: the amount they spend on us becomes a sign of their commitment; if they have funded us, we rely on their commitment. Each expression of enthusiasm becomes a reminder of a debt. I know how we are supposed to respond. We are supposed to be grateful. We are good objects at this point, but it is precarious. We know it is conditional on returning their commitment in the right way. What do they want? Will we do what they want?

Their commitment comes with conditions, but the conditions are not made explicit. Our task is to make the conditions explicit. We learn over time that the condition of their commitment is that we would in turn speak about their commitment in positive terms; which means we do not speak about anything that exposes the conditions of their commitment. As such, a condition of commitment becomes a demand to use happy words and a prohibition of unhappy words. "Racism" is heard as an unhappy word, as one that would get in the way of our capacity to fulfill our commitment. Prohibitions do not have to be made official; they can even function under the veil of permission. The permission to speak about racism becomes evidence of antiracism. The permission thus becomes prohibition: racism becomes something that we should not speak about, given that we have been given the freedom to speak of it.

The word "racism" is very sticky. Just saying it does things. Constantly, I am witnessing what the word "racism" does. We speak of racism in our papers, which we give at research meetings to an audience made up of other project teams. I can feel the discomfort. It is hard to know sometimes whether feelings are in the room or are a matter of our orientation, the impressions we have of the room by virtue of the angle at which we are placed. I feel uncomfortable, let's say that. We stop, and someone asks a question about class. It happens over and over again. We speak about racism, and they ask questions about class. Not just class but something more specific: they ask the same question about the complicity of middle-class black professionals, almost as if they have to reimagine black subjects as the ones with relative privilege.[12] They displace the attention. Discomfort shows the failure to fit.

After this particular session, someone from the audience comes up to me and puts her arm next to mine. "We are almost the same color," she says. No difference, no difference. "You wouldn't really know you were any different to me," she says. The very talk about racism becomes a fantasy that invents difference. She smiles, as if the proximity of our arms is evidence that the racism of which I was speaking is an invention, as if our arms tell another story. I say nothing. Perhaps my arm speaks by withdrawing.

I am speaking to one of my interviewees—a woman of color—about racism. It is the only such discussion I had in my formal interviews, although it took place after the interview. We are talking of those little encounters and their very big effects. It is off tape; we are just talking, recognizing each other, as you do, in how we recognize racism in those everyday encounters we have with people who can't handle it, the idea of it. She says, "They always say to me that you reduce everything to racism." A similar judgment has been implied to me or said to me many times. Why are you always bringing up racism? Is that all you can see? Are you obsessed? Racism becomes your paranoia. Of course, it's a way of saying that racism doesn't really exist in the way you say it does. It is as if we had to invent racism to explain our own feeling of exclusion, as if racism was our way of not being responsible for the places we do not or cannot go. It is a form of racism to say that racism does not exist. I think we know this.

But I am thinking more about paranoia and thinking about good reasons for bad feelings. I guess the problem is that I feel paranoid, even if I know that this paranoia is reasonable. I have a kind of paranoid anxiety about everything. I am never sure when x happens, whether x is about racism. I am not sure. If I am not sure, then x is lived as possibly about racism, as what explains how you inhabit the world you do. Racism creates paranoia; that's what racism does. Racism is reproduced both by the fantasy of paranoia (it doesn't "really" exist) and by the effect of the fantasy of paranoia, which is to make us paranoid.

When racism is understood as our creation, we become responsible for not bringing it into existence. The idea that race equality is a positive duty thus translates quickly into an institutional duty for people of color not to dwell on the "negative experiences" of racism. The institutional duty is a "happiness duty" (Ahmed 2010). Returning to the experience of doing the diversity research, we learned mostly about this duty in having been identified as failing it. We write our report as a critique of good practice, as a critique of how the emphasis on "positivity" (positive words, positive stories, and positive experiences) can make it harder to speak about racism, as well as other experiences of the intractability of institutional inequality. It doesn't take long for management enthusiasm to shift into hostility. In an audit panel, the auditors do not even address the findings of the research.[13] They focus on what the project has not offered. There are no numbers. There is too much theory. It will not be useful for practitioners. There is too much focus on racism (surely you are exaggerating, how can there be so much?). Elaine Swan (2010a) argues that these questions function as technologies of displacement: they block the message about racism from getting through. The hostility of the questions of the official audit is replicated in informal communications, a general sense of disappointment in the diversity research, repeated as murmur. They do not publish our report, which now can circulate only unofficially.[14] There are many different mechanisms for stopping the word "racism" from getting through. In chapter 3, I noted how performance culture is about generating friendly documents. Our report was written in a way that refused the demand to befriend the institution. When you are less friendly, you are more likely to be blocked.

To use the language of racism is to risk not being heard. We keep using the language of racism, whatever they say or do. But to keep on using the language does not mean you get the message through. No wonder that antiracist work can feel like banging your head against the brick wall. The wall keeps its place, so it is you who gets sore. Embodying diversity can be a sore point, but the soreness of that point is either hidden from their view, if we go along with the happiness of the image, which sometimes we "do do," or attributed to us (as if we talk about walls *because* we are sore).

Encountering Racism

It is important to stress here that going along with the happy image of an organization does not necessarily involve an act of identification with the organization. It can offer a way of protecting oneself from the consequences of being the sore point (although it does not always work as a form of protection). We could describe this "going along with" as a form of institutional passing: the labor of minimizing the signs of difference from institutional norms discussed in chapter 1. Passing here would not necessarily mean passing as white (a possibility not available to those who are visible as minorities) but passing as the "right kind" of minority, the one who aims not to cause unhappiness or trouble.

We can think of the pressure to pass as the pressure of visibility. I learned this lesson early on in my experience as a member of a race equality group. One of my ideas was to set up a working group for ethnic minority staff at the university.[15] With the kind of collaborative support system of Women's Studies in mind and showing a degree of political naiveté, I thought such a group would be a supportive device: it would enable minority staff to deal with all that whiteness. I had not realized that one of the effects of "all that whiteness" might be that minority staff would already feel hypervisible. At our second meeting hardly anyone turned up; the group was disbanded. I asked a colleague why he thought the initiative had failed. He said that most ethnic minority staff who arrive into the institutions of whiteness experience suspicion from their colleagues about whether they are there on merit. Because of the culture of equal opportunities, arriving as an ethnic minority person can risk being seen as advantaged *because* of your minority status. We know the political irony of how the structural advantages of whiteness are not noticed by those who are advantaged by them. But we still need to account for that "background" sense or feeling of illegitimacy that those who arrive into the institutions of whiteness, who are not white, experience as an institutional everyday. The need to legitimize your existence can require that you actively reduce rather than increase your visibility.

In the introduction to this book, I noted how when people of color turn up at equality and diversity committees, it is not scripted as a becoming.[16] Some people of color do not turn up for this reason. There is a political imperative not to become one of those who turn up *because* of their minority status. Institutional passing can thus refer to the political and emotional labor of being the right kind of minority—the ones who do not even think of themselves in these terms, as minorities. You pass into whiteness by passing out of the category that marks you as not white. The "right kind" is also the one who "can soften"—we might even say soften the blow—who aims not to cause trouble. "Institutional passing" can mean simply not being assertive or not asserting one's difference, as we can note from the following quote: "I think with a black person there's always a question of what's this woman going to turn out like, and maybe they think that about a white person I don't know, but I still think I don't want to use that word too often they're nervous about appointing black staff into senior positions. . . . Because if I went in my Sari and wanted prayer time off and started rocking the boat and being a bit different and asserting my kind of culture I'm sure they'd take it differently" (cited in Ahmed et al. 2006: 78). Some forms of difference are heard as assertive, as "rocking the boat." Some forms of difference become legible as willfulness and obstinacy, as if you are only different because you are insistent. The pressure not to "assert your culture" is lived as a demand to pass and integrate, not necessarily by becoming white but by being more alike. Note how this pressure can be affective: a command or demand does not have to be given, but you experience the potential nervousness as a threat; you try to avoid the nervous glance by not fulfilling its expectation.

The effects of racism make it difficult to bring racism up. Sometimes, we do not even need to bring the question of racism up. Women of color, bell hooks shows, do not have to say enough to cause tension: "A group of white feminist activists who do not know one another may be present at a meeting to discuss feminist theory. They may feel bonded on the basis of shared womanhood, but the atmosphere will noticeably change when a woman of color enters the room. The white women will become tense, no longer relaxed, no longer celebratory" (2000: 56). It is not just that feelings are "in tension," but that the tension is located somewhere. In being felt by some bodies, it is attributed as caused by another body, who thus comes to be felt as apart from the group, as getting in the way of its organic enjoyment and solidarity. The body of color is attributed as the cause of becoming tense, which is also experienced as the loss of a shared atmosphere. Just turning up can cause tension if your arrival is a reminder of histories that have receded from view.

The familiar figure of the "angry person of color" hovers in the background. When a person of color turns up, this figure is already there. The figure gets there before you do. When you do turn up, if things become tense, you become the cause of tension or even the one who is "tense." We can see how a personal experience of racism can also be the experience of being experienced as threatening in the following quote from a black diversity trainer:

> It becomes personal because in the feedback that I got from that person which was extremely forceful, it wasn't just, you know, I recognize that you are a younger teacher, it was worse than that because it was, it wasn't just the process of what I was doing, it was me as an individual, it was you know there is something wrong with you. You are a threat; you are aggressive in your actions and your motivations. And it's that kind of language that I think is racialised as well because it's no surprise to me that the terms aggression and forcefulness were being used to slate me. (Cited in Ahmed et al. 2006: 59)

The words "aggression" and "forcefulness" can stick: they assign the black body with a negative value. The words themselves can carry the weight of a history, becoming a form of racial baggage. The proximity of the black body is experienced as "forcing" something (onto individuals, onto the institution) and is experienced as forcefulness, such that the word itself can be assigned to you; when you become what is wrong, then you wrong what is.

The figure of the angry person of color has a defensive function: for example, if critiques of racism are "just" an expression of our anger, then our anger is heard as without reason. It is as if we talk about racism because we are angry, rather than being angry because of racism. Even if the figure is a defensive fantasy, people of color still have to relate to that figure, as if it corresponds to some truth or even our truth. Another black trainer describes the self-questioning entailed by living with this figure: "The other point as well about being a black trainer is that I've got to rapport build. Do I do that by being a member of the black and white minstrel show or do I do that by trying to earn respect with my knowledge? Do I do it by being friendly or do I do it by being cold, aloof and detached? And what does all this mean to the people now? From my point of view, it probably has nothing to do with the set of people that are in that room because actually the stereotype they've got in their heads is well and truly fixed" (cited in Ahmed et al. 2006: 59). Building rapport becomes a requirement because of a stereotype, as that which is fixed, no matter whom you encounter. The demand to build rapport takes the form of a perpetual self-questioning—the emotional labor of asking yourself what to do when there is an idea of you that persists, no matter what you do.

Indeed, the consequences of racism are in part managed as a question of self-presentation, of trying not to fulfill a stereotype:

> Don't give white people nasty looks straight in their eyes; don't show them aggressive body positions. I mean, for example I am going to go and buy a pair of glasses because I know the glasses soften my face and I keep my hair short because I'm going bald, so I need something to soften my face. But actually what I am doing, I am countering a stereotype, I'm countering the black male sexual stereotype and yes, I spend all my time, I counter that stereotype, I couch my language behaviour and tone in as English a tone as I can. I am very careful, just very careful. (Cited in Ahmed et al. 2006: 60)

Being careful is about softening the form of your appearance so you do not appear "aggressive" because you are already assumed to be aggressive before you appear.[17] The demand not to be aggressive might be lived as a form of body politics or as a speech politics: you have to be careful what you say, how you appear, to maximize the distance between you and their idea of you ("the black male sexual stereotype"). The *encounter* with racism is experienced as the intimate labor of *countering* their idea of you. We might note here the specificity of the experience of being a black man, and thus of the gendered nature of racial stereotypes. The quote recalls the writings of Frantz Fanon ([1952] 1986) and his powerful phenomenological description of the fright of being "the cause" of white fear as a black man (see Ahmed 2004: 62–63). A stereotype is a repetition (see Bhabha 2004: 153). The repetition of a stereotype allows it to accumulate negative affective value. A stereotype *is* a sticky sign.[18] The experience of being a black male subject in the institutions of whiteness is that of being on perpetual guard: of having to defend yourself against those who perceive you as someone to be defended against.

The experience of racism can involve self-censorship: because racism exists, people of color have to conceal its existence. The concealment of racism is understandable—it can be a way of coping with all that whiteness —but it still has far-reaching consequences. Those who do speak about racism are heard as all the more insistent. When people of color talk about racism, we are heard as the angry people they have already assumed us to be.

Feminists of color know very well the trouble it can cause just to bring racism up. If we talk about how racism affects us, then we are getting in the way of reconciliation, as if our talk is what prevents us all from "just" getting along. As Audre Lorde describes: "When women of Color speak out of the anger that laces so many of our contacts with white women, we are often told that we are 'creating a mood of helplessness,' 'preventing white women from getting past guilt,' or 'standing in the way of trusting communication and action'" (1984: 131). To preserve the possibility of getting on and moving on, we are asked to put racism behind us.

Another example: I publish an article on whiteness in the journal *Feminist Theory*, which also included a paper by Suneri Thobani (2007). I had previously written about Thobani's important critiques of the war against terrorism and the politics of how she was dismissed as an angry black woman (Ahmed 2004: 168–69). In this special issue, Thobani's article offers a critique of Phyllis Chesler, Zillah Eisenstein, and Judith Butler for how their writings are complicit with imperialism (albeit in very different ways). The journal publishes a response from Chesler alongside Thobani's article. The response draws on racist vocabularies with quite extraordinary ease. "It will be a good pedagogic tool," I say to a black feminist colleague at a conference. It will show students how racism works in academic practices. I don't convince myself or my colleague. We both know very well we have no need for any such tools. We have too many already.

What does Chesler say? She describes Thobani's article as "ideological, not scholarly" (2007: 228) and as trying "to pass for an academic or even intellectual work" (228). She describes the article as an "angry and self-righteous declaration of war" (228). She suggests "'white' folk have sorrows too" and then suggests that Thobani "is perfectly free to criticise, even to demonize the West, *in* the West because she is living in a democracy where academic freedom and free speech are (still) taken seriously" (230).[19]

The familiarity of these kinds of statements is exhausting. When I read them, I kept thinking of Audre Lorde and how I wished she were here to help us describe the moment. Description gets hard at this point. The woman of color isn't a real scholar; she is motivated by ideology. The woman of color is angry. She occupies the moral high ground. The woman of color declares war by pointing to the complicity of white feminists in imperialism. The woman of color is racist (and we hurt, too). The woman of color should be grateful, as she lives in our democracy. We have given her the right and the freedom to speak. The woman of color is the origin of terror, and she fails to recognize violence other than the violence of white against black. The exercising of this figure does more than make her work: *it is a defense against hearing her work.*

The stakes are indeed very high: to talk about racism is to occupy a space saturated with tension. History is saturation. It is because of how racism saturates everyday and institutional spaces that people of color often make strategic decisions *not* to use the language of racism. If you already pose a problem, or appear "out of place" in the institutions of whiteness, there can be good reasons not to exercise what is heard as a threatening or aggressive vocabulary. We learn also that hearing a language as a threat is a way of not hearing: if the organization has ears, it can block them, to stop the word "racism" from getting through.

If racism tends to recede from social consciousness, then it appears as if the ones who "bring it up" are bringing it into existence. A recession is possible if we make a concession. To recede is to go back or withdraw. To concede is to give way, yield. People of color are asked to concede to the recession of racism: we are asked to "give way" by letting it "go back." Not only that: more than that. We are asked to embody a commitment to diversity. We are asked to smile in their brochures. The smile of diversity is a form of political recession.

Diversity and Repair

One of my aims in this book has been to write about experiences of being included. Inclusion could be read as a technology of governance: not only as a way of bringing those who have been recognized as strangers into the nation, but also of making strangers into subjects, those who in being included are also willing to consent to the terms of inclusion. A national project can also be understood as a project of inclusion—a way others as would-be citizens are asked to submit to and agree with the task of reproducing that nation.[20]

Others have written of the current moment as a time in which the liberal promises of happiness and freedom have been extended to those who were previously excluded. For example, Jasbir Puar elegantly describes how a new class of (affluent, white, male) queer subjects are being "folded into life" (2007: xii, 24, 35, 36). The fold into life is an invitation to live; more than that, it is an invitation to live well, to flourish. The good ethnic as well as the good homosexual might be the ones who choose life, where life means being willing to become worthy of receiving state benevolence. To be included can thus be a way of sustaining and reproducing a politics of exclusion, where a life sentence for some is a death sentence for others.

I think this analysis provides an astute reading of both the politics of the state and those forms of politics premised on being willing to be the recipients of benevolence. If we start from our own experiences as persons of color in the institutions of whiteness, we might also think about how those benevolent acts of giving are *not what they seem*: being included can be a lesson in "being not" as much as "being in." The "folding into life" of minorities can also be understood as a national fantasy: it can be a "fantasy fold." We come up against the limits of this fantasy when we encounter the brick wall; we come up against the limits when we refuse to be grateful for what we receive. As Gail Lewis has convincingly shown, the inclusion of racial others by institutions implicit in the creation of the category "ethnic minorities" can mean, in practice, being "managed through a regime of governmentality in which 'new black subjects' were formed" (2000: xiii). "Being included" can thus be to experience an increasing proximity to those norms that historically have been exclusive; the extension of the norms might be not only a fantasy but also a way of being made increasingly subject to their violence.[21] We are not then simply or only included by an act of inclusion. In being "folded in," another story unfolds.

The smile of diversity is a fantasy fold. Diversity is often imagined as a form of repair, a way of mending or fixing histories of being broken. Indeed, diversity enters institutional discourse as a language of reparation; as a way of imagining that those who are divided can work together; as a way of assuming that "to get along" is to right a wrong. Not to be excluded becomes not simply an account of the present (an account of becoming included) but also a way of relating to the past. Racism is framed as a memory of what is no longer, a memory that if it was kept alive would just leave us exhausted. Fanon once commented very wisely how slavery had become "that unpleasant memory" ([1952] 1986: 115). It is almost as if it would be impolite to bring it up. In the book *Life in the United Kingdom*, on which British citizenship tests are based, there is one reference to slavery and that is to abolitionism (Home Office 2005: 31). The nation is remembered as the liberator of slaves, not as the perpetrator of slavery.

The empire has even been imagined as a history of happiness. In a speech given in 2005, Trevor Phillips describes empire as a good sign of national character: "And we can look at our own history to show that the British people are not by nature bigots. We created something called the empire where we mixed and mingled with people very different from those of this island." Happiness works powerfully here: the violence of colonial occupation is reimagined as a history of happiness (a story of hybridity, of mixing and mingling). The migrant who insists on speaking about racism becomes a rather ghostly figure. The migrant who remembers other, more painful aspects of such histories threatens to expose too much. The task of politics becomes one of conversion: if racism is preserved *only* in our memory and consciousness, then racism would "go away" if only we too would declare it gone.

The promise of diversity *is* the promise of happiness: as if in becoming happy or in wanting "just happiness" we can put racism behind us. We can use as an example here the film *Bend It Like Beckham* (2002, dir. Gurinder Chadha).[22] The film could be read as offering a narrative of repair. Reading this film in the context of an analysis of institutions is useful—a way of connecting an institutional story with a national story. The film is not only one of the most successful British films at the box office; it is also marketed as a feel-good comedy. It presents a happy version of multiculturalism. As one critic notes: "Yet we need to turn to the U.K. for the exemplary commercial film about happy, smiling multiculturalism. *Bend it like Beckham* is the most profitable all-British film of all time, appealing to a multicultural Britain where Robin Cook, former Foreign Secretary, recently declared Chicken Tikka Masala the most popular national dish. White Brits tend to love *Bend it like Beckham* because it doesn't focus on race and racism—after all many are tired of feeling guilty" (D. McNeil 2004). What makes this film "happy" is partly what it conceals or keeps from view. It might offer a relief from the negative feelings surrounding racism. We can note that these negative feelings are not identified with those who experience racism, but with "white Brits": the film might be appealing because it allows white guilt to be displaced by good feelings. The subjects for whom the film is appealing are given permission not to feel guilty about racism; instead, they can be uplifted by a story of migrant success.

The film offers a narrative of repair, a way of healing the injury of racism. The narrative is premised on the freedom to be happy, as the freedom of the daughter Jesminder (Jess) to do whatever makes her happy. Jess's idea of happiness is to play football, which is what puts her idea of happiness into proximity to a national idea. But her father won't let her play. How do we reach our happy resolution? We can consider two speeches the father makes in the film; the first takes place early on, the second toward the end:

> When I was a teenager in Nairobi, I was the best fast bowler in our school. Our team even won the East African cup. But when I came to

this country, nothing. And these bloody gora in the clubhouse made fun of my turban and sent me off packing. . . . She will only end up disappointed like me.

When those bloody English cricket players threw me out of their club like a dog, I never complained. On the contrary, I vowed that I would never play again. Who suffered? Me. But I don't want Jess to suffer. I don't want her to make the same mistakes her father made, accepting life, accepting situations. I want her to fight. And I want her to win.

The father's memory of racism on the cricket ground stops him from letting her play. A memory of racism can be what "gets in the way" of happiness. For the daughter to play, he must first let go of the memory. The desire implicit in both speech acts is the avoidance of the daughter's suffering. In the first speech, the father says she *should not play* so as not to suffer like him. In the second, he says she *should play* so as not to suffer like him. The gap between the speeches indicates a change of mind, a change of heart: to avoid history being repeated as suffering, he must let Jess play; he must let her go.

The second speech suggests that the refusal to play the national game is the "truth" behind the migrant's suffering: you suffer because you do not play the game. By implication, not only is he letting her go, he is letting go of his own suffering, the unhappiness caused by accepting racism, as the "point" of his exclusion. The exclusion of the migrant becomes readable as self-exclusion. Happiness becomes about "playing the game," about letting yourself be included. "Playing the game" would refer not simply to the sporting field but to the national field. The task of the migrants is to include themselves in the game.

In the first speech, being teased about the turban is what sends the father "off packing." We could think about the turban as a sticky sign.[23] We might say that the turban is what the migrant should give up to play the national game: the turban keeps an attachment to culture, to religion, to the homeland. Or if the migrant wants to keep the turban (the nation, after all, can incorporate some forms of difference under the happy sign of diversity), he must convert the turban into a happy object that can coexist with other objects, such as the flag. The father initially fails to make the conversion. He holds on not just to difference, to what keeps him apart, but to the unhappiness of difference as a historical itinerary. In other words, he is hurt by the memory of being teased about the turban, which is what makes the turban an unhappy object, tied to a history of racism.

The very memory of racism becomes an obstacle as that which stops the migrant from participating in the national game. Racism becomes readable as what the migrant is attached *to*, as an attachment to injury that allows migrants to justify their refusal to participate in the national game ("the gora in their clubhouse"). By implication, migrants exclude themselves if they insist on reading their exclusion *as* a sign of the ongoing nature of racism. The narrative implicit in the resolution of the father's trauma is not that migrants invent racism to explain our loss but that we preserve its power to govern social life by not getting over it. The moral task is thus "to get over it" as if when we are over it, it is gone.

In other words, the task is to put racism behind you. Jess is the one who *takes up this task*. We can note here that the father's experience of being excluded from the national game are repeated in Jess's encounter with racism on the football pitch (she is called a "Paki"), which leaves to the injustice of her being sent off. But in this case Jess's anger and hurt do not stick; she lets go of her suffering. How does she let go? She says to Joe, her football coach, "You don't know what it feels like." He replies, "Of course I know how it feels like, I'm Irish." This act of identification with suffering brings Jess back into the national game (as if to say, "we all suffer, it is not just you").[24] The film suggests that whether racism hurts depends on individual choice and capacity: we can let go of racism as something that happens, a capacity that is attributed to skill (if you are good enough, you will get by), as well as the proximate gift of empathy, where the hurt of racism is reimagined as a common ground.

It is important to note that the melancholic migrant's fixation with injury is read as an obstacle not only to their own happiness but also to the happiness of the generation to come and national happiness. This figure may even quickly convert in the national imaginary to the "could-be-terrorist" (Ahmed 2004). His anger, pain, misery (all understood as forms of bad faith insofar as they won't let go of something that is presumed to have gone) becomes "our terror." To avoid such a terrifying end point, the duty of the migrant is to attach to a different happier object, one that can bring good fortune, such as the national game. The film ends with the fortune of this reattachment. Jess goes to the United States to take up her dream of becoming a professional football player, a land that makes the pursuit of happiness an originary goal. Happiness becomes a vertical promise, the promise of mobility, of what allows you to move up and away.

The love story between Jess and Joe offers another point of reattachment. Heterosexuality becomes a form of happy return, promising to allow us to overcome injury. Love promises to overcome the injury or damage of racism. The acceptance of interracial heterosexual love is a conventional narrative of reconciliation as if love can overcome past antagonism and create what I call hybrid familiality: *white with color, white with another*. Such fantasies of proximity are premised on the following belief: if only we could be closer, we would be as one.[25]

The final scene is a cricket scene: the first of the film. As we know, cricket has been evoked in the father's memory of racism. Jess's father is batting. Joe, in the foreground, is bowling. He smiles as he approaches us. He turns around, bowls, and gets the father out. The implication is that it is Joe who enables the father to let go of his injury about racism and play cricket again. It is the white man who folds the migrant into the nation. Proximity becomes a promise: the happiness of the film is the promise of "the one," as if giving love to the white man as the ideal subject of the nation would allow us to have a share in this promise.

Recovery can not only re-cover an injury but demand that an injury be covered over. Implicit to the narrative is the concept of duty: migrants or strangers, those who are welcomed into the institutions of whiteness, must be loving and grateful in return. I would argue that diversity is exercised as a repair narrative in the context of institutions: a way of recentering on whiteness, whether as the subject of injury who must be protected or as the subject whose generosity is "behind" our arrival. To show our gratitude, we must put racism behind us. Even as memory, racism can be understood as an obstacle, as what "gets in the way" of our participation in institutions. Diversity is achieved when we show we are willing to participate: perhaps we must be happy as well as willing.

The happy signs of diversity become legible as signs of overcoming racism. Racism in turn is often reduced to bad feeling. The narrative of an injured whiteness is central to fascism: white people are represented as hurt by the proximity of racial others (see Ahmed 2004: 1–2). A version of this argument is also made by Julia Kristeva, who suggests that depression in the face of cultural difference provides the conditions for fascism: so we should eliminate the Muslim "head scarf" from the public sphere (1993: 37). There is a more sophisticated version of the argument in Ghassan Hage's *Against Paranoid Nationalism* (2003), which suggests that continued xenophobia has something to do with the fact that there is not enough hope to go around, although he does not, of course, attribute the lack of hope to cultural difference. Despite their obvious differences, the implication of such arguments is that antiracism is about making people feel better: safer, happier, more hopeful, and so on.

It might seem that happy, hopeful, and secure nonracist whites hardly populate our landscape. So we really should not bother too much about them. But I think we should. For this very promise—that antiracism resides in making whites happy or at least feeling positive about being white—has also been crucial to the emergence of pedagogy within Whiteness Studies.[26]

In Whiteness Studies, we can detect some anxiety about the place of "bad feeling" and "feeling bad." Even within the most "critical" literature, there is an implicit argument that Whiteness Studies should not make those who are white feel too bad about being white because bad feeling leads to racism. Such positions do respond to the work of bell hooks (2000) and Audre Lorde (1984), who both emphasize how feeling bad about racism or white privilege can function as a form of self-centeredness, which returns the white subject "back to" itself as the one whose feelings matter. Guilt can be a way of performing of rather than undoing of whiteness. Guilt certainly works as a "block" to hearing the claims of others as it "returns" to the white self. But within Whiteness Studies, does the refusal to make Whiteness Studies about bad feeling allow the white subject to "turn toward" something else? What is the something else? Does this refusal to experience shame and guilt work to turn Whiteness Studies away from the white subject?

Ruth Frankenberg has argued that if whiteness is emptied of any content other than that which is associated with racism or capitalism, then "this leaves progressive whites apparently without any genealogy" (1993: 232). I should note here that Frankenberg's work has been hugely important: offering us a feminist and critical geography of whiteness that attends to the complex ways that white women negotiate whiteness in time and in space. But the implications of this particular argument are somewhat unfortunate. It assumes the subjects of Whiteness Studies are "progressive whites" and that the task of Whiteness Studies is to provide such subjects with a genealogy. Joe L. Kincheloe and Shirley R. Steinberg make this point directly when they comment on "the necessity of creating a positive, proud, attractive antiracist white identity" (1998: 12). The shift from the critique of white guilt to claiming a proud antiracism is not a necessary one. But it is a telling shift. The white response to the black critique of shame and guilt has enabled here a turn toward pride, which is not, then, a turn away from the white subject and toward something else but another way of returning to whiteness. Indeed, the most astonishing aspect of this list of adjectives (positive, proud, attractive, antiracist) is that antiracism becomes just another white attribute or even a quality of whiteness (this rather likable whiteness would be one in which antiracism can be assumed). Antiracism even becomes a discourse of white pride.

Here, antiracism becomes a matter of generating a positive white identity that makes the white subject feel good. The declaration of such an identity sustains the narcissism of whiteness and allows Whiteness Studies to make white subjects feel good about "their" antiracism. One wonders what happens to bad feeling in this performance of good, happy whiteness. If bad feeling is partly an effect of racism (rather than its origin) and racism is accepted as ongoing in the present (rather than what happened in the past), then who gets to feel bad about racism? One suspects that happy whiteness, even when this happiness is *about* antiracism, is what allows racism to remain the burden of racialized others. Indeed, I suspect that bad feelings of racism (hatred, fear, and so on) are projected onto the bodies of unhappy racist whites, which allows progressive whites to be happy with themselves in the face of continued racism toward racialized others.

Audre Lorde has taught me so much about the politics of emotion and about how institutional spaces are saturated. Bodies that come and go leave traces behind, as signs of former occupations. Our bodies can re-member these histories, even when we don't. Lorde invites us to use the anger we might have about racism creatively or even to identify our anger as a creative response to histories of racism that are unfinished. Addressing herself to white women, she suggests that "she cannot hide" her anger "to spare" their guilt (1984: 130). Indeed, Lorde asks us to claim anger and to hear in anger a certain claim. As she writes so powerfully: "My response to racism is anger. I have lived with that anger, ignoring it, feeding it, learning to use it, before it laid my visions to waste, for most of my life. Once I did it in silence, afraid of the weight. My fear of anger taught me nothing . . . anger expressed and translated into action in the service of our vision and our future is a liberating and strengthening act of clarification. . . . Anger is loaded with information and energy" (1984: 127). Anger is constructed in different ways: as a response to the injustice of racism, as a vision of the future, as a translation of pain into knowledge, and as loaded with infor-mation and energy. Crucially, anger is not simply defined in relationship to a past, but as opening up the future. In other words, being against some-thing does not end with "that which one is against." Anger can open up the world. This is not to say that anger is our only response to racism—after all, if anger is creative, then it gives us room to do other things. Nor is anger our duty; I am not obliged to keep hitting that wall, sometimes I will, and sometimes I won't. But not to speak anger because it is pointless is not the answer. After all, even if we use softer language, we are already sore points. We might as well do things with these points. To speak about racism is to labor over sore points.

A Phenomenological Practice

In this conclusion, I offer a way of thinking about diversity work as a phenomenological practice. Diversity work does not simply generate knowledge *about* institutions (in which the institution becomes a thematic); it generates knowledge of institutions in the process of attempting to transform them. We could also think of diversity as praxis, drawing on a Marxist understanding of the point of intellectual labor: as Marx argues in *Theses on Feuerbach*, "Philosophers have only interpreted the world differently but *the point* is to change it" ([1845] 2009: 97; emphasis added). Drawing on this radical tradition, Paulo Freire defines praxis as "reflection and action upon the world *in order to* transform it" ([1970] 2000: 51; emphasis added).[1] I want to offer a different way of thinking about the relationship between knowledge and transformation. Rather than suggesting that knowledge leads (or should lead) to transformation, I offer a reversal that in my view preserves the point or aim of the argument: transformation, as a form of practical labor, leads to knowledge.

The very labor of transforming institutions, or at least aiming for transformation, is how we learn about institutions *as* formations. We can thus think of diversity work as a "phenomenological practice." What do I mean by this? Edmund Husserl in his Vienna lecture (presented in 1935 and published in the appendix of *The Crisis of European Sciences and Transcendental Phenomenology*) offers an important redescription of the phenomenological method. He suggests that phenomenology has its roots in classical Greek philosophy as *theôria* or theoretical attitude. A theoretical attitude is a reorientation of a previous attitude, defined as "a habitually fixed style of willing life comprising directions of the will or interests that are prescribed by this style" ([1936/ 54] 1970: 280). An attitude is thus not simply a reflection on the world but is worldly: an attitude could even be thought of as institutionality, in which a norm is also prescribed as a style of life. A norm is how we are immersed in a life. For Husserl, phenomenology is defined as reorientation: "The theoretical attitude, in its newness, refers back to a previous attitude, one which was earlier the norm: [with reference to this] it is characterized as a *reorientation*" (280; emphasis added). The phenomenological attitude in reflecting on the previous attitudes is thus a new style; a theoretical attitude is new in relation to what already exists because *in* reflecting on what exists, it withdraws from an immersion, such that an existence is transformed. In this new attitude the world becomes thematic, as what consciousness is directed toward. Husserl argues explicitly that such a new attitude is theoretical: it must, at least in the first instance, be "totally unpractical" (282).[2]

We can offer a different angle on the task at hand by thinking about how phenomenology can work as a practice or even "practically." It is not simply that diversity workers are philosophers—in the sense of being reflexive and critical—in their attitude toward institutions (though they can be). It is not simply that they become conscious of what recedes from view. Rather, diversity workers acquire a critical orientation to institutions in the process of coming up against them. They become conscious of "the brick wall," as that which keeps its place even when an official commitment to diversity has been given. Only the practical labor of "coming up against" the institution *allows this wall to become apparent*. To those who do not come up against it, the wall does not appear—the institution is lived and experienced as being open, committed, and diverse.

Diversity workers thus generate knowledge not only of what institutions are like but of how they can reproduce themselves, how they become like and keep becoming alike. We come up against the force and weight of something when we attempt to alter the conditions of an existence. But we can also come up against something in our experience of an existence. Doing diversity work is institutional work in the sense that it is an experience of encountering resistance and countering that resistance. Each new strategy or tactic for getting through the wall generates knowledge of what does or does not get across. Perhaps diversity workers aim to transform the wall into a table, turning the tangible object of institutional resistance into a tangible platform for institutional action. Thinking of diversity work in this way allows us to understand how speaking in the happier languages of diversity does not necessarily mean an identification with the institution but can be understood as a form of practical knowledge of the difficulty of getting through.

Getting people to the table by not speaking of the wall (by not speaking about what does get across) does not mean the wall disappears. Even if the wall is a metaphor for immobility, it can move. When practitioners overcome resistance, it seems to reappear elsewhere. Institutional immobility thus requires a mobile defense system. I described in chapter 1 how diversity workers have to be mobile: embedding diversity requires inhabiting different kinds of institutional spaces. The experience of physical mobility also involves the feeling of coming up against the same thing, *wherever* you come up against it. One of my primary aims has been to describe the physical and emotional labor of "banging your head against a brick wall."

I want to expand the terms of my argument here by thinking of diversity work in two distinct but related ways. First, diversity work can refer to work that has the explicit aim of transforming an institution; second, diversity work can be what is required, or what we do, when we do not "quite" inhabit the norms of an institution.[3] When you don't quite inhabit the norms, or you aim to transform them, you notice them as you come up against them. The wall is what we come up against: the sedimentation of history into a barrier that is solid and tangible in the present, a barrier to change as well as to the mobility of some, a barrier that remains invisible to those who can flow into the spaces created by institutions.

Feminist and race theorists over generations have taught us that to inhabit a category of privilege is not to come up against the category. What makes a lesson hard is what makes a lesson worth repeating. When we fail to inhabit a category (when we are questioned or question ourselves whether we are "it"), then that category becomes more apparent, rather like the institutional wall: a sign of immobility or what does not move.[4] There is an implicit relation between categories and mobility that we can make more explicit. When a category allows us to pass into the world, we might not notice that we inhabit that category. When we are stopped or held up by how we inhabit what we inhabit, then the terms of habitation are revealed to us. We need to rewrite the world from the experience of not being able to pass into the world. In *Queer Phenomenology* I called for a phenomenology of "being stopped," a description of the world from the point of view of those who do not flow into it (2006: 140). I suggested that if we begin with the body that loses its chair, the world we describe will be quite different (139).

Diversity work can take the form of description: it can describe the effects of inhabiting institutional spaces that do not give you residence. An example: we are at a departmental meeting with students to introduce our courses. One after the other, we come up to the podium. A colleague is chairing, introducing each of us in turn. She says: this is Professor So-and-So; this is Professor Such-and-Such. On this particular occasion, I happen to be the only female professor in the room.[5] And I am the only professor introduced without using the title. She says, "This is Sara." In taking up the space that has been given to me, I feel like a girl, and I giggle. It is a "girling" moment, to use Judith Butler's evocative term (1993: 7). Girling moments do not stop happening, even after we have been pronounced girls. We can feel an assignment as atmosphere. When you look like what they expect a professor to be, you are treated like a professor. A somber and serious mood follows those who have the right kind of body, the body that allows them to pass seamlessly into the category, when the category has a certain affective value, as somber and serious.

Diversity work can involve an experience of hesitation, of not knowing what to do in these situations. There is a labor in having to respond to a situation that others are protected from, a situation that does not come up for those whose residence is assumed. Do you point it out? Do you say anything? Will you cause a problem by describing a problem? Past experience tells you that to make such a point is to become a sore point. Sometimes you let the moment pass because the consequences of not letting it pass are too difficult.

Some have to "insist" on belonging to the categories that give residence to others.[6] If you point out the failure to be given the proper title, or if you ask to be referred to by the proper name, then you have to insist on what is simply given to others. Not only that, you are heard as insistent, or even as self-promotional, as insisting on your dues. If you have to become insistent to receive what is automatically given to others, your insistence confirms the improper nature of your residence. We don't tend to notice the assistance given to those whose residence is assumed, those informal networks that are often behind arrivals into and occupations of institutional space as I discussed in chapter 4.[7] When assistance is assumed, insistence is not required.

I could add here that I was the only professor of color in the room (as the only professor of color in the department, this detail was not so surprising). Other critics have documented what it means to occupy the place and position of a professor of color. Pierre W. Orelus, for example, offers an account of how being a professor of color causes trouble, as if being one thing makes it difficult to be seen as the other: "After I formally introduce myself in class, I have undergraduate students who ask me, in a surprised tone of voice, 'Are you really the professor?' I have overheard some of them asking their peers, 'Is he really the professor?'" (2011: 31). Orelus compares this mode of questioning, this sense of curiosity and astonishment, with the questions typically asked of immigrants about "funny accents." Or we could think of the question typically asked to strangers, "where are you from?" as if to say, or more accurately, which is to say, "you are not from here." When we are asked questions, we are being held up, we become questionable. Being asked whether you are the professor is a way of being made into a stranger, of not being at home in a category that gives residence to others.

To catalogue these incidents is not a melancholic task. To account for experiences of not being given residence is not yet another sad political lesson, a lesson of what we have had to give up in order to keep going. I suspect there is a loss at stake here, but it is not ours. The failure to inhabit the categories that give order to an existence or bring an existence into order can be understood as beneficial, not in the sense that this failure might propel us forward but that it might give us insight into the very system of propulsion, into what does and does not move forward. I realize how much we come to know about institutional life because of these failures of residence, how the categories in which we are immersed as styles of life *become explicit when you do not quite inhabit them.*[8]

When the restrictions governing who can occupy a category become explicit, you are noticing what is around you, what gathers, but what does not ordinarily come into view. When you realize that the apparently open spaces of academic gatherings are restricted, you notice the restriction: you also notice how those restrictions are either kept out of view or defended if they come into view. Over and over again, it is revealed to me: this institutional lesson, which is also a life lesson, of coming up against a category *in the very attempt to make the restrictions more explicit.* How many times have I had male colleagues defending all-male reading lists, all-male speaker lists, all-male reference lists? To give an account of these defenses is to give an account of how worlds are reproduced.

An open call comes out for an academic event on power and resistance. A number of speakers are named on the call: all male speakers but one, all white speakers but one (is this "but one" a way of holding onto the "all"?). Some of us point out the restriction. A wall comes up in the very denial of a wall. We begin with a friendly openness. It's an open call, they say. Come along, they say. Take our places, they even say. Note here how the gesture of inclusion, which is also a promise of inclusion, can be offered in a way that negates a point about exclusion. To suggest incorporation as potential (come along as you *can* come along) prevents any acknowledgment that the open call was restricted as a call. How to respond? We point out publicly that the publicity of the call suggests the event is not open.[9] We didn't mean anything by it, they say; it's unfair to assume we did, they say.

You have hurt our feelings; you have presumed knowledge of our intentions. That's just who turned up. I respond: if privilege means going the way things are flowing, then letting things flow will mean that's who ends up going. The friendly tone ceases. You are the problem, they say. In assuming we have a problem, you are the problem.

It is not noticeable, this "all" to those who pass through this "all," until you point it out, becoming a feminist killjoy, making a sore point, being a sore point, assumed to be sore because of your point. I do not usually bother to point out that "all male" is often "all white," though I could make that point, becoming an angry person of color. Sometimes we have to take the risk of fulfilling the fantasies other people have of us! I should note as well that I have experienced the most defensive reactions to such points from white male academics who think of themselves as "critical." When criticality becomes an ego ideal, it can participate in not seeing complicity. Perhaps criticality as an ego ideal offers a fantasy of being seeing.[10] As I suggested in chapter 5, critical whiteness might operate as a way of not seeing in the fantasy of being seeing: the critical white subjects, by seeing their whiteness, might *not* see themselves as participating in whiteness in the same way.

At one moment I express my fatigue at the repetition of these gatherings, where the all is hidden by the assumed generality of a particular ("open to all" often translating into all male, all white, or all but one). I express a sense of what is lost when academic gatherings are restricted to certain kinds of bodies. Someone replies that he thought I sounded "very 1980s," and he thought we had "got over" identity politics. Not only might we want to challenge the use of identity politics here as a form of political caricature, we might want to think of this as "over." What does it mean to assume we have "gotten over" something? This claim participates in the genre of argumentation that I describe as "overing." In assuming that we are over certain kinds of critique, they create the impression that we are over what is being critiqued. Feminist and antiracist critique are heard as old-fashioned and outdated, as based on identity categories we are assumed to be over. We are even heard as the ones who are oppressive, in our influence or existence, because we point out the existence of oppression.

Diversity work could be described as a very practical refusal of the theoretical argument about overing. The very practical work of doing diversity work brings a wall to the surface. A wall can be defined as that which you do not get over. It is not over if you don't get over it.

It is not always the case that overing arguments are made explicitly. I would say that in the landscape of contemporary critical theory there is a sense—sometimes spoken, sometimes not—that we need to "get beyond" categories like gender and race: as if the categories themselves have restricted our understanding, as if the categories themselves are the blockage points. Those who point out restrictions and blockages become identified with the restrictions and blockages they point to, as if we are creating what we are describing. The hope invested in new terms (mobilities, becomings, assemblages, capacities) can thus be considered a way of overing, as if these terms allow us to get over the categories themselves. In turn, academic work that works on questions of gender or race or that works with existing social categories (whether or not these categories are the starting points, and whether or not the categories are assumed in advance of starting) becomes associated with stasis.

An example of how categories are understood as "blockages of thought" is offered in the following statement by the geographer Susan Ruddick:

> for instance for those of us who want to build on struggles in a way that embraces and amplifies the capacity to act instead of storying every momentary gain as "cooptation,"—no wonder there is still a lingering melancholia of the left in some corners!—or those who want to think beyond the narrow categorizations of gender race and class (and ableism, ageism, et cetera) to new configurations and alliances I think *Hegel or Spinoza* provides a kind of metaphysics that helps us move beyond current blockages in thought. (2011, n.p.)[11]

Here race, gender, and class (and all that is relegated to the bracket, as well as all that is pointed to by the "et cetera") enter theoretical discourse as "narrow categorizations." The implication is that to exercise such categories would be to restrict not only the "capacity to act" but our capacity to think that capacity. Category thinking becomes seen as a narrowing of vision, associated with a lingering melancholia, as what is holding us back, stopping us from moving on. Perhaps those who point to such categories are the ones who linger, who are stopping the forward movement we might attach to progression. This is how those who "stay behind" can get in the way of a forward progression. I am not saying that we need to dismiss these new theoretical vocabularies: we need resources to think differently as we encounter worlds.[12] I am suggesting that the hope invested in new terms can mean *turning away* from social restrictions and blockages by identifying restriction and blockages with the old terms that we need to move beyond.[13] Indeed, we need to note that the *narrowing* of the descriptive or analytic potential of the old terms is part of this narrative of overcoming; a caricature of the work done by these terms allows the terms to be, as it were, "given up."

In giving up these terms, we give up more than the terms: we give up on a certain kind of intervention into the world. It is not that the categories described as "blockages of thought" introduce blockages into our thought; rather, we need to account for blockages and restrictions within institutional worlds. Maybe we could redescribe social categories as blunt instruments. It could be the case that by exercising their bluntness we might lose a certain precision. Or we could say that institutional life is full of blunt instruments. Stop and search, for example, is a technology that makes this bluntness into a point: stop! You are brown! The blunter the edges of political instruments, the sharper their points. Being sharp in our descriptions of this world requires a certain willingness to be blunt.

The very tendency to "look over" how everyday and institutional worlds involve restrictions and blockages is how those restrictions and blockages are reproduced. It is not the time to be over it, if it is not over. It is not even the time to get over it. Social categories are sediments: they go all the way down, and they weigh some of us down. They might even appear lighter and more buoyant to those who can float, as if they are "above" them. Perhaps the experience of aboveness creates the impression of overness. Perhaps lightness and buoyancy are the affects of privilege — the affective worlds inhabited by those whose bodies don't weigh them down or hold them up.

We can also consider the language of critique and how it is assumed to be dated. I think even within some feminist writing, the idea that we should be critical of sexism has indeed become understood as rather dated and even as a habit that is blocking us, holding us down, or keeping us back: stopping us from reading or engaging most positively, affirmatively, and creatively with the texts that are the objects of critique.[14] It would be timely to restate the arguments that sexism and racism are not incidental but structural, and thus to understand sexism and racism requires better, closer readings of what is being gathered. To account for a situation—which is to account for the situated nature of knowledge—means we can offer "a better account of the world" (Haraway 1997: 187).[15] Attending to the restrictions in the apparently open spaces of a social world brings us into closer proximity to an actual and material world. We need feminist and antiracist critique because we need to understand how it is that the world takes shape by restricting the forms in which we gather. The time for this is now. We need this critique now if we are to learn *how not to reproduce what we inherit.*

A critical task is thus to attend to categories given that they do not have any ontological ground (we do not assume there is such a thing called white or black in advance, as it were). We attend to categories to understand how what is ungrounded can become a social ground (we know there is such a thing as being called white or black, and we know that the call "calls us" into different places). A phenomenological approach shows how a critique of the ontological basis of categories does not mean that the categories themselves disappear (see Alcoff 2006: 185). I would thus not argue, as Paul Gilroy (2000) does, that our problem is with the category of race itself and the solution is to unlearn the habit of using the category.[16] To proceed as if the categories *do not matter* because *they should not matter* would be to fail to show how the categories continue to ground social existence.

An account of diversity as a phenomenological practice is an account of how racism is reproduced by receding from view, becoming an ordinary feature of institutional life. My critique of this disappearance can be related to wider critiques of the contemporary as postracial, or critiques in the United States of the discourse of color blindness (see Street 2007: 37; Eng 2010: x; Wise 2010).[17] The very idea that we are beyond race, that we can see beyond race, or that we are "over race" is how racism is reproduced; it is how racism is *looked over*. Diversity work as phenomenological practice is a refusal to look away from what has already been looked over. Not all diversity work works this way, as I have shown in this book. Indeed, diversity work itself can allow institutions to "look over" racism. A practical phenomenology is also about witnessing labor: noticing how the responses to what we come up against can also cover over the signs of againstness. A recovery can be to re-cover, a covering over. At the very moment of "overing," a category is redone. The reproduction of a category can happen at the moment in which it is imagined as overcome or undone. This is why the very promise of inclusion can be the concealment and thus extension of exclusion. This is why a description of the process "of being included" matters.

We are not just talking of the bigger categories, those that are reified as or in forms of life.[18] What we need is an account of how smaller categories can become grounds of an existence. I might also be tempted to describe this book as offering a phenomenology of social perception. When given out or communicated, perceptions have a social life. Even ways of perceiving somebody as having certain kinds of qualities become objects in the world, tangible things. This could be about the perception of an individual, that tricky matter of reputation, how some individuals are given certain attributes (sometimes independently of what they do, sometimes not), and how the institutional life of an individual person is partly about the value of that attribution. These little perceptions do stick to bigger categories or might be how those categories stick. A feminist colleague who attends her university's promotions committee tells me how you can "hear" how male and female staff are valued differently just by the kinds of adjectives used in the letters to describe their performances: descriptive words for men are upward, energetic, and thrusting, whereas for women they are quieter, more sedentary, closer to the ground.[19] That gender becomes wordy should not surprise us. We can do gender through words, although this is not, of course, the only way we do gender.

Furthermore, the perception of individual subjects is not only what matters here. My experience of doing the research for this project, as well as my involvement in Women's Studies, has taught me a great deal about the politics of perception. When I was co-director and director of Women's Studies in the early 2000s, I was told by the dean that Women's Studies was a problem because it was perceived as a problem: we were "not viable." This judgment of being "not" viable might be more about the "not" than the "viable." This "not" seemed to float quite freely, becoming attached to whatever criteria for viability could be exercised. But of course the mobility of this "not" is more about stickiness than freedom. When we could establish our viability in terms of one set of criteria (student numbers, research activity and income), the criteria changed, so that we were not. What mattered was this not, *being not.*

It seems obvious what we should do: we should challenge the perception. But I was told that this response to being perceived as not viable would not be viable. We had to accept the judgment that we were not viable, in other words, to go along with the perception of not being viable if we were to become seen as viable. We were told that the "best response" was to act as if that perception was true by self-modification. Because we were not perceived as being viable, any disagreement with the perception would simply become a symptom of the truth of the judgment. So the institutional task became to modify ourselves as an agreement with the perception. You will notice in this book how some diversity practitioners accept this task. As I showed in chapter 2, some agree with the judgment that there is a problem with the "equity office," and thus their task is not to change perceptions of what they do but change what they do. In accepting this task, there is a sense of alienation from the predecessors, a belief that they (and not the institution) were the problem.

Contrast this account with another account offered in chapter 1 of what is called in the diversity world "perception research." One project finds that external communities perceive the university as being white. Rather than responding by accepting this perception (and thus assuming the task of modifying the thing perceived as white) the perception becomes the problem. The task becomes changing the perception of whiteness rather than changing the whiteness of the organization. Contrasting accounts: in one, the perception is taken as truth and the demand is for self-modification; in the other, the perception is taken as false and the demand is for a new truth. How can we account for this difference?

Diversity practitioners have helped me understand how perceptions can have quite different social or institutional careers. A difference of perception can be the difference that matters. Whether it is the perception that is treated as the problem is a way of distributing a problem. Whether or not a perception is of a problem, it is about making some and not others into the problem. I have learned so much about how even the language of inclusion and repair makes those who are to be included into the problem. And once the "to be included" or "not yet included" are the problem, those who are already given a place by the institution are not only not the problem but can become the solution to the problem.

To account for the affective distribution of problems is and must be more than what is described (and perhaps dismissed) as "ideology critique," as a critique of what the surface hides. It would be to describe how what "comes up" as a problem is already dependent on interests that cannot and will not be declared. In other words, it is a critique of *how things surface*, which is to say, a critique of what recedes. So, for example, whiteness recedes when diversity becomes a solution to the problem of whiteness. Note again, when institutions are working, the wall is what does not surface. The wall describes the tangibility of recession, a blockage point that is not seen when things are (assumed to be) flowing.

I have suggested that when description becomes hard, we need description. One of my aims has certainly been to offer a description of what recedes when diversity becomes the view. But I do not simply want to give a descriptive content to this recession. I also argue that to account for what recedes is to offer a different kind of account. In contemporary social theory, the primary motifs for the social are of fluidity. Social theory now tends to emphasize movement or mobilities (Urry 2007) or liquidity (Bauman 2005). At one level, the emphasis is part of an effort to depict social changes: the fast speeds of late capitalism, the precarious conditions of labor, the loosening of social ties. But these metaphors also carry social theory in a certain direction. For example, Zygmunt Bauman has argued: "One attribute that liquids possess but solids do not, an attribute that makes liquids *an apt metaphor for our times*, is the intrinsic inability of fluids to hold their shape for long on their own" (in Gane 2004: 19; emphasis added). Doing the research for this book has taught me about solidity, about how what appears as mobile and changing can *hold its shape*.

In the introduction to this book, I suggested that to account for racism is to offer a different account of the world. What are we accounting for? We are accounting for how a "holding pattern" becomes intrinsic. We are accounting for the difficulty of social transformation. We are also offering a different way of understanding the relationship between fluidity and solidity. An understanding can be practical. Diversity workers as institutional plumbers are the ones who point out what is getting blocked. To point out what is blocked is to be experienced as the blockage point, as the ones who are getting in the way of a flow. The flow, in other words, is a fantasy that is protected by blocking the exposure of the blockage.[20] Diversity practitioners not only come up against the wall, as that which does not move, they are often themselves encountered as the wall, as obstructing the movement of others.

We can think more about institutional flows. Institutions are crowded. In noticing the crowds, we also notice the orientation devices that direct the flow of human traffic in particular ways. We all know the experience of "going the wrong way" in a crowd. Everyone seems to be going the opposite way than the way you are going. No one person has to push or shove for you to feel the collective momentum of the crowd as pushing and shoving. To keep going, you have to push harder than any of those individuals who are going the right way. The body who is "going the wrong way" is the one experienced as "in the way" of a will that is acquired as momentum. For some, mere persistence, "to continue steadfastly," requires great effort, an effort that might appear to others as stubbornness, willfulness, or obstinacy. This book has been written from the experience of "going against" and "coming up against." Diversity work thus requires insistence. You have to become insistent to go against the flow, and you are judged to be going against the flow because you are insistent. A life paradox: you have to become what you are judged as being.

Things might appear fluid if you are going the way things are flowing.

When you are not going that way, you experience a flow *as* solidity, as what you come up against. In turn, those who are not going the way things are flowing are experienced *as* obstructing the flow. We might need to be the cause of obstruction. We might need to get in the way if we are to get anywhere. We might need to become the blockage points by pointing out the blockage points.

I end this book with a maxim: *don't look over it, if you can't get over it.*

Introduction

1. Reflecting back, I find it interesting that I looked around for an object in the room in which I was writing for inspiration. Many years later, I turned such an object into my subject: the writing table in *Queer Phenomenology* (2006). I began writing about tables as orientation devices in part as I caught sight of Edmund Husserl's table in his phenomenological writing. Objects can indeed become our subject.

2. For further details about the event see Ahmed (1998). In my earlier writing, I attended to the specificity of the address (the use of Aboriginality to figure criminality) as well as the conditions under which I received it (the disavowal of Aboriginality gave me a certain freedom to leave the address behind). I also explore the question of passing and whiteness (the second policeman asked if "it" was "just" a suntan) in my account of the significance of the event.

3. I have made the decision to adopt the U.S. phrase "of color" in this book, even though the data I draw on is from Australia and the United Kingdom. I find this term less problematic than other terms, including the dominant term in the United Kingdom, which is "Black and Minority Ethnic" or, more recently, "Black Asian and Minority Ethnic." In policy discourse Black and Minority Ethnic or Black Asian and Minority Ethnic are usually abbreviated as BME and BAME. I think the abbreviations can work to conceal the "trouble" of race. I think "of color" works better to include those who are not white (to inhabit this "not" is shared experience even if we don't share the same experiences). The terms "majority/minority" in implying quantities (more/less)

seem more disembodied, and less able to address the experiential aspects of inhabiting "the not."

4. The document I refer to here is *Equality, Diversity and Excellence: Advancing the National Higher Education Framework* (Higher Education Council [HEC] 1996).

5. My location in Women's Studies matters to this research and not simply in terms of resources. As a member of the Institute for Women's Studies, I was already working on the "edges" of academic legitimacy and was thus very conscious of the politics of legitimation. I could also note here that some of the debates about mainstreaming diversity and equality echo earlier feminist debates about the politics of incorporation and resistance within the academy. As Hilary Rose argues, the entry of feminism into the academy meant that a largely "outsider knowledge" was changed into "one that constantly speaks of itself as being both outside and inside, precariously balanced between the academy and the movement" (1994: 53). My critiques of how diversity and equality become embedded within performance culture in this book can also be heard as echoes of earlier discussions in Women's Studies. Louise Morley argues that "the existence of Women's Studies can signify a performance indicator of an organization's commitment to change" (1995: 177). To offer a genealogy of Women's Studies would be another way of telling the story of diversity and the academy. For a more recent discussion of Women's Studies in relation to institutional change in the United States, see Robyn Wiegman (2002).

6. The individuals who made up the diversity team all had independent research projects, although we worked together to analyze data and present the material to a range of audiences. We also attended some of the same policy conferences, participating together in "the diversity world." My project was the only one based in the higher education sector; the other projects were based in further education and adult and community learning. It was very fruitful for us as a team to work across these sectors because they have quite distinctive cultures and histories in relation to equality and diversity. For those interested in an account of equality and diversity practices in further education and adult and community learning, please see our joint report, Ahmed et al. (2006).

7. I want to explain the delayed interview briefly. Like many stories of delay, the reasons are institutional as well as personal. In 2006, when we submitted our final report, we began to experience some serious problems as a project team that led to the report not being published. I give a partial account of these experiences in chapter 5 (see also Swan 2010a). Suffice to say here that some of the problems practitioners talked to us about (diversity pride translating quickly into hostility toward diversity workers) were replicated by our own

experience of doing the research. I found the experience so difficult that I "dropped" the data in 2006 and instead wrote *The Promise of Happiness* (Ahmed 2010), a book that was partly inspired by my realization that diversity was being offered as a discourse of happiness and institutional flourishing. After completing this book, I decided to return to the data I had gathered. I did a supplementary interview as a way of reengaging myself with the project. I should note as well that the research draws on my experience doing diversity work between 2000 and 2010. I did not, at any point, stop doing this work. Having a decade of "doing diversity" has given me the time and space to think about what it means to be doing this kind of work.

8. I think it is important to acknowledge here that although this book draws on interviews with practitioners in Australia and the United Kingdom, and while I am both Australian and British (in the sense of personal identification as well as citizenship), this book has been written "out of" the British political and educational context, as this is where I have been primarily based as both a diversity practitioner and an academic. In Australia, the discourse of diversity has been shaped by the (ongoing, unfinished) colonial experience and is used to denote indigenous as well as migrant or non–English-speaking background (NESB) experience. For important critiques of diversity discourse in relation to the experiences of indigenous and NESB women in Australia, see Adele Murdolo (1996), as well as Aileen Moreton-Robinson (2000). For engagements with the politics of Australian multiculturalism, see Ien Ang (2001) and Sneja Gunew (2004). For critiques of whiteness in the Australian context, see the collections edited by Aileen Moreton-Robinson (2004) and Claire McLisky (2009). For an account of diversity leadership within higher education in Australia, see Jill Blackmore and Judyth Sachs (2003), and of gender and diversity mainstreaming in Australia see Carol Bacchi and Joan Eveline (2010). I also acknowledge here the importance of the Australian Critical Race and Whiteness Studies Association. The creation of a space for conversation about whiteness and racism in the Australian academic context has been hugely important for me personally and for many others. See http://www.acrawsa.org.au/.

9. Most of the data from my interviews in Australia is drawn on in the first two chapters, and most of the data from my interviews in the United Kingdom is drawn on in the fourth and fifth chapters. However, the book is not as tidy as this summary suggests; some material from Australia appears in chapter 4 on commitment, and some material from the United Kingdom appears in chapters 1 and 2. I should note here that research is "messy" (even if there are stages, the stages are not always containers), and capturing this process requires a certain messiness in turn.

10. I include only these acts in the main body of the text because they all follow the form of the RRAA by defining equality as a positive duty. Since 2000, other equalities legislation has been introduced in the United Kingdom to extend the protection of particular groups of people from workplace discrimination, including the Employment Equality Age Regulation (2006), the Employment Equality (Sex Discrimination) Regulations (2005), the Employment Equality (Religion or Belief) Regulations (2003), and Employment Equality (Sexual Orientation) Regulations (2003). Two additional equality acts have taken the form of offering legal recognition: the Gender Recognition Act (2004), which gave legal recognition to transsexual people in an acquired gender, and the Civil Partnership Act (2004), which provides legal recognition and parity of treatment for same-sex couples, including employment benefits and pension rights.

11. The concept of thick description is central to American cultural anthropology. Ryle's term was adopted and given new meaning in the work of Clifford Geertz (1973).

12. See Michael H. Agar (1980) for a description of ethnographers as "professional strangers," as well as chapter 2 in *Strange Encounters* (Ahmed 2000), which interrogates the idea of ethnography as the transformation of strangerness into a profession. For a discussion of phenomenology and strangers, see the classic essay by Alfred Schutz (1944). A good account of the relationship between phenomenology and ethnography on strangers is offered by Ilja Maso (2007).

13. Although race is central to this ethnography of diversity, it is not a study of a racialized group per se, although it is a study of racialization as an institutional process. For excellent discussions of how ethnography can be used as a research method to analyze the experience of racialized groups, see Claire Alexander (2004) and Yasmin Gunaratnam (2003).

14. The CRE and other equality bodies in the United Kingdom have merged to form a new single body: the Human Rights and Equality Commission, which is headed by Trevor Phillips, the former head of the CRE. I refer to some of Phillips's writing and speeches in this book. I should note here that the language of intersectionality was used to justify merging the equality commissions. When intersectionality becomes a cost-cutting exercise, we know we are in trouble! See also note 18.

15. A note on translation: In the United Kingdom, "Black feminism" would refer to the work by women of Asian as well as African descent and has become an important affiliation. In the United States, "Black feminism" would refer to the work of women of African descent. In respect of these differences, I use "Black feminism" in this British sense only when I am talking about Black

British feminism. I will otherwise use "black" in the U.S. sense and adopt the term "feminism of color."

16. For important reflections on the experience and practices of Black feminists in higher education in the United Kingdom, also see Cecily Jones (2005) and Suki Ali (2009).

17. There is a huge and important body of feminist literature on the gendering of institutions as well as organizations. One particularly influential approach is offered by Joan Acker (1990), who shows how organizations are not gender neutral and how this lack of neutrality is masked by obscuring the embodied nature of organizational work. The critique of diversity as an obscurant could be understood as a continuation of the feminist critique of the neutrality of organizational processes.

18. "Intersectionality" is a key contribution of Black feminist scholarship. The term was coined by Kimberlé W. Crenshaw (1989) and is further developed in the work of Patricia Hill Collins (1990). An important elaboration of how intersectionality can be used to challenge "additive models" is offered by Rose M. Brewer (1993). For an excellent "cartographic" approach to intersectionality, see Avtar Brah (1996). For a useful description of intersectionality as a "bottom-up" concept, see Ann Phoenix (2011). The term has now been taken up not only within Black feminism but also more widely within feminist theory, critical race studies, social theory, and cultural studies. I think that the term itself is now often used in a way that forgets its genealogy within Black feminism and neutralizes its critical potential. I would also suggest that the term "intersectionality" can be used as a method of deflection. When I give talks on race and racism a common question is "but what about intersectionality?" or "what about gender/sexuality, class?" I am not suggesting these are not legitimate questions. But given how hard it is to attend to race and racism, these questions can be used as a way of redirecting attention. In other words, when hearing about race and racism is too difficult, intersectionality can be deployed as a defense against hearing. For a good discussion of the history of the uses of intersectionality, see Carolyn Pedwell (2010).

19. Research that draws on interviews with diversity and equal opportunities practitioners based in universities includes Dua's (2009) research in the Canadian context and Blackmore and Sachs (2007) in the Australian context (their interviews include equality officers among a much wider data set of academic managers and leaders). In the U.K. context, in addition to material cited in this paragraph, research based on interviews with diversity trainers is also relevant, including Hamaz (2008) and Swan (2009). In the U.S. context, most of the qualitative research on diversity in universities appears to be based on interviews

with faculty, which may reflect differences in how diversity work is organized. In addition to Brown-Glaude (2009), see Brayboy (2003) and Moody (2004): the latter is not based on interviews but offers an account of programs to "diversify faculty" as well as the author's own experience of faculty diversity initiatives.

20. I think the location of research in terms of "sectors" is very important. In the United Kingdom, given the impact of the new equality legislation, more research is needed that draws on the experience of practitioners, particularly given the increasing mobility of practitioners across the public sectors (in the United Kingdom many of the practitioners I interviewed came into higher education from other sectors, including health and local government). Moving across sectors means that diversity practitioners are in a good position to reflect on the institutional norms, values, and rules that can be enforced by not being stated.

21. Some (but not all) of the practitioners I spoke to fit this description of the "tempered radical" offered by Meyerson and Scully. I decided not to use this term because it risks creating an image of the diversity practitioner as *a certain kind of type*. However, see Swan and Fox (2010) for a useful extension of the idea of the "tempered radical" to describe the complexity of diversity work.

22. The website for Diversity in Organizations, Communities and Nations is http://ondiversity.com/.

23. I should note that not all the practitioners I spoke to would even be described or describe themselves as "diversity practitioners." This is a term I have used throughout the book as shorthand, a decision I made for pragmatic reasons of simplicity and clarity, but which I do acknowledge can create the problematic impression of consistency across a range of practices. I note as well that there can be a difference between an official title and self-description. One practitioner I spoke to was officially an "equality and diversity officer" but refused to use the term "diversity" because she thought it was a "cop-out." She had even taken the word "diversity" off her business cards. For discussion of this example, see chapter 2.

24. There are no major national studies of diversity practitioners as a professional and social group in either the United Kingdom or Australia. There is one report by the ECU (2006) that was based on online questionnaires (seventy fully completed questionnaires from Higher Education Institutions, which was a response rate of 41 percent). They include as an appendix the equality profile of respondents: 87 percent female and 82.5 percent white. In the United Kingdom, it seems the majority of diversity practitioners in HE are white women. See also Kirton and Greene (2009: 164) for similar data. Because of the relatively small number of formal interviews I completed for this project, I decided not to identify practitioners in terms of their social backgrounds to

avoid any oversimplistic interpretations of the material. I am interested, however, in exploring at a more speculative level the relationship between "doing diversity" and "being diversity" in the context of race: those of us of color *are* already diversity before we *do* diversity, such that our doing is often read as being. Some of us might not *do* diversity precisely because we *are* diversity. Perhaps white practitioners, in *doing* diversity without *being* diversity, can experience institutions in ways that are similar and dissimilar to those who *are* diversity no matter what they *do*.

1. Institutional Life

1. My approach to institutions could be compared to an actor-network approach with its focus on how effects (including effects we might denote as institutional) are generated by alliances between humans and nonhuman entities (for an excellent use of actor-network theory [ANT] to describe institutional work, see Lawrence and Suddaby 2006). However, I argue that ANT tends to focus on social and institutional phenomena as verbs *rather than* nouns. John Law describes an ANT approach as assuming "that social structure is not a noun but a verb" (1992: 385). I agree that institutionalization is a process, but would also argue that institutions acquire solidity, regularity, and stability over time; they refer to a settling down (and can thus be nouns as well as verbs). As I argue in the conclusion, it is through praxis (the labor of trying to change institutions) that *we encounter what settles*. Actor-network approaches such as Law's (1992) focus on the precarity of institutions or institutional precarity. My work with diversity practitioners has shown me how some features of institutionality are quite far from precarious (I would even say that if institutions are precarious, institutionalization is the protection of some more than others from precarity). I also decided not to use ANT because I find the language of "actors" and "networks" rather flattening (even if anything can become an actor or network, the use of these terms firmly ties the acquisition of significance to the terms themselves, such that they can operate as containers of significance). However, this is not to say that an actor-network approach to diversity would not have its uses. For a good example of how ANT can be used to examine diversity work, see Hunter and Swan (2007). See also Marilyn Strathern for an anthropological engagement with the question of how ANT focuses on "fragile temporality" (1996: 523).

2. The following texts are useful. For the new institutionalism in sociology of organizations, see DiMaggio and Powell (1991) and Brinton and Nee (2001); for the new institutionalism in political science, see Rhodes, Binder, and Rockman (2008); for the new institutionalism in education, see Meyer and Rowan (2006); for a feminist engagement with "the new institutionalism" literature,

see Gatens (1998). We can note the proliferation of new institutionalisms—for example, we now have "discursive institutionalism" (Schmidt 2006) and "constructionist institutionalism" (Hay 2006). Although these proliferating knowledges might share the institution as an object, they are heterogeneous because "the institution" is defined in quite different ways.

3. Neil Gross suggests that one of the sources of "phenomenology's continuing influence is the program of neo-institutionalism in the sociological analyses of organizations" (2007: 222). As he explains, "neo-institutionalists drew important lessons from Berger and Luckmann insofar as institutionalization, for them too, had referred to the process by which shared taken-for-granted schemata become obdurate and invisible, and thus determinative of an agent's behavior" (222). DiMaggio and Powell draw on phenomenology and ethnomethodology in attending to "the ongoing efforts of agents at the micro level to achieve intelligibility through the operation of practical reason" (1991: 223). DiMaggio and Powell draw on the work of Garfinkel and Giddens in addition to Berger and Luckmann. In my own work on phenomenology, I draw on an earlier philosophical tradition, including the work of Husserl, Heidegger, and Merleau-Ponty (see Ahmed 2006), as well as the social phenomenologist Alfred Schutz, as they provide conceptual tools for thinking about the significance of what recedes from consciousness, or becomes background.

4. In this book I use "over" as a verb (to over, overing) to indicate both a genre of academic argument as well as a style of institutional life.

5. I return to this description of diversity as a phenomenological practice—and develop it into an argument—in the conclusion.

6. In the United Kingdom, the vast increase in diversity posts in the public sector is a direct result of the changes to the equality regimes, beginning with the Race Relations Amendment Act of 2000, discussed in the introduction. As I explore in chapters 3 and 4, this meant that many practitioners were appointed not only to express an organizational commitment to diversity but also to comply with the law.

7. Jacoby is discussing second nature as individual incorporation. In this book, I am exploring what we can call institutional incorporation. This concept of institutional incorporation could be related to Bourdieu's understanding of the habitus: "embodied history, internalized as second nature and so forgotten as history" (1990: 56). The institution has an embodied history, as I show throughout this book, which is exercised in the ways that bodies gather. For a good use of Bourdieu to discuss institutions and race, see Puwar (2004). I will not be adopting Bourdieu's terminology (habitus, field, cultural capital, social capital) because I want to write more experientially, using the language of the everyday to reflect on the everyday experience of institutions, but my argu-

ments can nevertheless be related to his central insights as a social theorist of incorporation.

8. It is interesting to consider the brick wall in relation to the glass ceiling. Both are metaphors for institutional limits that derive their sense by analogy not only to physical objects but also to the means by which internal spaces are delineated and contained. The glass ceiling refers to the institutional processes that stop certain categories of people from moving up (vertical mobility), whereas the brick wall refers to the institutional processes that stop certain values from moving across (horizontal mobility). Both metaphors point to the significance of visibility and invisibility: the point of the ceiling being made of glass is that you can't see it. The transparency of glass means, however, that you can see through it; you see above to the places you cannot reach. With the brick wall, you cannot see it unless you come up against it. The metaphor of the brick wall points to how what is tangible and visible to some subjects, something so thick and solid that *you cannot see through it*, does not even appear to others. What some cannot see through, others cannot see. See the conclusion for a fuller discussion of the phenomenological and political significance of the brick wall.

9. James's approach to habit as a form of conservation (a way of conserving energy and also in the sense of a conservative agent of society; [1890] 1950: 121) is hugely influential. He cites a passage from the work of M. Leon Dumont, which I find particularly useful: "Everyone knows how a garment, after having been worn a certain time, clings to the shape of the body better than when it was new. A lock works better after being used some time; at the outset more force was required to overcome certain roughness in the mechanism. The overcoming of their resistance is a phenomenon of habituation. It costs less trouble to fold a paper when it has been folded already. This saving of trouble is due to the essential nature of habit, which brings it about that, to reproduce the effect, a less amount of the outward cause is required" (105–6). Institutional habits could also be thought of as saving trouble: less energy is required to bring about what is intended. For those who are struggling against a habit, *more force is required*. See the final section of chapter 4 on pressure and the conclusion on diversity work as insistence.

10. For an interesting use of Berger and Luckmann's model to describe how race inequality becomes institutionalized in schools in the United States, see Colleen L. Larson and Carlos Julio Ovando (2001).

11. I explore the metaphor of the organic body to describe the social body in my current research on the will and willfulness. I am especially interested in how parts that do not perform in a way that is in sympathy with other parts (and thus the whole) are attributed with willfulness.

12. Arendt is referring here to Henri Bergson's work to show how when something has been accomplished, it seems necessary or inevitable. Admittedly, I am quoting out of context as Arendt is referring to acts that have been performed by individuals. I suggest that institutional givens are rather like individual accomplishments; when something becomes given, it loses the air of contingency, appearing as necessary and inevitable.

13. The RAE refers to the Research Assessment Exercise, a national research exercise that takes place periodically in the United Kingdom to measure research contributions of departments and institutions to allocate funding. The RAE has since been replaced by the Research Assessment Framework (REF), which is scheduled to be completed in 2014. The suggestion made here—that research is given higher priority than teaching within many higher educational institutions—is uncontroversial. Practitioners who do not work at research-led institutions (who work at universities that have a more vocational or teaching focus) typically describe diversity as relatively intrinsic to their university's missions but also suggest that this intrinsic status can be a problem. See chapter 2 for further discussion.

14. There are a number of recent studies on whiteness as a habit: in addition to Sullivan (2006), see also MacMullan (2009).

15. These policy events in the United Kingdom were for all public sectors, that is, they were not specific to higher education, where it is much harder to encounter a "sea of brownness." There have been some exceptional times when I have attended academic events that I experienced as "seas of brownness." They include inaugural lectures for women of color professors, as well as events that are specifically on race or racism or events set up to address the work of scholars of color.

16. I cite our collectively written report for any quotes that derive from the research of my fellow team members rather than my own research. I thank all members of the team as well as all those who gave us their time and insight into their experiences of "the diversity world."

17. In *Strange Encounters* (2000) I drew on Derrida's concept of conditional hospitality to address the politics of multiculturalism, reflecting on how multicultural hospitality imagines the nation as "ours to give," thus transforming guests into hosts, those who assume the right to be welcoming or not (190). For further discussion, see also Molz and Gibson (2007).

18. The term "professor" in the United Kingdom is used for the most senior rank of academic appointment (equivalent to the U.S. full professor), which means that only academics who have this rank are addressed with the title "professor." I should note as well that the response referred to in this anecdote is not the only or even the typical response to women of color becoming pro-

fessors. When another woman of color became a professor, a white male professor said, "They give professorships to anyone these days." As with the figure of the stranger discussed earlier, this "anyone" points to some bodies more than others (if we can, anyone can: the value of "can" depends on it not being open to others). When we become professors, the value of professorship diminishes. One of the values of feminism of color is the opportunity it gives us to catalogue these institutional encounters. See also the conclusion for further discussion of "the professor" as a gendered and racialized category.

19. I am extending the argument I made in *The Cultural Politics of Emotion* about how shame—and the apology as shame given form in words—can as recovery also "re-cover" or cover over an injury (see Ahmed 2004: 112). I noted there how the desire for an apology (the desire for the Australian government to apologize to indigenous Australians on behalf of nonindigenous Australians for the Stolen Generation) can take the form of a desire to move on by putting the past behind us. The apology is thus assumed to have a magical form: as if saying it, is being over it.

20. Dominic Casciani, "Phillips Clears Police of Racism," BBC News, January 19, 2009, http://news.bbc.co.uk/1/hi/uk_politics/7836766.stm.

2. The Language of Diversity

1. I address the question of how we can understand "institutional will" in chapter 4.

2. When considering how diversity replaces phrases such as "equal opportunities" and "social justice," we might want to ask what the replacements are doing. A replacement can also be understood as a way of forgetting the histories of struggle that surround these terms. In the U.K. context, it is noticeable that much of the recent literature on diversity does not reference earlier debates on antiracism and multiculturalism within education. For examples of these earlier works, see Sarup (1991) and Rattansi (1992). For a more recent discussion of racism and education, see Gillborn (2008).

3. For analyses of how brands emerge as complex social as well as symbolic forms, see Lury (2004) and Moor (2007).

4. The critical reading of diversity within institutions offered in this book can be situated within the wider literature on multiculturalism. Stuart Hall argues that multiculturalism in the substantive sense "references the strategies and policies adopted to govern or manage the problems of diversity and multiplicity which multicultural societies throw up" (2000: 209). Sneja Gunew suggests that "multiculturalism deals with the often compromised management of contemporary geopolitical diversity in former imperial centres as well as their ex-colonies" (2004: 15). For another critical engagement with

official and liberal multiculturalism that draws on an analysis of policy documents, see Stratton and Ang (1998). It is worth noting that in many parts of Europe, multiculturalism has now been declared dead and even blamed for terrorism and the disintegration of the social, as explored by Lentin and Titley (2011). As I have discussed elsewhere, the shift away from multiculturalism at the level of official policy in the United Kingdom has kept in place some of the ideas that informed how multiculturalism was exercised in policy: in particular, the use of diversity as a binding agent or diversity as a way of integrating or creating a common culture (Ahmed 2004, 2010). The idea that multiculturalism placed "too much" emphasis on diversity, leading to segregation, is a retrospective fantasy that justifies the withdrawal of political commitment to multiculturalism, however it is understood.

5. However, it is important to note that statistical data is not always useful. For example, at a conference I attended on further education in 2005, discussions centered on the limitations of data as a technology. As one speaker suggested, "You don't fatten a pig by weighing it." Another speaker suggested that "people need to be empowered to read the data." Although data can be a useful way of capturing inequality, it is not an end in itself; when it is treated as such, it can actually become an obstacle. If "the weighing" is assumed to be "the fattening," then to weigh can be not to fatten. Data as with other technologies can be useful in diversity work by supporting arguments, rather than making them.

6. Austin notes that the trouble of statements is akin to the trouble of performative utterances: "some troubles that have arisen in the study of statements recently can be shown to be simply troubles of infelicity" (1970: 248). The failure of the performative / constative distinction to hold in Austin's work is followed by the failure of the distinction between the locutionary, illocutionary, and perlocutionary distinctions. These failures are productive in the sense that they demonstrate the impossibility of locating "trouble" in particular kinds of speech acts. I find that some of the critiques of Austin's distinction between the constative and performative do not recognize how much Austin himself acknowledged the instability of these distinctions as a source of trouble and potentiality.

7. As Derrida suggests, all speech acts are citations: "Could a performative utterance succeed if its formulation did not repeat a 'coded' or iterable utterance . . . if it were not then identifiable in some way as a 'citation' " (1988: 18). Judith Butler develops Derrida's insight on the relation between citationality and performativity, as I discuss further in chapter 4. What interests me here is not simply that the speech act "we are diverse" is a citation but also how the

performative success of the speech act depends on whether it is *re-cited* by others within an institution.

8. Thinking of words as pathways also helps us to understand how they are orientation devices: in following a trail we are directed a certain way. In *Queer Phenomenology* I explored what I called "the paradox of the footprint." I noted: "A path is made by the event of the ground 'being trodden' upon. We can see the path as a trace of past journeys. The path is made out of footprints—traces of feet that 'tread' and in 'treading' create a line on the ground. When people stop treading the path may disappear. And when we see the line of the path before us, we tend to walk upon it, as a path 'clears' the way. So we walk on the path as it is before us, but it is only before us as an effect of being walked upon" (2006: 16). Words are material, like pathways: once they leave a trail, they clear a way and we tend to follow them, and in following them, we are directed that way.

9. This tool model of language was offered by the philosopher Ludwig Wittgenstein: "think of the tools in the tool-box: there is a hammer, pliers, a saw, a screw driver, a rule, a glue-pot, glue, nails, and screws—the functions of words are as diverse as the functions of these objects" ([1953] 2009: 9). Wittgenstein stresses that it is not clear what the words themselves do or are being used to do: "their *use* is not that obvious" (10). I consider the utility of words in terms of affect (the "sticky" associations between words).

10. The phenomenon of "diversity fatigue" has indeed been reported. This phenomenon is not particularly new, although none of the practitioners I interviewed used this expression. Most uses of the expression "diversity fatigue" that I have found are from media sources in the United States. For example in 2006, Po Bronson with Ashley Merryman published an article in *Time*, "Are Americans Suffering Diversity Fatigue?" They state: "It's clear people are tired of walking on eggshells, afraid to offend those with different beliefs, ideas, and lifestyles. It's grown exhausting, and they want their lives back. The idea of diversity seems to have worn out its welcome. It is now like a house guest who has stayed too long." The unwelcome nature of diversity signals the limits of what people are willing to incorporate, taking the form of being exhausted by the demand not to be racist. Diversity fatigue has also been offered as an alternative explanation to that of racism. For example, in an article, "Americans Aren't Racist, They Just Have Diversity Fatigue" (2010), John Derbyshire argues, "Could it be that this phase of our history is coming to a close? It seems to me that in the recent arguments over Arizona's immigration law and the Ground Zero mosque, I detect a whiff of diversity fatigue. Could it be that the mindset of Congressman Vaile is still to be found, in quantity, among the

American public? A mindset not of racial superiority or privilege, still less of 'hate,' but of satisfaction with one's country the way it is, with the ethnic balance it has, and a reluctance to countenance the indefinite continuation of headlong demographic change?" When diversity fatigue replaces racism as an explanation, it becomes a *justification* of the limits of what a nation is willing to incorporate. Diversity fatigue is described here as a satisfaction with one's situation, where the situation becomes definable as sameness. Note that even if "diversity" appears as if it is a lighter or happier word, as buoyant, it can still be sticky; it can still be associated with the arrival of others who are "not like us," and thus be heard as a threat to the continuation of that us. What seems light in one context can seem weighed down with negative associations in another. For further discussion of light and heavy words, see also chapter 5.

11. Personal communication (via Facebook). I want to acknowledge my debt to Sirma Bilge for directing me to the poster *Enjoy Diversity* and for her thoughtful remarks on edible diversity. The slogan referred to can be found online at the United for Intercultural Action website, http://www.unitedagainstracism .org/pages/InfoARW_10.htm#2.

12. For a more detailed discussion of the distinction between digestible and indigestible differences, or between assimilable and inassimilable differences, which draws on bell hooks's work, see chapter 4 in Ahmed (2000). I also discuss how multiculturalism as a national body "takes some others in" by defining the limits of what can be digested. There is a long history of what we might call "consumer multiculturalism," in which the primary analogy is between multiculturalism and food. The national dish is imagined as a way of combining ingredients, and the bodies of racial others become the ingredients to be combined. As Angela Davis describes, "The metaphor that has replaced the melting pot is the salad. A salad consists of many ingredients, is colorful and beautiful, and it is to be consumed by someone. Who consumes multiculturalism is a question begging to be asked" (1996: 45). See also Ghassan Hage's analysis of the metaphor of stew in "celebrating diversity" in the Australian context (2000: 119–23), as well as Anita Mannur's account of how multiculturalism "accords a special status" to food (2010: 224).

13. We can relate "happy diversity" as a management discourse to a wider social discourse of "feel good" multiculturalism. See Gargi Bhattacharyya's convincing analysis of this discourse, in which she shows how the imperative to feel good about the multicultural city means racism does not become part of the picture. As she notes, "One version of the translation of multiculturalism into 1990s Britain is the assertion that feeling good about your city is about feeling comfortable with different people. Unlike some calls to rally around your

location, here racism cannot be part of the deal" (1998: 258). For a more recent critique of multiculturalism as a "feel good politics," see Fortier (2008).

14. However, the strategic decision to "go native" is not without risks or limitations. For example, one member of a diversity committee spoke to me about how she could never get hold of the diversity officer because that person was always in conversation with leaders and managers. The reorientation of diversity workers as institutional friends can mean becoming less attentive to those within the institution who are more critical of it.

15. Global Nomads International has a "virtual village" website at http://www.gnvv.org/. "Global nomads" is used primarily to refer to children "who work, or worked, in the diplomatic corps, the military, international businesses, missionary organizations and intergovernmental or voluntary service agencies, such as the UN or the Peace Corps, and various other organisations." The description is from http://www.globalnomads-dc.org/. For further discussion of global nomads see Ahmed (2000: 84–86).

3. Equality and Performance Culture

1. The ECU was established in 2001 to promote equality for staff employed in the higher education sector. See http://www.ecu.ac.uk/.

2. I need to explain why I use the term "a culture of performance" rather than "performativity," especially given that scholars in educational studies have generally used "performativity" in developing Lyotard's work (see Ball 1998, 2004; Blackmore and Sachs 2003, 2007). In a note in *The Postmodern Condition*, Lyotard locates his understanding of performativity with reference to Austin: "The term *performative* has taken on a precise meaning in language theory since Austin. Later in this book, the concept will reappear in association with the term *performativity* (in particular, of a system) in the current sense of efficiency measured according to an input/output ratio. The two meanings are not far apart. Austin's performative realizes the optimal performance" (1984: 88). However, I would question the assumption of kinship between the two senses of performative. Austin's performatives are not really about the achievement of optimal performance; their efficacy or felicity, whether or not they succeed, is determined within a speech situation, rather than being about the optimal performance of a system. Furthermore, Lyotard seems more invested than Austin in performativity as having a denotative function, that is, as referring to a specific class of things or as a way of classing things. Because I am working specifically with the idea of "institutional speech acts," I restrict my use of "performativity" to refer to speech acts. I thus use "a culture of performance" or "performance culture" to refer to the qualitative changes that Lyotard offered such an astute (and prophetic) analysis of in the late 1970s.

3. An audit culture could be described as a coercive form of "institutional isomorphism," to use a key and influential concept first offered by Paul J. DiMaggio and Walter W. Powell to explain the "startling homogeneity of organizational forms of practices" (1983: 148). Organizations become more alike, at the level of fabrication or appearance, when the documents they are required to write are measured in terms of their consistency with an external system. If diversity and equality become performance indicators, they participate in institutional isomorphism. Although I agree with Pushkala Prasad's (1997) argument that institutional isomorphism could be understood as "institutional monoculturalism," as involving a lack of diversity, we could also note here how diversity, when institutionalized, can generate institutional likeness, if only at the level of appearance.

4. Note also how it might only be at the level of appearance that documents are agentic. To treat documents as agents with a life of their own would be to assume that an appearance of agency is an adequate sign of agency. It might even be that giving agency to documents—as if by moving around, they are doing something—allows us *not to see* how things are stuck. Furthermore, if the point of the document is to create a trail, it suggests that in following the trail we are not necessarily getting anywhere. All we are following are the signs of where documents have been. See also chapter 2, note 8. If documents as well as words are pathways, then we can be directed in such a way that the point becomes to keep them going.

5. See the Quality Assurance Agency for Higher Education website at http://www.qaa.ac.uk/.

6. The Equality and Human Rights Commission (EHRC) defines itself as "a modern regulator" and thus has a checking role of some kind for the public sectors: "The primary objective for the Commission is to achieve better outcomes in equality human rights and good relations. We aim to achieve regulatory compliance with the relevant legislation in order to support that; however sometimes it will be necessary to take formal enforcement action to achieve this. As a statutory regulator the Commission has a wide range of tools available. The Commission will aim to choose an enforcement method which is relevant and proportionate to a particular breach." The EHRC does have the power to serve compliance notices to public sector authorities and lists some anonymized examples on its website. See Equality and Human Rights Coalition, "A Legal Enforcement Update from the Equality and Human Rights Commission," August 2009, http://www.equalityhumanrights.com/uploaded_files/enforcement_update_aug09.pdf. However the EHRC (and the CRE before it) is very remote from the day-to-day situations of most universities. Although there is a mechanism for ensuring compliance, it falls short of an audit.

7. Their website (http://www.ecu.ac.uk/about-us) states: "The Equality Challenge Unit (ECU) supports the higher education sector to realise the potential of all staff and students, whatever their race, gender, disability, sexual orientation, religion and belief, or age, to the benefit of those individuals, higher education institutions (HEIS) and society." In my interview with Joyce Hill (December 10, 2004), she describes their role as a "critical friend." Maybe the discourse of friendship makes the ECU fall short of an auditor.

8. One might note the contrast with the argument that diversity is useful because it is more positive than equality, which is associated with compliance and sticks. We learn that in some scenarios, the sticks are given more value as compulsion. The stick might be viewed as having more efficacy for institutions (particularly when a policy is inconsistent with existing institutional priorities and values) and less efficacy for individuals (particularly when a policy is inconsistent with their own desires). In other words, for individuals, the aim is to create the impression of consistency between diversity and their own desires; whereas for institutions, the aim is to replace desire with the law as the motor of action. However, I have also shown that diversity can be used in a happier way for institutions (diversity as consistency with institutional desire). Perhaps the implication is that while sticks *can be* useful for institutions, they are less likely to be useful for individuals.

9. Arthur Scargill is currently the head of the Socialist Labour Party in the United Kingdom. He is a key figure in British left-wing political history, particularly as a leader of the miners' strike in 1984–85.

10. See "May Drops 'Simplistic' Clause in Equality Law," FT.com, November 17, 2010, http://www.ft.com/intl/cms/s/%f84bbc8-f281–11df-a2f3–00144feab49a.html#axzz1V7qsXuS9.

4. Commitment as a Non-performative

1. To describe them as "statements of commitment" suggests they involve constative and performative elements: they *report* on a commitment as well as *making* a commitment. As I have already pointed out, Austin eventually gives up on the distinction between the performative and constative. We might note here that many speech acts that appear as performatives have constative elements (they can report on a situation, as well as create a situation, by being offered in a situation). A statement of commitment can thus be treated as false (as an inadequate report of a situation) as well as unhappy (as not having force).

2. I thank Lauren Berlant, who helped me recognize the performativity of my own gesture of describing these speech acts as non-performatives.

3. One could relate this discursive occupation to Bourdieu's concept of social

capital: those "networks of connection" that are behind how subjects arrive into and occupy certain spaces, which he describes aptly as "an endless effort at institution" (1986: 245). Some forms of capital are more convertible in casual domains. We can note that what allows entry into and occupation of institutional spaces (including formal and informal networks) is often invisible.

4. This argument is counterintuitive insofar as will and habit are often assumed as distinct aspects of human experience: will is mostly used to refer to conscious and deliberate acts of volition, while habit is mostly used to refer to behaviors that have become automatic. I develop my arguments on habits and will in my current research project on the will and willfulness.

5. I thank Sarah Franklin for posing the question of the relationship between institutional will and institutional wall.

6. I am not suggesting here that individual actors are unimportant. I just suggest that resistance to diversity and equality work does not require an individual subject to act as a blocking agent (though individuals can and do act in this way). See the next section of this chapter for a discussion of individual actors as distributors of commitment.

7. For more discussion of diversity leadership, see our report (Ahmed et al. 2006: 55–58, 107–20). There is a burgeoning body of literature on diversity and leadership that includes reflections on the importance of having diverse leaders, as well as discussions of the impact of diversity on leadership as both practice and theory. See Jean Lau Chin's (2010) introduction of a special issue of *American Psychologist* on diversity and leadership for a recent discussion of these themes. Although our project was funded by a leadership center, I decided not to frame my own work around leadership. This is partly because diversity leadership often works as a call to certain individuals to become diversity leaders, and I think we need to resist that call, as it can locate responsibility for diversity in the bodies of those individuals. However, this is not to say that individual leadership does not matter.

8. My focus here is on some of the practical problems that follow when mainstreaming is used by institutions to justify closure. We should not, however, reduce the idea of mainstreaming to these problems. For a feminist discussion of mainstreaming that focuses on how this concept can be elaborated as feminist theory as well as policy or practice, see Sylvia Walby (2005). For a consideration of the idea of diversity mainstreaming in relation to deliberative democracy, see Judith Squires (2005). For an account of the relationship between gender mainstreaming and diversity mainstreaming, see Carol Bacchi and Joan Eveline (2010).

9. Although, as I point out in the conclusion, you can feel the "force" of the mainstream if you are not going in its direction.

10. This idea of making institutions catch up with their commitments to diversity is evident in Indigo Violet's reflection on feminist of color activism at the New School. As she describes: "We demanded that the New School live up to its promises of progressivism and diversity" (2002: 491). We need to reflect on the political labor required to transform a promise or commitment to diversity. However, as Violet shows in this article, even if the institution still does not live up to its promises, the political labor of demanding that it do so can generate something: "It enabled spaces of critique, dissent and direct action to expose the university's unfulfilled promise of progressivism and diversity" (491). Political labor, as feminist of color activism has shown, can generate new life-worlds. Not all diversity work helps create such alternatives. But it can.

5. Speaking about Racism

1. I am indebted here to Shona Hunter, who introduced this quote from Haraway to describe diversity work in our report (Ahmed et al. 2006: 24).
2. The contexts drawn on in the chapter are LGBTQ politics and feminist politics. It is worth noting that racism might cause a particular kind of trouble in both contexts not only because they have historically been dominated by whiteness (though not exhausted by this dominance) but also because feminist and queer subjects often have a sense of political identity based on being progressive. When individuals have an idea of themselves as progressive, they might be more likely to hear the critique of racism as self-injury (as injuring their sense of themselves as progressive).
3. This definition can be found on the CIPR's website: http://www.cipr.co.uk/.
4. Nick Griffin is the chairman of the British National Party, a far Right political party in the United Kingdom. The party is gradually acquiring political legitimacy with members elected to European parliament. The increase in far Right politics is, of course, a noticeable phenomenon across Europe. It would be easy to overstate the legitimacy of the BNP: the galvanization of opposition to the prospect of their legitimacy is probably a more significant trend. In my view, the more sinister political reality in the United Kingdom is the extent to which anti-immigrant discourses inform more "moderate" Left- and Right-wing politics, including New Labour as well as the Conservative Party.
5. Whether or not Tatchell and his team threatened the publisher with the law, the use of the language of libel to describe the article constitutes a threat. Tatchell later argued that he and his lawyers did not threaten litigation; my point is that they did not need to, whether or not they did.
6. All of Tatchell's writings referred to in this chapter can be downloaded from his website: http://www.petertatchell.net.

7. In this supplementary response, Tatchell refers directly only to Erel and Klesse; however, the article also uses terms like "my detractors" and "my critics," suggesting the object of the response is more generalized, as well as anticipatory as a mode of defense ("my critics" easily becomes "anyone" who would agree with the criticisms made in the original chapter).

8. My argument does not rest on a semantic distinction between "accusation" and "critique" but on the suggestion that the word "accusation" is heard in a particular way (or is a way of hearing). Indeed, the two words "racism" and "accusation," when stuck together, tend to conjure up a scene of an individual subject who is under attack by a collective. This distinction between critique and accusation is thus subtle but effective.

9. I thank Katie King for directing me to Ward's excellent critique of diversity in queer politics.

10. I suspect identification takes place at a number of levels. First, white sexual minorities can identify with the racial sexual minorities as a way of not identifying their own whiteness. This identification is a performing of whiteness in the mode of disavowal (whiteness from the point of view of the white subject does not appear). Second, white sexual minorities *overidentify* with whiteness. Given the phenomena that Jin Haritaworn, Tamsila Tauqir, and Esra Erdem (2006) call "gay imperialism," and Jasbir Puar (2007) calls "homonationalism," white sexual minorities identify with the project of nation and empire in an almost compensatory way, performing an allegiance to the nation by disidentifying from those that are identified as national threats (such as Islam, which appears as a threat not only to the national body but to queer bodies specifically, by being identified *as* homophobic). This overidentification with the nation could be described as melancholic: white sexual minorities, in identifying with the national and imperial project, are identifying with that which repudiates them (see Crimp 2002: 6, for a discussion of gay melancholia). The psychic economy can be compared with the overidentification that follows when the beloved does not love the lover back in the way the lover loves the beloved: the lover more desperately wants the love of the beloved as the lover senses the withdrawal of that love. White sexual minorities "show" how much they love the nation; they might aim to demonstrate their love *even more forcefully* given their previous exclusion from the national body. This showing of love, which is all the more desperate when homosexual bodies remain on the borders of the abject (becoming less abject can still mean to be unbecoming), can thus take the form of performing whiteness against racialized others. On the one hand, white sexual minorities identify with the oppression of racial minorities by assuming outsiderness, and on the other, they disidentify from racialized sexual minorities by overperforming their whiteness. No won-

der the affective spaces of queer space in a world of state and empire building are saturated!

11. Mirza used this suggestive formulation in her comments during the Narratives of Feminism workshop at the Gender Institute, London School of Economics, November 20, 2010. I am indebted to Mirza's wisdom in many ways. The comment is especially suggestive because it relates the way bodies can become targets in performance culture to how bodies can be targets in a military sense. Following Martin Heidegger, Rey Chow observes, "We may say then in the age of bombing, the world has also been transformed into—is essentially concerned and grasped as—a target" (2006: 31). If the world becomes target, then some more than others become the referent, what the world in becoming target is aimed at. In relating these different senses of target, we need to be cautious: we cannot and should not make the domain of performance culture equivalent to the domain of war. But we could think about how racialized bodies as targets become objects of life and death.

12. I am *not* suggesting in any way that the question of class is not important. But I would add that there is a political economy in attention: at times, I have sensed a sigh of relief in the return to class as "the core business" of the social sciences as if gender and race have been rather irritating distractions. We can witness this positioning of diversity (often as code for identity) as a distraction from the real concerns of the Left in Walter Benn Michaels's *The Trouble with Diversity* (2010), which ends up as a denial of the material and systematic aspects of racial experience. This is an extreme articulation of what I sense elsewhere: not only the argument that class is material and that race and gender are not (somehow these are "merely" about culture or identity), but that the concern with race and gender are distractions from more-pressing real and material concerns. See Butler for an excellent critique of the "tendency to relegate new social movements to the sphere of the cultural, and indeed to dismiss them for being preoccupied with what is called 'merely' cultural" (1997: 265).

13. For a discussion of the audit panel, which I could not go to and was attended only by Elaine Swan as co-director of the project, please see Swan (2010a). Swan shows how responses in the panel displaced attention from the findings: "Several of the questions seemed to imply that the project team had been duplicitous on a number of fronts. One of the panel members asked why there was not more good news in the report on diversity; in spite of the focus of the research on race, another asked why there was so much focus on race when we could have focused on disability. The panel did not ask any questions about the actual findings or the recommendations. There was no discussion among the panel about the findings. There was no attempt to listen responsively or

responsibly to the voices in the data or their narratives. This engagement with actual findings could have been a legitimate aim of the panel as its remit was to examine the quality and impact of the research in relation to the programme objectives" (494–95). In the auditors' report, Swan points out, the critique softens somewhat, but there was still no discussion of the substance of the arguments offered in the report: "Again it did not go into any detail on the findings. There was no mention of racism or whiteness" (495).

14. They never published our report, and despite numerous emails, we were not given an explanation for this decision. See Ahmed et al. (2006).

15. I use the U.K. term "ethnic minorities" in this example, as these were the terms we used in the conversation.

16. I have already discussed how when people of color become diversity workers it is not scripted as a becoming. This means that when people of color turn up at equality and diversity meetings, we are doing what we are supposed to be doing, but when white subjects turn up, they are doing something exceptional: this is how "critical white subjects" can end up being congratulated for doing the kinds of work that people of color are routinely asked to do. A parallel example would be when men are congratulated for doing the housework: the very stance implicit in the congratulation keeps in place the status of this event as exceptional, thus also keeping in place the expectation of who is and should be doing the banal forms of housework. See also my conclusion to this chapter and the conclusion of the book for further discussions of critical whiteness.

17. We might contrast the labor of softening undertaken by black diversity workers with the efforts of making diversity appear harder, discussed in chapter 2. The problem of trying to appear harder as diversity workers might be specific to those workers who are white (and probably, given the gendered as well as racialized nature of such metaphors, this experience might be specific to white women). For those who are not white, you might already appear as harder because of the body you have. The relative values of softness and hardness might be one way we could explore the difference between doing diversity and being diversity, depending on the body you have, or on how your body is apprehended.

18. In my previous work, I have explored language as stickiness. In *The Cultural Politics of Emotion* (2004), I suggest we can repose the *question* of history by rethinking history in terms of stickiness rather than repetition, which I would suggest is somewhat different from claiming that history is the *answer* to the question, "what sticks?" (Puar 2007: 190). I suggested that signs accumulate affective value through repetition. I would now qualify my argument somewhat. The nature of affective accumulation might depend on the kind of value

being given to signs. For example, positive affective value can make signs appear lighter or buoyant, whereas negative affective value can make signs seem heavy. Stickiness, I suggest, relates specifically to negative affective value, which is in turn how bodies associated with such signs also become stuck. There is a feedback loop between bodies and signs rather than a causal relation; if weighty bodies can make signs sticky through proximity, then the weight of signs can be experienced as the weighing down or holding up of bodies. Note also that in chapter 2 I suggested that the repetition of some words can mean they become tired, thus becoming less rather than more affective. We need to account for the complex relation between repetition and affect, which recognizes the complexity of the biography of words as an institutional biography.

19. It seems that Chesler did not realize how much this "academic freedom" did not protect Thobani from the consequences of her own critical work. After a speech that showed how "the war on terror" is a form of imperialism, Thobani describes how she "began to receive hate mail, harassing phone calls, and death threats. . . . In this climate, the Royal Canadian Mounted Police chose to make public through an announcement in the media, that I was the subject of a 'hate-crime' investigation, an offence under the criminal code" (2003: 403). The freedom of speech becomes a form of subject-constitution for the West (what we have, what the other lacks). It also becomes evident that this freedom is a fantasy, or at least that it is restricted as an idea (the fantasy is that freedom is unrestricted). Those who speak of racism and imperialism can find that they are *not* protected by this freedom: whether or not they are accused of hate crime, such speech is often heard as disloyal to the nation that supposedly guarantees freedom. I also noted earlier in this chapter how the permission to speak about racism (under the sign of being given the freedom to speak) becomes an unofficial prohibition on speaking about racism (the gift of this permission becomes evidence of not having a problem with racism). Understanding the relationship between the idea of freedom of speech and racism is important; it is indeed a complicated history. We might note how freedom of speech can be translated into the freedom to be offensive. As I argued in chapter 4 of *The Promise of Happiness* (2010), Muslims are often represented as "offended" by the freedom of speech, where their offendability becomes evidence of how Muslims impose a restriction on "our freedom." Another twist in this complicated history is how political correctness within political discourse operates to create the illusion that people are "no longer free to be racist"—a position, in other words, that racism is the new minority position.

20. It is worth noting that the new equality regime discussed throughout this

book has been introduced at the same time as the "war on terror" has been conducted and new laws enshrined to extend state racism under the rubric of national security. There is no paradox in this if we think of the equality regimes as a project of managing racism, as a project that demands allegiances from those who are to be included *under* or *as* the sign of diversity. For some relevant and interesting observations on the historical coincidence of increasing racial violence and a discourse of diversity, see Rey Chow (2002: 14).

21. There is a limitation to my argument here: I am associating diversity as a politics of including racial minorities with queer liberalism as a politics of including sexual minorities. The analogy helps me give an account of why we should not read such inclusions "literally." We should also note that diversity can be understood as liberalism (queer or not): as a way of including or enveloping those marked as other. I agree very much with the critiques of queer liberalism offered by scholars such as Jasbir Puar (2007), Lisa Duggan (2003), and David L. Eng (2010). At the same time, I would add that the *promise* of being "folded in" can also take the form of a *threat* (be in—or else!). Of course, some more than others will be promised inclusion and thus threatened with exclusion (other others are not threatened with exclusion, they threaten *as* the already excluded). If we hear a threat in the promise, we might note that being "folded in" by the nation might only be at the level of an appearance (a promise is made as a way of making others subject to a threat, as subjects *who acquire something to lose*). The nation appears to include queers and other others, where the appearance of inclusion becomes a requirement to identify with the national promise (which is not to say that queer liberals do not actively collude with the appearance and benefit from it; they most certainly do).

22. I offer a longer reading of this film in *The Promise of Happiness* (2010), attending to the figure of melancholic migrant. The experience of seeing this film, just as I was beginning the diversity research, first captured my interest in exploring the intimacy of happiness and diversity.

23. For an excellent consideration of the affectivity of the turban, see Puar (2007). We can relate the anxiety about the turban to the veil. Take Jack Straw's comments about Muslim women who wear "the full veil" made when he was British home secretary in 2006. He suggested that the wearing of the niqab made him feel uncomfortable and that the failure of the covered woman to show her face was a refusal to communicate. When defending his comments to a Muslim woman he said, "If we bumped into each other in the street, you would be able to say hello to me. I would not be able to do the same. The obvious reason is that I cannot see your face. Chance conversations make

society stronger." The Muslim woman becomes the stranger; she prohibits our capacity to say hello, as a happily weak signifier of social solidarity. We might say that the Muslim woman is constituted as unfriendly, as refusing the very grounds of friendship. She becomes the blockage point, the point where communication stops, where community fails to deliver its social promise. Note also how discomfort is used here as a demand that the white body be made more comfortable. To keep whiteness comfortable, the Muslim woman must unveil.

24. By reading Joe's speech act in terms of identification and whiteness, it could appear that I am negating the significance of his Irishness, with its postcolonial history, as not quite being white in the white/right way. It is of course significant that empathy is offered by an Irishman, as a kind of shared recognition of what it means to be the butt of an insult. However, what is significant is how Joe's joke is what allows us to pass over the insult (to put it "behind us"). It is as if an act of identification (the sharing of hurt) can allow an injury to be healed.

25. For a longer explanation of the ethics of proximity in multiculturalism, see Ahmed (2004: 133–41).

26. Although I offer a critique here of how Whiteness Studies, when presuming progressive whites as its proper subjects, can recenter on white agency, I should state that I do support the critical interrogation of whiteness. For an important critique of whiteness and how it is secured by not being seen, see Dyer (1997). For a useful introduction to Whiteness Studies (with a focus on the social sciences), see Garner (2007). For a historical account of the emergence of whiteness in the United States, see Roediger (1991, 2006).

Conclusion

1. Freire draws on Husserl in developing his model of praxis: "That which had existed objectively but had not been perceived in its deeper implications (if indeed it was perceived at all) begins to 'stand out,' assuming the character of a problem" ([1970] 2000: 83). Freire's pedagogy could thus be described as a "practical phenomenology."

2. I indicate "in the first instance" because Husserl argues for an eventual synthesis between theoretical and practical, such that the former can be called on "to serve . . . mankind in a new way, mankind which, in its concrete existence, lives first and always in the natural sphere" ([1936/54] 1970: 283).

3. I am not claiming that norms simply hold their place. Inclusion can destabilize norms by extending them. At the same time, an extension can be an experience of "coming up against." To inhabit norms that have historically excluded you can mean coming up against those norms in ways that might not be

experienced by those whose inclusion is already given. Take, for example, the extension of family norms to include queer families. Queers who become proximate to such norms by virtue of their life choices (by having marriages, civil partnerships, children) might be the ones who most come up against them in their everyday life-worlds (experienced as a querying or questioning of whether *you* are *that*). See chapter 7 in *The Cultural Politics of Emotion* (Ahmed 2004) for an argument that inhabiting social forms as bodies that are not quite the norms can both extend and destabilize those norms. I thank Lauren Berlant for her inspirational question "how do norms become forms?" which I first heard her ask during a talk at Lancaster University and from which I have learned so much.

4. I acknowledge here that it is possible not to inhabit fully a category of privilege even if one is privileged by a category. For example, if men do not inhabit the category of masculinity properly or fully, *then the category appears as an institutional wall*, as a barrier that is revealed in coming up against it. I should also note that it is possible not to inhabit fully a category without becoming conscious of the restriction of that category: the psychic work of accommodating to a world that does not take your body as a norm can involve *not* registering those norms as a way of protecting oneself from them.

5. Please note that in this example I am using "professor" in the British sense of the word. See chapter 1, note 18, for explanation. In the following citation, Orelus uses "professor" in the U.S. sense. I would suggest that being the professor in either sense (as faculty or as senior faculty) can involve a crisis of seeing, when your body and voice *do not line up with an expectation*. In these examples, I am attending to forms of address (when you become questionable by how you are or are not addressed). The experience of not fulfilling an expectation of how professors appear (and we can broaden the category of professor to include other professions) can involve more subtle forms of questioning. For example, if you enter the room with someone who fulfills an expectation of what a professor is like, the gaze will tend to slide over you and settle on that person. The audience will wait for him to speak as the professor. You can even disappear from the room. Those who fulfill an expectation of what a professor is like are unlikely to notice what is going on. This is how just walking into a room, or sharing a podium, can mean taking up some space at the expense of others.

6. I am theorizing insistence as a political grammar in my current research on will and willfulness. There are many feminist, queer, transgender, and antiracist stories that can be heard as stories of insistence, of having to insist on what is given to others or having to become insistent just to keep going the

way you are going. We could think of trans and gender queer experiences of having to insist on a personal pronoun (which is often an experience of correction, of having to correct an assignment by reassigning oneself as "he" or "she"), as well as lesbian and gay experiences (again, often an experience of correction, of having to correct an assignment by reassigning one's partner "he" or "she"). Insistence thus becomes an everyday form of labor.

7. The assistance given to minorities is visible precisely because assistance given to the majority is not (which is how the majority can point to assistance given to minorities as evidence that a minority is being favored). The perception that equality has meant the privileging of minorities is an expression of privilege.

8. The argument I am making here—that not inhabiting the categories of privilege can generate knowledge of the categories themselves—can be related directly to the central thesis of standpoint feminism that the experience of oppression has epistemic significance. We do not necessarily have to assume the coherence of a group—or the experience of a group—as grounds to validate the central claim of standpoint. See Nancy Hartsock's classic *Money, Sex, and Power* (1983) for one of the strongest statements of standpoint feminism.

9. I use "we" because a colleague of mine was the first to point out the problems of listing only one female speaker. Given some of my past experiences of the loneliness of being a feminist killjoy, I thanked her for speaking up and reiterated her point about the problem of having such a listing of speakers in the official announcement of an event, whether or not there was an intention to have or ask more women speakers. At this point, on the virtual wall of a Facebook event page, I felt interpellated into further posting: the responses to our responses put the wall up *by the very appearance of bringing it down*. By the responses to our responses to the responses, it became clear that the wall could not be a table (that resistance could not be made into a platform), so I withdrew from the wall. Both of us subsequently received hostile private communications from one of the organizers, who described us as "feminist police." Please note, as with all the anecdotes in this book, the account is my own; it's certainly an account from the point of view of how I experience the institutions I inhabit. That others will disagree with my account (and disagree with the description of there being a wall in the first place) would be my starting point.

10. I would be tempted to name the phenomena I describe here as "critical sexism" and "critical racism": the kind of sexism and racism reproduced by critical subjects who do not see the reproduction because of their self-assumed criticality. I would note here that my own college, in which many academics have a critical self-identity (the college even identifies itself as critical), there

are regularly events, often organized under the rubric of critical theory, in which speakers are all male and all white (there is not even a "but one"). We need to point out the places where criticality itself becomes complicit with the reproduction of the same. I should also note that many practitioners suggested to me that universities are particularly hard institutions in which to do diversity and equality work because academics tend to think of themselves as "critical subjects," and thus tend not to see themselves as part of a problem.

11. I read this interview with Susan Ruddick while revising the conclusion of this book. It is a very good illustration of what I was trying to show by way of anecdote. I think the account she offers makes explicit what is often an implicit tendency in critical theory. I thus treat the narrative here as an exemplification of a wider trend. It does not follow that Ruddick's own work is not important and interesting on its own terms.

12. There are important works that exercise new vocabularies to account for how race works: see, for example, Jasbir Puar's excellent book *Terrorist Assemblages: Homonationalism in Queer Times* (2007), which draws on theories of assemblage to account for race without assuming the category of race as a stabilizing point. My own concern about this use of assemblage is the extent to which it is produced as a good theoretical object (and even a hope technology) by being contrasted with intersectionality, which becomes a bad object. It is noticeable that intersectionality is associated with stasis and assemblage with movement (see esp. pp. 211–12). The intersectionality/assemblage distinction is thus converted into a progress narrative. When assemblage becomes a way of progressing, what happens? Categories then reappear as what blocks movement or progression: "intersectional identities are the byproducts of attempts to still and quell the perpetual motion of assemblages, to capture and reduce them, to harness their threatening mobility" (213). The aim of my work has been to think of mobility not as what is threatened but what is enabled (for some) by the very restriction of categories. I do, however, agree with Puar's critique of how the language of intersectionality can be taken up as a mode of governance (for further discussion, see my introduction), although I would add that any terms we employ can be taken up as governing strategies.

13. I first learned this lesson as a Ph.D. student working on my thesis as the tide in critical theory was turning toward Deleuze. I remember numerous conversations when I would speak about whiteness and be accused of "being molar" such that "becoming molecular" became a way of not speaking about whiteness. This experience made it difficult for me to encounter Deleuze as a philosopher: I witnessed what the turn toward Deleuze was turning away from before I could turn to Deleuze myself. I have since worked more closely

with Deleuze. I have to confess it took me some time to recover from De-
leuzianism and to find my way to Deleuze! See the conclusion to Ahmed
(2010) for a response to Deleuze's reading of Spinoza, which, though critical, is
very much engaged with the spirit of his encounter by offering a different
angle on what is at stake in good and bad encounters.

14. See, for example, Elizabeth Grosz's association of feminist critique with the
exposure of error in her defense of Darwin's value for feminism (2005: 27). We
can link this questioning of the language of feminist critique to the affirmative
turn within feminism. See Maureen McNeil (2010) for an account of this turn
and Angela McRobbie (2008) for a critique of affirmative feminism.

15. A feminist practical phenomenology can be understood as an offspring of
Donna Haraway's model of "situated knowledges" given her emphasis on the
located and embodied nature of knowledge practice. It can also be considered
an extension of feminist work on "the politics of location," including the
writings of Adrienne Rich (1986). For an excellent formulation of a feminist
politics of location in relation to transnational practice, see Kaplan (1994).

16. I agree with many parts of Gilroy's argument in *Against Race* (2000), and it is
important to note here that his vision is of the future: specifically, one in which
the category "race" no longer has a future. My difference of view could be
described as a difference in strategy. I think evoking the future in this way is
too consistent with the argument that we can move beyond race by not seeing
race. This is why his argument can be understood as complicit with fantasies
of being "postracial," even though Gilroy does not use the term "postracial"
(as we can note, for example, in the review by Thomas West 2002). For a
critical reading of Gilroy's arguments "against race," see Alana Lentin (2008:
496–97).

17. The idea of the United States as postracial became particularly significant, of
course, with the election of President Barack Obama. The desire to read his
arrival into the White House (which henceforth acquires color) as a sign of
overcoming racism has been evident in media debates. There are many critiques of this discourse of postracial post-Obama. A good example is offered
by Bonilla-Silva and Ray (2009).

18. The phrase "forms of life" is used by Ludwig Wittgenstein to denote "what
has to be accepted—the given" ([1953] 2009: 223). For Wittgenstein, when we
agree in what we say, we are agreeing in language and in "forms of life" (94). I
suggest here, admittedly by bringing Wittgenstein's words into a different
context, that social categories can be thought as norms or even as a set of
agreements, which in becoming "forms of life" disappear from view as norms.
As what has been given, they also then define a field of intelligibility (what we

can say, what we can do). I thank Christine Wieseler, who asked me a question about how my use of this expression relates to Wittgenstein during a workshop at Miami University.

19. These observations were offered to me in the early 2000s. They were borne out by a recent U.S. study comparing descriptions of male and female performances in recommendation letters. See Madera, Hebl, and Martin (2009).

20. I thank Elaine Miller, whose question about flows and blockages during a workshop at Miami University prompted the formulation in this sentence.

Acker, Joan (1990). "Hierarchies, Jobs, Bodies: A Theory of Gendered Organizations," *Gender and Society*, 4, no. 2: 139–58.

—— (2006). "Inequality Regimes: Gender, Class, and Race in Organizations," *Gender and Society*, 20, no. 4: 441–64.

Agar, Michael H. (1980). *The Professional Stranger: An Informal Introduction to Ethnography*. New York: Academic Press.

Ahmed, Sara (1998). *Differences That Matter: Feminist Theory and Postmodernism*. Cambridge: Cambridge University Press.

—— (2000). *Strange Encounters: Embodied Others in Postcoloniality*. London: Routledge.

—— (2004). *The Cultural Politics of Emotion*. Edinburgh: Edinburgh University Press.

—— (2006). *Queer Phenomenology: Orientation, Objects, Others*. Durham: Duke University Press.

—— (2010). *The Promise of Happiness*. Durham: Duke University Press.

Ahmed, Sara, Shona Hunter, Sevgi Kilic, Elaine Swan, and Lewis Turner (2006). *Race, Diversity and Leadership in the Learning and Skills Sector*. Unpublished report. Available at http://www.gold.ac.uk/media/finaldiversityreport.pdf.

Aizura, Aren Z. (2009). "Racism and the Censorship of Gay Imperialism," *MR Zine*, October 23. Available at http://mrzine.monthlyreview.org/2009/aizura231009.html.

Alcoff, Linda Martín (2006). *Visible Identities: Race, Gender, and the Self*. Oxford: Oxford University Press.

Alexander, Claire (2004). "Writing Race: Imagination and the Writing of *The*

Asian Gang," in *Researching Race and Racism*, ed. Martin Bulmer and John Solomos. London: Routledge, 134–49.

Alexander, Jacqui M. (2005). *Pedagogies of Crossing: Meditations on Feminism, Sexual Politics, Memory, and the Sacred*. Durham: Duke University Press.

Ali, Suki (2009). "Black Feminist Praxis: Some Reflections on Pedagogies and Politics in Higher Education," *Race, Ethnicity and Education*, 12, no. 1: 79–66.

Althusser, Louis (1971). *Lenin and Philosophy and Other Essays*, trans. Ben Brewster. London: New Left Books.

Ang, Ien (2001). *On Not Speaking Chinese: Living between Asia and the West*. London: Routledge.

Anzaldúa, Gloria, and AnaLouise Keating (2009). *The Gloria Anzaldúa Reader*. Durham: Duke University Press.

Arendt, Hannah (1978). *The Life of the Mind*. Orlando, FL: Harcourt Brace and Company.

Austin, John Langshaw (1970). *Philosophical Papers*. Oxford: Clarendon Press.

—— (1975). *How to Do Things with Words*. Oxford: Oxford University Press.

Bacchi, Carol, and Joan Eveline (2010). *Mainstreaming Politics: Gendered Practices and Feminist Theory*. Adelaide: University of Adelaide Press.

Back, Les (2004). "Ivory Towers? The Academy and Racism," in *Institutional Racism in Higher Education*, ed. Ian Law, Deborah Phillips, and Laura Turney. Stoke on Trent: Trentham Books, 1–6.

Ball, Stephen J. (1998). "Performativity and Fragmentation in 'Postmodern Schooling,'" in *Postmodernity and the Fragmentation of Welfare*, ed. John Carter. London: Routledge, 187–203.

——. (2004). "Performativities and Fabrications in the Education Economy: Towards the Performative Society," in *The Routledge Falmer Reader in Sociology of Education*, ed. Stephen Ball. London: Routledge, 143–55.

Bannerji, Himani (2000). *The Dark Side of the Nation: Essays on Multiculturalism, Nationalism and Gender*. Toronto: Canadian Scholars Press.

Bauman, Zygmunt (2005). *Liquid Life*. Cambridge: Polity.

Bell, Joyce M., and Douglas Hartmann (2007). "Diversity in Everyday Discourse: The Cultural Ambiguities and Consequences of 'Happy Talk,'" *American Sociological Review*, 72: 895–914.

Benschop, Yvonne (2001). "Pride, Prejudice and Performance: Relations between HRM, Diversity and Performance," *International Journal of Human Resources Management*, 12, no. 7: 1166–81.

Berger, Peter, and Thomas Luckmann (1967). *The Social Construction of Reality: A Treatise in the Sociology of Knowledge*. London: Penguin Books.

Bhabha, Homi (2004). *The Location of Culture*. London: Routledge (Classics Edition).

Bhattacharyya, Gargi (1998). "Riding Multiculturalism," in *Multicultural States: Rethinking Identity and Difference*, ed. David Bennett. London: Routledge, 252–66.

Blackmore, Jill, and Judyth Sachs (2003). "Managing Equity Work in the Performative University," *Australian Feminist Studies*, 18, no. 41: 141–62.

—— (2007). *Performing and Reforming Leaders: Gender, Educational Restructuring, and Organizational Change*. Albany: State University of New York Press.

Bonilla-Silva, Eduardo, and Victor Ray (2009). "When Whites Love a Black Leader: Race Matters in Obamerica," *Journal of African-American Studies*, 13, no. 2: 176–83.

Bourdieu, Pierre (1986). "The Forms of Capital," in *Handbook of Theory and Research for the Sociology of Education*, ed. John G. Richardson, trans. Richard Nice. New York: Greenwood Press, 242–58.

—— (1990). *The Logic of Practice*, trans. Richard Nice. Stanford: Stanford University Press.

Brah, Avtar (1996). *Cartographies of Diaspora: Contesting Identities*. London: Routledge.

Brayboy, Brian McKinley Jones (2003). "The Implementation of Diversity in Predominantly White Colleges and Universities," *Journal of Black Studies*, 3, no. 1: 72–86.

Brewer, Rose M. (1993). "Theorizing Race, Class and Gender: The New Scholarship of Black Feminist Intellectuals and Black Women's Labor," in *Theorizing Black Feminisms: The Visionary Pragmatism of Black Women*, ed. Stanlie Myrise James and Abena P. A. Busia. London: Routledge, 13–30.

Brinton, Mary C., and Victor Nee, eds. (2001). *The New Institutionalism in Sociology*. Stanford: Stanford University Press.

Bronson, Po, with Ashley Merryman (2006). "Are Americans Suffering Diversity Fatigue?" *Time*, May 26. Available at http://www.time.com/time/nation/article/0,8599,1199702,00.html.

Brown-Glaude, Winnifred R., ed. (2009). *Doing Diversity in Higher Education: Faculty Leaders Share Challenges and Strategies*. New Brunswick, NJ: Rutgers University Press.

Butler, Judith (1993). *Bodies That Matter: On the Discursive Limits of "Sex."* New York: Routledge.

—— (1997). "Merely Cultural," *Social Text*, 52, no. 53: 265–77.

—— (2004). *Undoing Gender*. New York: Routledge.

Carby, Hazel (1999). *Cultures in Babylon: Black Britain and African America*. London: Verso.

Chesler, Phyllis (2007). "Response," *Feminist Theory*, 8, no. 2: 227–34.

Chin, Jean Lau (2010). "Introduction to the Special Issue on Diversity and Leadership," *American Psychologist*, 65, no. 3: 150–56.

Chow, Rey (2002). *The Protestant Ethnic and the Spirit of Capitalism*. New York: Columbia University Press.

—— (2006). *The Age of the World Target: Self-Referentiality in the Age of War, Theory, and Comparative Work*. Durham: Duke University Press.

Cockburn, Cynthia (1991). *In the Way of Women: Men's Resistance to Sex Equality in Organizations*. Basingstoke: Macmillan.

Collins, Patricia Hills (1990). *Black Feminist Thought: Knowledge, Consciousness and the Politics of Empowerment*. London: Routledge.

Couldry, Nick, and Angela McRobbie (2010). "The Death of the University, English Style," *Culturemachine*, November. Available at http://www.culturemachine.net/index.php/cm/article/view/417/430.

Crenshaw, Kimberlé W. (1989). "Demarginalizing the Intersection of Race and Sex: A Black Feminist Critique of Antidiscrimination Doctrine, Feminist Theory, and Antiracist Politics," *University of Chicago Legal Forum*: 139–67.

Crimp, Douglas (2002). *Melancholia and Moralism: Essays on AIDS and Queer Politics*. Cambridge: MIT Press.

Davis, Angela (1996). "Gender, Multiculturalism, and Class: Rethinking 'Race' Politics," in *Mapping Multiculturalism*, ed. Avery Gordon and Christopher Newfield. Minneapolis: University of Minnesota Press, 40–48.

De Bary, Brett, ed. (2009). *Universities in Translation: The Mental Labor of Globalization*. Hong Kong: Hong Kong University Press.

Deem, Rosemary, and Jenny Ozga (1997). "Women Managing for Diversity in a Postmodern World," in *Feminist Critical Policy Analysis: A Perspective from Post-Secondary Education*, ed. Catherine Marshall. London: Falmer, 25–40.

Derbyshire, John (2010). "Americans Aren't Racist, They Just Have Diversity Fatigue," *Taki's Magazine*, August 26. Available at http://takimag.com/article/americans_arent_racist_they_just_have_diversity_fatigue/.

Derrida, Jacques (1988). *Limited Inc.*, trans. Samuel Weber. Evanston, IL: Northwestern University Press.

—— (2000). *Of Hospitality*, trans. Rachel Bowlby. Stanford: Stanford University Press.

DiMaggio, Paul J., and Walter W. Powell (1983). "The Iron Cage Revisited: Institutional Isomorphism and Collective Rationality in Organizational Fields," *American Sociology Review*, 48, no. 2: 147–60.

——, eds. (1991). *The New Institutionalism in Organizational Analysis*. Chicago: University of Chicago Press.

Douglas, Mary (1986). *How Institutions Think*. Syracuse: Syracuse University Press.

Dua, Enakshi (2009). "On the Effectiveness of Anti-Racism Policies in Canadian Universities: Issues of Implementation of Policies by Senior Administration," in *Racism in the Canadian University: Demanding Social Justice, Inclusion and Equity*, ed. Frances Henry and Carol Tator. Toronto: University of Toronto Press, 160–96.

Du Bois, W. E. B. [1903] (2003). *The Souls of Black Folk*. New York: Barnes and Noble Classics.

Duggan, Lisa (2003). *The Twilight of Equality: Neoliberalism, Cultural Politics, and the Attack on Democracy*. Boston: Beacon Press.

Durkheim, Émile [1901] (1982). "On the Objective Method in Sociology," in *The Rules of Sociological Method and Selected Texts on Sociology and Its Method*, trans. W. D. Halls. London: Macmillan.

Dyer, Richard (1997). *White*. London: Routledge.

Elgström, Ole (2000). "Norm Negotiations. The Construction of New Norms Regarding Gender and Development in EU Foreign Aid Policy," *Journal of European Public Policy*, 7, no. 3: 457–76.

Eng, David L. (2010). *The Feeling of Kinship: Queer Liberalism and the Racialization of Intimacy*. Durham: Duke University Press.

Equality Challenge Unit (2004). "Good Talking: The HE Communicators Equality and Diversity Toolkit." London: Higher Education Funding Council for England.

—— (2006). "The Role of the Equality Specialist in Higher Education Institutions." Available at http://www.ecu.ac.uk/publications/role-of-the-equality-specialist-in-he#.

Erel, Umut, and Christian Klesse (2009). "Out of Place: Silencing Voices on Queerness/Raciality," *MR Zine*, October 24. Available at http://mrzine.monthlyreview.org/2009/ek241009.html.

Essed, Philomena (1996). *Diversity: Gender, Color, and Culture*, trans. Rita Gircour. Amherst: University of Massachusetts Press.

Falzon, Mark-Anthony (2009). "Introduction: Multi-sited Ethnography: Theory, Practice and Locality in Contemporary Research," in *Multi-sited Ethnography: Theory, Praxis and Locality in Contemporary Research*, ed. Mark-Anthony Falzon. Farnham, Surrey: Ashgate, 1–24.

Fanon, Frantz [1952] (1986). *Black Skin, White Masks*, trans. C. L. Markmann. London: Pluto.

Fleras, Augie (2011). "'Cooling Out Troublesome Constituents': The Politics of Managing 'Isms' in the Antipodes," in *Managing Ethnic Diversity*, ed. Reza Hasmath. Farnham, Surrey: Ashgate, 119–40.

Fortier, Anne-Marie (2008). *Multicultural Horizons: Diversity and the Limits of the Civil Nation*. London: Routledge.

Frankenberg, Ruth (1993). *White Women, Race Matters: The Social Construction of Whiteness*. Minneapolis: University of Minnesota Press.

Freire, Paulo [1970] (2000). *Pedagogy of the Oppressed*, trans. Myra Bergman Ramos. New York: Continuum.

Friedan, Betty (1965). *The Feminine Mystique*. Harmondsworth: Penguin.

Gane, Mike (2005). "Introduction" to Marcel Mauss's *The Nature of Sociology: Two Essays*, Oxford: Berghahn Press, ix–xxii.

Gane, Nicholas (2004). *The Future of Social Theory*. London: Continuum.

Garner, Steve (2007). *Whiteness: An Introduction*. London: Routledge.

Gatens, Moira (1998). "Institutions, Embodiment and Sexual Difference," in *Gender and Institutions: Welfare, Work and Citizenship*, ed. Moira Gatens and Alison Mackinnon. Cambridge: Cambridge University Press, 1–18.

Geertz, Clifford (1973). *The Interpretation of Culture: Selected Essays*. New York: Basic Books.

Gillborn, David (2008). *Racism and Education: Coincidence or Conspiracy?* London: Routledge.

Gilroy, Paul (2000). *Against Race: Imagining Political Culture beyond the Color Line*. Cambridge: Belknap Press of Harvard University Press.

Gross, Neil (2007). "Pragmatism, Phenomenology, and Twentieth-Century American Sociology," in *Sociology in America: A History*, ed. C. Calhoun. Chicago: University of Chicago Press, 183–224.

Grosz, Elizabeth (2005). *Time Travels: Feminism, Nature, Power*. Durham: Duke University Press.

Gunaratnam, Yasmin (2003). *Researching "Race" and Ethnicity: Methods, Knowledge and Power*. London: Sage.

Gunew, Sneja (2004). *Haunted Nations: The Colonial Dimensions of Multiculturalism*. London: Routledge.

Hage, Ghassan (2000). *White Nation: Fantasies of White Supremacy in a Multicultural Society*. London: Routledge.

—— (2003). *Against Paranoid Nationalism*. Annandale, NSW: Pluto Press.

Hall, Stuart (2000). "Conclusion: The Multicultural Question," in *Un/settled Multiculturalisms: Diasporas, Entanglements, Transruptions*, ed. Barnor Hesse. New York: Zed, 209–41.

Hamaz, Sofia (2008). "How Do Diversity Trainers and Consultants Embody Antiracism? Constructions of Antiracism in the United Kingdom," *International Journal of Sociology*, 38, no. 2: 30–42.

Haraway, Donna (1997). *Modest_Witness@ Second_Millennium.FemaleMan© _Meets_OncoMouse™: Feminism and Technoscience*. Routledge: New York.

Haritaworn, Jin, Tamsila Tauqir, and Esra Erdem (2008). "Gay Imperialism: Gender and Sexuality Discourse in the 'War on Terror,'" in *Out of Place: Silences in Queerness/Raciality*, ed. Esperanza Miyake and Adi Kuntsman. York: Raw Nerve Books, 9–33.

Hartsock, Nancy (1983). *Money, Sex, and Power: Toward a Feminist Historical Materialism*. Boston: Northeastern University Press.

Hay, Colin (2006). "Constructivist Institutionalism," in *The Oxford Handbook of Political Institutions*, ed. R. A. W. Rhodes, Sarah A. Binder, and Bert A. Rockman. Oxford: Oxford University Press, 56–74.

Hegel, Georg Wilhelm Friedrich [1827–28] (2007). *Lectures on the Philosophy of Spirit*, trans. Robert R. Williams. Oxford: Oxford University Press.

Hesse, Barnor (2004). "Discourse on Institutional Racism: The Genealogy of a Concept," in *Institutional Racism in Higher Education*, ed. Ian Law, Deborah Phillips, and Laura Turney. Stoke on Trent: Trentham, 131–48.

Higher Education Council (HEC) (1996). *Equality, Diversity and Excellence: Advancing the National Higher Education Framework*. Canberra: Australian Government Publishing Service.

Hill, Mike (2004). *After Whiteness: Unmaking an American Majority*. New York: New York University Press.

Home Office (2005). *Life in the United Kingdom: A Journey to Citizenship*. Norwich: Stationery Office Books (TSO).

hooks, bell (1992). *Black Looks: Race and Representation*. London: Turnaround

—— (2000). *Feminist Theory: From Margin to Centre*. London: Pluto Press.

Hunter, Shona (2008). "Living Documents: A Feminist Psychosocial Approach to the Relational Politics of Policy Documentation," *Critical Social Policy*, 28: 506–28.

—— (forthcoming). *Power, Politics and the Emotions: Impossible Governance*. London: Taylor and Francis.

Hunter, Shona, and Elaine Swan (2007). "Oscillating Politics and Shifting Agencies: Equalities and Diversity Work and Actor Network Theory," *Equal Opportunities International*, 26, no. 5: 402–19.

Hurtado, Aida (1996). *The Color of Privilege: Three Blasphemies on Race and Feminism*. Ann Arbor: University of Michigan Press.

Husserl, Edmund [1913] (1969). *Ideas: General Introduction to Pure Phenomenology*, trans. W. R. Boyce Gibson. London: George Allen and Unwin.

——. [1936/54] (1970). *The Crisis of the European Sciences and Transcendental Phenomenology: An Introduction to Phenomenological Philosophy*, trans. David Carr. Evanston, IL: Northwestern University Press.

Jacoby, Russell (1975). *Social Amnesia: A Critique of Contemporary Psychology*. New Brunswick: Rutgers University Press.

James, William [1890] (1950). *The Principles of Psychology*, vol. 1. New York: Dover.

Jones, Cecily (2005). "Falling between the Cracks: How Equality and Diversity Policies Fail Black Women Academics," *Policy Futures in Education*, 4, no. 2: 154–59.

Kandola, Rajvinder, and Johanna Fullerton (1994). *Diversity in Action: Managing the Mosaic*. London: Institute for Personnel and Development.

Kaplan, Caren (1994). "The Politics of Location as a Transnational Feminist Practice," in *Scattered Hegemonies: Postmodernity and Transnational Feminist Practices*, ed. Inderpal Grewal and Caren Kaplan. Minneapolis: University of Minnesota Press, 137–52.

Kincheloe, Joe L., and Shirley R. Steinberg (1998). "Addressing the Crisis of Whiteness: Reconfiguring White Identity in a Pedagogy of Whiteness," in *White Reign: Deploying Whiteness in America*, ed. Joe L. Kincheloe, Shirley R. Steinberg, Nelson M. Rodriguez, and Ronald E. Chennault. New York: St. Martin's Press, 3–29.

Kirton, Gill, and Anne-Marie Greene (2000). *The Dynamics of Managing Diversity: A Critical Approach*. Oxford: Heinemann.

—— (2009). "The Costs and Opportunities of Doing Diversity Work in Mainstream Organisations," *Human Resource Management Journal*, 19, no. 2: 159–75.

Kirton, Gill, Anne-Marie Greene, and Deborah Dean (2007). "British Diversity Professionals as Change Agents—Radicals, Tempered Radicals or Liberal Reformers?," *International Journal of Human Resource Management*, 18, no. 11: 1979–94.

Kristeva, Julia (2003). *Nations without Nationalism*, trans. Leon S. Roudiez. New York: Columbia University Press.

Kuokkanen, Rauna Johanna (2007). *Reshaping the University: Responsibility, Indigenous Epistemes, and the Logic of the Gift*. Vancouver: University of British Columbia Press.

Larson, Colleen L., and Carlos Julio Ovando (2001). *The Color of Bureaucracy: The Politics of Equity in Multicultural School Communities*. Belmont, CA: Wadsworth.

Law, John (1992). "Notes on the Theory of the Actor Network: Ordering, Strategy and Heterogeneity," *Systemic Practice and Action Research*, 5, no. 4: 379–93.

Lawrence, Thomas B., and Roy Suddaby (2006). "Institutions and Institutional Work," in *The Sage Handbook of Organization Studies*, ed. Stewart R. Clegg, Cynthia Hardy, Thomas B. Lawrence, and Walter R. Nord. London: Sage, 215–54.

Lentin, Alana (2008). "Europe and the Silence about Race," *European Journal of Social Theory*, 11, no. 4: 487–503.

Lentin, Alana, and Gavan Titley (2011). *The Crises of Multiculture: Racism in a Neo-Liberal Age*. London: Zed.

Lewis, Gail (2000). *"Race," Gender, Social Welfare: Encounters in a Postcolonial Society*. Cambridge: Polity Press.

Lorbiecki, Anna (2001). "Changing Views on Diversity Management," *Management Studies*, 32, no. 3: 345–61.

Lorde, Audre (1982). *Zami: A New Spelling of My Name*. London: Sheba Feminist Publishers.

—— (1984). *Sister Outsider: Essays and Speeches*. Trumansburg, NY: Crossing Press.

Luft, Rachel E., and Jane Ward (2009). "Toward an Intersectionality Just out of Reach: Confronting Challenges to Intersectional Practice," in *Perceiving Gender Locally, Globally, and Intersectionally*, ed. Vasilikie Demos and Marcia Texler Segal. Bingley, U.K.: Emerald Group Publishing, 9–38.

Lury, Celia (2000). "The United Colours of Diversity," in *Global Nature, Global Culture*, by Sarah Franklin, Celia Lury, and Jackie Stacey. London: Sage, 147–87.

—— (2004). *Brands: The Logos of the Global Economy*. London: Routledge.

Lyotard, Jean-François (1984). *The Postmodern Condition: A Report on Knowledge*, trans. Geoff Bennington and Brian Massumi. Manchester: Manchester University Press.

MacMullan, Terrance (2009). *Habits of Whiteness: A Pragmatist Reconstruction*. Bloomington: Indiana University Press.

Macpherson, William (1999). *The Stephen Lawrence Inquiry*. London: HMSO.

Madera, Juan M., Michelle R. Hebl, and Randi C. Martin (2009). "Gender and Letters of Recommendation for Academics: Agentic and Communal Differences," *Journal of Applied Psychology*, 94: 1591–99.

Mannur, Anita (2010). *Culinary Fictions: Food in South Asian Diasporic Culture*. Philadelphia: Temple University Press.

March, James G., and Johan P. Olsen (1989). *Rediscovering Institutions: The Organizational Basis of Politics*. New York: Free Press.

Marcus, George E. (1998). *Ethnography through Thick and Thin*. Princeton: Princeton University Press.

Marx, Karl [1845] (2009). *Theses on Feuerbach*, trans. Austin Lewis. Ellicott City, MD: Mondial Press.

Maso, Ilja (2007). "Phenomenology and Ethnography," in *Handbook of Ethnography*, ed. Paul Atkinson. London: Sage, 136–44.

McCaig, Norma (1996). "Understanding Global Nomads," in *Strangers at Home: Essays on the Effects of Living Overseas and Coming "Home" to a Strange Land*, ed. Carolyn D. Smith. New York: Aletheia Publications, 99–120.

McLisky, Claire, ed. (2009). *Creating White Australia*. Sydney: Sydney University Press.

McNeil, Daniel (2004). "Dancing across Borders: Blackness That Isn't (African) American," *Bright Lights Film Journal*, 44. Available at http://www.brightlightsfilm.com/44/pan.htm.

McNeil, Maureen (2010). "Post-Millennial Feminist Theory: Encounters with

Humanism, Materialism, Critique, Nature, Biology and Darwin," *Journal for Cultural Research*, 14, no. 4: 427–37.

McRobbie, Angela (2008). *The Aftermath of Feminism: Gender, Culture and Social Change*. London: Sage.

Merleau-Ponty, Maurice (2002). *Phenomenology of Perception*, trans. Colin Smith. London: Routledge.

Meyer, Heinz-Dieter, and Brian Rowan (2006). "Institutional Analysis and the Study of Education," in *The New Institutionalism in Education*, ed. Heinz-Dieter Meyer and Brian Rowan. Albany: State University of New York Press, 1–14.

Meyerson, Deborah E., and Maureen A. Scully (1995). "Tempered Radicalism and the Politics of Ambivalence and Change," *Organization Science*, 6, no. 5: 585–600.

Michaels, Walter Benn (2010). *The Trouble with Diversity: How We Learned to Love Identity and Ignore Inequality*. New York: Metropolitan.

Milton, Nicholas (2009). "Anti-Racism Initiatives by Universities Are Failing to Have an Effect Off-Campus," *The Guardian*, November 24.

Mirza, Heidi, ed. (1996). *Black British Feminism*. London: Routledge.

—— (2009). *Race, Gender and Educational Desire: Why Black Women Succeed and Fail*. London: Routledge.

Mohanty, Chandra Talpade (2003). *Feminism without Borders: Decolonizing Theory, Practicing Solidarity*. Durham: Duke University Press.

Molz, Jennie Germann, and Sarah Gibson (2007). "Introduction: Mobilizing and Mooring Hospitality," in *Mobilizing Hospitality: The Ethics of Social Relations in a Mobile World*, ed. Jennie Germann Molz and Sarah Gibson. Farnham, Surrey: Ashgate, 1–26.

Moody, JoAnn (2004). *Faculty Diversity: Problems and Solutions*. New York: Routledge Falmer.

Moor, Liz (2007). *The Rise of Brands*. Oxford: Berg.

Moreton-Robinson, Aileen (2000). *Talkin' up to the White Woman: Aboriginal Women and Feminism*. St. Lucia: University of Queensland Press.

——, ed. (2004). *Whitening Race: Essays in Social and Cultural Criticism*. Canberra: Aboriginal Studies Press.

Morley, Louise (1995). "The Micropolitics of Women's Studies: Feminism and Organizational Change in the Academy," in *(Hetero)sexual Politics*, ed. Mary Maynard and June Purvis. London: Taylor and Francis, 171–85.

Murdolo, Adele (1996). "Warmth and Unity with All Women? Historicising Racism in the Australian Women's Movement," *Feminist Review*, 52: 69–86.

Neal, Sarah (1998). *The Making of Equal Opportunities Policies in Universities*. Philadelphia: Open University Press.

Nee, Victor (1998). "Sources of the New Institutionalism," in *The New Institu-

tionalism in Sociology, ed. Mary C. Brinton and Victor Nee. Stanford: Stanford University Press, 1–16.

Nicoll, Fiona (2004). "'Are You Calling Me a Racist?' Teaching Critical Whiteness Theory in Indigenous Sovereignty," *borderlands*, 3, no. 2.

Orelus, Pierre W. (2011). *Courageous Voices of Immigrants and Transnationals of Color: Counter Narratives against Discrimination in Schools and Beyond*. New York: Peter Lang.

Pai, Hsiao-Hung (2005). "Anxiety in the UK," *The Guardian*, February 8.

Pedwell, Carolyn (2010). *Feminism, Culture and Embodied Practice: The Rhetorics of Comparison*. London: Routledge.

Phillips, Trevor (2005). "A New Highway Code for Multi-Ethnic Britain," speech given to the Conservative Party Muslim Forum in Blackpool.

———. (2008). "Fairness and Respect in an Integrated Society." Available at http://www.thefreelibrary.com/Fairness+and+respect+in+an+integrated+society.-a0178071394

Phoenix, Ann (2011). "Psychosocial Intersections: Contextualizing the Accounts of Adults who Grew up in Visibly Ethnically Different Households," in *Framing Intersectionality: Debates on a Multi-Faceted Concept in Gender Studies*, ed. Helma Lutz, Maria Teresa Herrera Vivar, and Linda Supik. Farnham, Surrey: Ashgate, 137–54.

Poovey, Mary (1995). Making a Social Body: British Cultural Formation, 1830–1864. Chicago: University of Chicago Press.

Power, Michael (1994). *The Audit Explosion*. London: Demos.

——— (1997). *The Audit Society: Rituals of Verification*. Oxford: Oxford University Press.

Prasad, Pushkala (1997). "The Protestant Ethic and the Myths of the Frontier: Cultural Imprints, Organizational Structuring, and Workplace Diversity," in *Managing the Organizational Melting Pot—Dilemmas of Workplace Diversity*, ed. Pushkala Prasad, Albert J. Mills, Michael Elmes, and Anshuman Prasad. Thousand Oaks, CA: Sage, 129–48.

Prasad, Pushkala, and Albert J. Mills (1997). "From Showcase to Shadow: Understanding the Dilemmas of Managing Workplace Diversity," in *Managing the Organizational Melting Pot: Dilemmas of Workplace Diversity*, ed. Pushkala Prasad, Albert J. Mills, Michael Elmes, and Anshuman Prasad. Thousand Oaks, CA: Sage, 3–30.

Prior, Lindsay (2003). *Using Documents in Social Research*. London: Sage.

Probyn-Ramsey, Fiona (2009). "Putting Complicity to Work for Accountability," in *Commitment and Complicity in Cultural Theory and Practice*, ed. Begüm Özden Firat, Sarah De Mul, and Sonja van Wichelen. Hampshire: Palgrave Macmillan, 154–66.

Puar, Jasbir K. (2007). *Terrorist Assemblages: Homonationalism in Queer Times*. Durham: Duke University Press.

Puwar, Nirmal (2004). *Space Invaders: Race, Gender and Bodies out of Place*. Oxford: Berg.

Rattansi, Ali (1992). "Changing the Subject? Racism, Culture and Education," in *Race, Culture and Difference*, ed. James Donald and Ali Rattansi. London: Sage, 11–48.

Readings, Bill (1996). *The University in Ruins*. Cambridge: Harvard University Press.

Rhodes, R. A. W., Sarah A. Binder, and Bert A. Rockman, eds. (2008). *The Oxford Handbook of Political Institutions*. Oxford: Oxford University Press.

Rich, Adrienne (1986). *Blood, Bread, and Poetry: Selected Prose, 1979–1985*. New York: W. W. Norton.

Riles, Annelise (2006). "Introduction: In Response," in *Documents: Artifacts of Modern Knowledge*, ed. Annelise Riles. Ann Arbor: University of Michigan Press, 1–40.

Roediger, David R. (1991). *The Wages of Whiteness: Race and the Making of the American Working Class*. London: Verso.

—— (2006). *Working toward Whiteness: How America's Immigrants Became White: The Strange Journey from Ellis Island to the Suburbs*. New York: Basic Books.

Rose, Hilary (1994). *Love, Power, and Knowledge: Towards a Feminist Transformation of the Sciences*. Cambridge: Polity.

Rosello, Mireille (2001). *Postcolonial Hospitality: The Immigrant as Guest*. Stanford: Stanford University Press.

Rothe, Johanna (2009). "Out of Place, Out of Print: On the Censorship of the First Queerness/Raciality Collection in Britain," *MR Zine*, October 15. Available at http://mrzine.monthlyreview.org/2009/rothe151009.html.

Ruddick, Susan (2011). "Interview with Susan Ruddick." *Society and Space: Environment and Planning D*, April 1. Available at http://societyandspace.com/2011/04/01/interview-susan-ruddick/.

Ryle, Gilbert (1971). *Collected Papers: Volume 2*. New York: Barnes and Noble.

Sarup, Madan (1991). *Education and the Ideologies of Racism*. Stoke-on-Trent: Trentham Books.

Schmidt, Vivien A. (2006). "Discursive Institutionalism: The Explanatory Power of Ideas and Discourse," *Annual Review of Political Science*, 11: 303–26.

Schutz, Alfred (1944). "The Stranger: An Essay in Social Psychology," *American Journal of Sociology*, 49, no. 6: 499–507.

Shore, Cris, and Susan Wright (2000). "Coercive Accountability: The Rise of Audit Culture in Higher Education," in *Audit Cultures: Anthropological Studies in Accountability, Ethics and the Academy*, ed. Marilyn Strathern. London: Routledge, 57–89.

Singh, Val (2002). *Managing Diversity for Strategic Advantage*. London: Council for Excellence in Management and Leadership.

Smith, Dorothy E. (2005). *Institutional Ethnography: A Sociology for People*. Lanham, MD: AltaMira Press.

Solomos, John (1999). "Social Research and the Stephen Lawrence Inquiry," *Sociological Research Online*, 4, no. 1. Available at http://www.socresonline.org.uk/4/lawrence/solomos.html.

Spivak, Gayatri Chakravorty (2000). "Claiming Transformation: Travel Notes with Pictures," in *Transformations: Thinking through Feminism*, ed. Sara Ahmed, Jane Kilby, Celia Lury, Maureen McNeil, and Beverley Skeggs. London: Routledge, 119–30.

Squires, Judith (2005). "Is Mainstreaming Transformative? Theorizing Mainstreaming in the Context of Diversity and Deliberation," *Social Politics*, 12, no. 3: 366–88.

Strathern, Marilyn (1996). "Cutting the Network," *Journal of the Royal Anthropological Institute*, 2, no. 3: 517–35.

—— (2000). "Introduction: New Accountabilities," in *Audit Cultures: Anthropological Studies in Accountability, Ethics and the Academy*, ed. Marilyn Strathern. London: Routledge, 1–19.

—— (2004). *Commons and Borderlands: Working Papers on Interdisciplinary, Accountability and the Flow of Knowledge*. Wantage: Sean Kingston Publishing.

—— (2006). "Bullet-Proofing: A Tale from the United Kingdom," in *Documents: Artifacts of Modern Knowledge*, ed. Annelise Riles. Ann Arbor: University of Michigan Press, 181–205.

Stratton, Jon, and Ien Ang (1998). "Multicultural Imagined Communities: Cultural Difference and National Identity in the USA and Australia," in *Multicultural States: Rethinking Difference and Identity*, ed. David Bennett. London: Routledge, 135–62.

Street, Paul Louis (2007). *Racial Oppression in the Global Metropolis: A Living Black Chicago History*. Plymouth: Rowland and Littlefield.

Sullivan, Shannon (2006). *Revealing Whiteness: The Unconscious Habits of White Privilege*. Bloomington: Indiana University Press.

Swan, Elaine (2009). "Putting Words in Our Mouths: Diversity Training as Heteroglossic Organisational Spaces," in *Equality, Diversity and Inclusion at Work: A Research Companion*, ed. Mustafa F. Özbilgin. Cheltenham: Edward Elgar, 308–21.

—— (2010a). "States of White Ignorance, and Audit Masculinity in English Higher Education," *Social Politics*, 17, no. 4: 477–506.

—— (2010b). "Commodity Diversity: Smiling Faces as a Strategy of Containment." *Organization*, 17, no. 1: 77–100.

Swan, Elaine, and Steve Fox (2010). "Playing the Game: Strategies of Resistance and Co-optation in Diversity Work," *Gender, Work and Organization*, 17, no. 5: 565–89.

Thobani, Sunera (2003). "War and the Politics of Truth Making in Canada," *Journal of Qualitative Studies in Education*, 16, no. 3: 399–414.

—— (2007). "White Wars: Western Feminisms and the 'War on Terror.'" *Feminist Theory*, 8, no. 2: 169–85.

Titley, Gavan, and Alana Lentin (2008). "More Benetton than Barricades: The Politics of Diversity in Europe," in *The Politics of Diversity in Europe*, ed. Gavan Titley and Alana Lentin. Strasbourg: Council of Europe, 9–30.

Urry, John (2007). *Mobilities*. Cambridge: Polity Press.

Violet, Indigo (2002). "Linkages: A Personal-Political Journey into Feminist with Color Politics," in *This Bridge We Call Home: Radical Visions for Transformation*, ed. Gloria Anzaldúa and AnaLouise Keating. London: Routledge, 486–94.

Walby, Sylvia (2005). "Gender Mainstreaming: Productive Tensions in Theory and Practice," *Social Politics*, 12, no. 3: 321–43.

Ward, Jane (2008). *Respectably Queer: Diversity Culture in LGBT Activist Organizations*. Nashville: Vanderbilt University Press.

Warner, Michael (2002). *Publics and Counterpublics*. Brooklyn: Zone Books.

Weber, Samuel (2001). *Institutions and Interpretation*. Stanford: Stanford University Press.

West, Thomas (2002). "Review of Paul Gilroy, *Against Race: Imagining Political Culture beyond the Color Line*," *JAC*, 22, no. 1, n.p.

Wiegman, Robyn, ed. (2002). *Women's Studies on Its Own: A Next Wave Reader in Institutional Change*. Durham: Duke University Press.

Wise, Tim (2010). *Colorblind: The Rise of Post-Racial Politics and the Retreat from Racial Equity*. San Francisco: City Lights.

Wittgenstein, Ludwig [1953] (2009). *Philosophical Investigations*. Oxford: Blackwell.

Yancy, George (2008). *Black Bodies, White Gazes: The Continuing Significance of Race*. Lanham, Maryland: Rowman and Littlefield.

51–52; disassociation from equality of, 63–65, 79; food metaphors for, 69–70, 204nn11–12; maintaining the status quo with, 57–58, 66, 71–72; newness of, 61–63, 77, 203n10; normative uses of, 52; in official speech acts, 54–60, 202nn6–7; positive appeal of, 65–72, 131, 156, 204n13, 207n8; public relations uses of, 143–52; as self-referential, 108; as a tool, 60–62, 203n9; value accrued by use of, 58–60, 75–78, 203n8. *See also* language of diversity

diversity champions, 131–35, 208n7

diversity fatigue, 203n10

Diversity in Organizations, Communities and Nations, 16

diversity practitioners. *See* practitioners of diversity

Diversity Weeks, 32f

diversity work. *See* work of diversity

documents of diversity, 6, 83, 85–97; accessibility and circulation of, 95–97; associations with excellence of, 105–11; external preparation of, 104–5; group authorship of, 90–95; legal requirements of, 87–89, 111, 114–15; measurement functions of, 85–86, 97–100, 103–5, 111, 206n3, 206n6; as paper trails, 97, 206n4; practitioner detachment from writing of, 86–87; self-referential nature of, 89–90; statements of commitment in, 114–21; as substitutes for action, 100–105, 115–21; as unpopular required reading, 116–17

doing. *See* gap between saying and doing

Doing Diversity in Higher Education (Brown-Glaude), 16

Douglas, Mary, 25

Dua, Enakshi, 195n19

Du Bois, W. E. B., 152–53

Duggan, Lisa, 214n21

Dumont, M. Leon, 199n9

Durkheim, Emile, 19–20

Eisenstein, Zillah, 161

Elgström, Ole, 25

embodiment. *See* bodies of color

Employment Equality regulations, 194n10

Eng, David L., 214n21

Enjoy Diversity poster, 69–70, 204n11

Equality, Diversity and Excellence: Advancing the National Higher Education Framework, 192n4

Equality Act of 2006, 8

Equality Act of 2010, 8; documentation requirements of, 86; socioeconomic obligations under, 111

Equality and Human Rights Commission (EHRC), 206n6

equality (as term): disassociation of diversity from, 63–65, 79; legal frameworks of, 68–69

Equality Challenge Unit (ECU), 93, 196n24, 205n1; auditing role of, 98–101; on communication through documents, 94–95; "Good Talking" toolkit of, 107–8; mission of, 98, 207n7; ranking of institutions by, 83–84, 98, 102–5, 108–9

equal opportunities practices, 15, 195n19

Erdem, Esra, 147, 210n10

Erel, Umut, 148–49, 210n7

Essed, Philomena, 153

Eveline, Joan, 208n8

excellence, 57, 105–11

failure to inhabit categories, 176–82, 216nn4–5, 217n8

Falzon, Mark-Anthony, 11

Fanon, Frantz, 3, 161, 164

fatigue, 37, 94, 149, 179; diversity fatigue, 203n10; document fatigue, 86; equity fatigue, 90, 94

Fauconnet, Paul, 19–20

feminism: critical practices in, 181–82, 219nn14–15; on experiencing oppression, 217n8; killjoys in, 52, 179, 217n9; overing in, 179–80, 183 feminism of color, 13–14, 194n15, 209n2; blurred intersectionality within, 14–15, 195n18; on white feminists, 161–62, 213n19

Feminism without Borders (Mohanty), 13–14

fluidity, 185–87

Fox, Steve, 196n21

Frankenberg, Ruth, 169–70

freedom of speech, 162, 212n19

Freire, Paulo, 173, 215n1

Friedan, Betty, 72

gap between saying and doing: through documents, 100–105, 115–21; through language of diversity, 57–58, 66, 71–72, 151–52, 166–69, 210n10, 214n23; through mainstreaming of responsibility for diversity, 135–40, 208nn8–9; through official speech acts, 54–60, 83–84, 116, 121, 202nn6–7, 205n2; through practitioner writing obligations, 86–87, 101

Gates, Bill, 109–10

gay and lesbian contexts. *See* LGBTQ contexts

"Gay Imperialism: Gender and Sexuality Discourse in the 'War on Terror,'" 148, 209n5, 210n10

Geertz, Clifford, 194n11

gendering processes, 13, 195n17

Gender Recognition Act of 2004, 194n10

Gilroy, Paul, 182, 219n16

global citizenship, 77–78

good practices, 105–11

"Good Talking: The HE Communicators Equality and Diversity Toolkit" (ECU), 107–8

Greene, Anne-Marie, 15

Griffin, Nick, 145, 209n4

Gross, Ned, 198n3

Grosz, Elizabeth, 219n14

Gunaratnam, Yasmin, 194n13

Gunew, Sneja, 193n8, 201n4

habitual behavior of institutions, 24–27, 198–99nn7–9; committees as, 122; embodied nature of, 127–29

Hage, Ghassan, 169

Hall, Stuart, 201n4

Hamaz, Sofia, 195n19

happiness, 14, 72, 192–93n7, 204n13; as duty, 155–56; in inclusion projects, 163–68, 214n22; of institutions, 10, 71, 146–47, 152–53; in Whiteness Studies programs, 169–70, 215n26; and words, 67, 154

Haraway, Donna, 142, 219n15

Haritaworn, Jin, 147, 210n10

Hartmann, Douglas, 72

Hartsock, Nancy, 217n8

Hegel, Georg, 128–29

Heidegger, Martin, 198n3, 211n11

Hill, Joyce, 90; on ECU rankings, 102–3, 108; on ECU's role, 207n7; on good practices, 105–6

Hill, Mike, 52

hooks, bell: on causing tension, 158–59; eating metaphors of, 69, 204n12; on guilt, 169

hopeful performatives, 67

How to Do Things with Words (Austin), 54–56, 121

Human Rights and Equality Commission, 194n14

Hunter, Shona, 46, 209n1

Hurtado, Aida, 152

Husserl, Edmund, 191n1, 198n3; on attitudes and praxis, 23–24, 174, 215nn1–2; on the experienced world, 21–22

image management, 33–35, 102

inclusion projects, 163–71, 178–79, 214nn21–23; language of happiness in, 164–65, 214n22; phenomenological practice of, 183–87

individual commitment, 130–35; distribution through networking of, 133–34, 208n6; of institutional leaders, 131–33,

208n7; overreliance on individual bodies in, 134–35

inequality regimes, 8

insistence, 186–87, 216n6

institutional passing, 157–63, 176–82, 216nn4–5

institutional racism, 44–50, 147; language of, 48–49; Macpherson's definition of, 44–45, 49; politics of recognition in, 45–49; recovering from, 47, 201n19. *See also* racism

institutional whiteness, 33–43; as an unmarked expectation, 35–36, 41–43; countering with images of diversity of, 33–35, 102; importance of likability in, 38–42; as requiring labor to inhabit, 36–38, 41–43, 200nn17–18; somatic norms in, 38

institutional will, 128–29, 208n4, 208n6

institutions, 19–32, 49–50; background of habitual activity in, 24–27, 122, 127–29, 175, 198–99nn7–9, 215n3; circulating diversity in, 29–32; confirmation of whiteness through, 33–43; diversity officers in, 23, 25–26, 198n6; explicit goals and values in, 23–24; hospitality to the other in, 42–43, 200n17; language of happiness in, 146–47, 153, 156, 192–93n7; leadership on diversity in, 131–33, 208n7; new institutionalism of, 20–22, 197n1; as objects of sociological inquiry, 19–20; offices of diversity in, 27–28; official speech acts of, 54–60; phenomenological perspectives on, 21–22, 24, 198n3; as physical bodies, 28–29, 113, 199n11; presumed stability of, 20–21; reputation of, 103–5, 107–9, 151; resistance (brick walls) in, 26–27, 52, 129, 173–75, 186–87, 199n8, 208n5; transformation within, 173–82, 215n3

Institutions and Interpretation (Weber), 20

intersectionality, 14–15, 194n14, 195n18, 218n12

Jacoby, Russell, 198n7

James, William, 26, 199n9

Kaplan, Caren, 219n15

Kincheloe, Joe L., 170

Kirton, Gill, 15

Klesse, Christian, 148–49, 210n7

Kristeva, Julia, 169

Kuokkanen, Rauna Johanna, 43

La Grand Encyclopédie, 19–20

language of diversity: associated values in, 75–78; conversational spaces created by, 78–81; in defense of reputation, 151; global citizenship discourse in, 77–78; maintaining the status quo with, 57–58, 66, 71–72; in official speech acts, 54–60; in public relations work, 143–52; reproducing whiteness with, 151–52, 166–69, 210n10, 214n23; strategic switching in, 73–78, 205n14; as tools, 60–62, 203n9; using data in, 55, 75–76, 202n5. *See also* diversity (as term)

Larson, Coleen L., 199n10

Law, John, 197n1

Lawrence, Stephen, 44–45, 47

legislation, 4, 8, 10–11, 194n10; on creation and sharing of documents, 86–89, 97, 114–15; on diversity officer roles, 23, 87, 198n6; on positive spirit, 105–6; tick box approaches of, 106–8, 111, 153

Lentin, Alana, 52, 219n16

Lewis, Gail, 163–64

LGBTQ contexts, 148–49, 209n2; identification strategies of, 152, 210n10, 216n6; inclusion experiences in, 163–64, 214n21, 216n3

libel, 148, 209n5

Life in the United Kingdom (UK Home Office), 164

lip service conventions, 57–58

liquidity, 185–87

literature on diversity, 15

Lorde, Audre, 152, 161–62, 169–71
Lourau, René, 20
Luckmann, Thomas, 26, 198n3
Luft, Rachel E., 14
Lyotard, Jean-François, 6, 84–85, 205n2

Macpherson (William) Report, 44–45, 47, 49
mainstreaming policies, 135–40, 208nn8–9
"Malcolm X Was Bisexual. Get Over It"
    (Tatchell), 151
Managing the Organizational Melting Pot
    (Prasad and Mills), 107
Mannur, Anita, 204n12
March, James G., 21
Marx, Karl, 173
Mauss, Marcel, 19–20
May, Theresa, 111
McCaig, Norma, 78
McLisky, Claire, 193n8
McNeil, Maureen, 219n14
McRobbie, Angela, 219n14
Merleau-Ponty, Maurice, 127–28, 198n3
Merryman, Ashley, 203n10
Meyerson, Deborah E., 15, 196n21
Michaels, Walter Benn, 211n12
Mills, Albert J., 107
minority terminology, 65
Mirza, Heidi, 13, 153, 211n11
mission statements, 24, 57, 90
Mohanty, Chandra Talpade, 13–14
Money, Sex, and Power (Hartsock), 217n8
Moreton-Robinson, Aileen, 193n8
Morley, Louise, 192n5
multiculturalism (as term), 53, 201n4,
    204nn12–13
Muslim headscarves, 169, 214n23

Neal, Sarah, 15
Nee, Victor, 20
new institutionalism, 20–22, 198n3
Nicoll, Fiona, 150
non-performatives, 116–21, 126–27,
    207nn1–2
normative white bodies, 3–5

Obama, Barack, 219n17
obscured by diversity, 14–15
offices of institutional diversity, 27–28. *See
    also* practitioners of diversity
official diversity, 54–60
Olsen, Johan P., 21
Orelus, Pierre W., 177, 216n5
*Out of Place: Interrogating Silences in Queer-
    ness / Raciality* (Haritaworn, Tauquir,
    and Erdem), 147, 209n5
OutRage! 147
Ovando, Carlos Julio, 199n10
overing, 179–80, 183
Ozga, Jenny, 53

passing. *See* institutional passing
Pedagogies of Crossing (Alexander), 13–14
Pedwell, Carolyn, 195n18
perception: challenges to, 183–85, 219n18;
    measurement of, 34–35, 184
performance culture, 205n2; documents of
    diversity in, 6, 83, 85–97; equality indica-
    tors in, 85; good practice and excellence
    in, 105–11; hopeful performatives in, 67;
    official speech acts in, 54–60, 83–84, 116,
    121, 202nn6–7; of public relations work,
    144–53; tick box approaches of, 106–8, 111,
    113–14, 118–19, 153; utility and efficiency
    goals in, 84–85
performativity, 54–56, 58, 116, 202n6,
    205n2; constative elements of, 207n1;
    futurity in, 126–27; vs. non-
    performatives, 116–21
persistence, 25–27, 29–32, 140, 186–87
phenomenological practice, 173–87; in
    color-blind discourses, 182–83, 219nn16–
    17; fluidity vs. solidity in, 185–87; habit-
    ual bodies in, 127–29; inhabiting of cate-
    gories in, 176–84, 216nn4–5, 217n8; per-
    ception of inclusion in, 183–87, 219n18;
    in study of institutions, 21–22, 24, 198n3;
    transformation in, 173–75, 215n3; work
    of diversity as, 14–15, 22

Warner, Michael, 56
war on terrorism, 167–68, 212nn19–20
Weber, Samuel, 20
whiteness, 5; antiracist whiteness, 169–70;
criticality in, 169–70, 179, 215n26,
217n10, 218n13; disidentification from,
151–52, 210n10. *See also* institutional
whiteness
Whiteness Studies programs, 169–70,
215n26, 217n10
willfulness, 158, 186, 199n11, 208n4, 216–
17n6
Wittgenstein, Ludwig, 203n9, 219n18
Women's Studies programs, 183–84, 192n5
work of diversity, 4–6; ambivalence in, 15,

196n21; government (UK) cuts in, 111;
knowledge communities in, 15–16,
196n20; in offices of institutional diversity, 27–28; persistence required for, 25–
27, 29–32, 140, 186–87; as phenomenological practice, 14–15, 22; as public relations, 143–52; shift from equal opportunity framework to, 15. *See also*
practitioners of diversity
Wright, Susan, 99–100

Yancy, George, 41–42

Zami: A New Spelling of My Name (Lorde),
152

SARA AHMED is a professor of race and cultural studies
at Goldsmiths College, University of London.

Ahmed, Sara
On being included : racism and diversity in institutional
life / Sara Ahmed.
p. cm.
Includes bibliographical references and index.
ISBN 978-0-8223-5221-1 (cloth : alk. paper)
ISBN 978-0-8223-5236-5 (pbk. : alk. paper)
1. Minorities in higher education. 2. Racism in higher
education. 3. Education, Higher—Social aspects.
4. Cultural pluralism. 5. Universities and colleges—
Sociological aspects. I. Title.
LC212.4A398 2012
378.1'9829—dc23   2011041895